DIVERSIFYING THE TEACHER WORKFORCE

D0223564

Diversifying the Teacher Workforce critically examines efforts to diversify the teaching force and narrow the demographic gap between who teaches and who populates U.S. classrooms. Although the demographic gap is often invoked to provide a needed rationale for preparing all teachers, and especially White teachers, to work with students of color, it is far less often invoked in an effort to examine why the teaching force remains predominantly White in the first place. On the basis of work engaged in by the National Association for Multicultural Education on this phenomenon, this edited collection brings together leading scholars to look closely at this problem. They examine why the teaching force is predominantly White from historical as well as contemporary perspectives, showcase and report available data on a variety of ways this problem is being tackled at the preservice and teacher credentialing levels, and examine how a diverse and high-quality teaching force can be retained and thrive. This book is an essential resource for any educator interested in exploring race within the context of today's urban schools.

Christine E. Sleeter is Professor Emerita in the College of Professional Studies at California State University Monterey Bay, USA.

La Vonne I. Neal is Dean of the College of Education at Northern Illinois University, USA.

Kevin K. Kumashiro is Dean of the School of Education at the University of San Francisco, San Francisco, USA.

DIVERSIFYING THE TEACHER WORKFORCE

Preparing and Retaining Highly Effective Teachers

Edited by
Christine E. Sleeter, La Vonne I. Neal, and
Kevin K. Kumashiro

Routledge
Taylor & Francis Group

NEW YORK AND LONDON

First published 2015
by Routledge
711 Third Avenue, New York, NY 10017

and by Routledge
2 Park Square, Milton Park, Abingdon, Oxon, OX14 4RN

Routledge is an imprint of the Taylor & Francis Group, an informa business

Library of Congress Cataloging-in-Publication Data

Diversifying the teacher workforce : preparing and retaining highly
   effective teachers / edited by Christine E. Sleeter, La Vonne I. Neal,
   Kevin K. Kumashiro.
      pages cm
   Includes bibliographical references and index.
   1. Minority teachers—Recruiting—United States.   2. Minority
teachers—Training of—United States.   3. Teaching—United States—
Regional disparities.   4. Culturally relevant pedagogy—United States.
5. Diversity in the workplace—United States.   I. Sleeter, Christine E.,
1948– editor of compilation.   II. Neal, La Vonne Isabelle, 1955– editor
of compilation.   III. Kumashiro, Kevin K., 1970– editor of compilation.
   LB2835.25.D58 2015
   371.100973—dc23
   2014006296

ISBN: 978-0-415-73671-8 (hbk)
ISBN: 978-0-415-73672-5 (pbk)
ISBN: 978-1-315-81832-0 (ebk)

Typeset in Bembo
by Apex CoVantage, LLC

Printed and bound in the United States of America by Publishers Graphics,
LLC on sustainably sourced paper.

CONTENTS

PREFACE

This book originated through work of the National Association for Multicultural Education (NAME). In 2012, NAME held a very successful summer institute entitled "Addressing the Demographic Imperative: Recruiting and Preparing a Diverse and Highly Effective Teaching Force." We held it on the campus of Northern Illinois University, where La Vonne, a member of the NAME board at the time, is dean. Christine, NAME president at the time, was the main session organizer. Kevin, who participated, is NAME president as of this writing. The institute was designed to address a core concern of NAME: that all children and youth, and particularly those from historically marginalized communities, experience an education that fully embraces their intellectual abilities and identities. With the growing demographic gap between teachers and students, recruiting and preparing a more diverse teaching force, especially teachers who are from the same communities as their students, is one important prong in addressing this concern.

We wanted to actively counter an objection we had heard for years: that teacher educators can prepare those who choose to go into teaching but cannot do much about who chooses to do so. Therefore, we organized the institute such that leaders and directors of programs that were intentionally designed to recruit and prepare racially and ethnically diverse teachers would provide workshops for teams of people wanting to figure out how to do this work. In advertising the institute, we suggested that attendees come in teams of up to five that include someone from teacher education, from the school district, and from the community.

And people came. We realized that there is hunger for this kind of shift in thinking and practice about teaching in relationship to multicultural education, culturally responsive pedagogy, the "achievement gap," and the student demographics. The 2 1/2 days of the institute were filled with rich conversations, sharing, preliminary planning, and networking.

Toward the end, the three of us were sitting over the dinner table in La Vonne's home, strategizing next steps for NAME to take. One of the steps we agreed on was to capture and share as much of the work of the institute as possible in the form of a book. We put out a call for chapters, and again, people came.

We extend our appreciation to the NAME Board of Directors for supporting this project and to the Northern Illinois University School of Education's conference planning team for hosting the event. We applaud the teams around the country who are engaging in the day-to-day work it takes to recruit, prepare, and support a strong and diverse teaching force. We thank particularly those who took time out of their work "on the ground" to share what they are doing by offering a workshop and/or writing about it. May the results of your work continue to thrive!

INTRODUCTION

Why a Diverse Teaching Force Must Thrive

La Vonne I. Neal, Christine E. Sleeter,
and Kevin K. Kumashiro

> *What we see in the children is what they have seen in us—or more accurately perhaps, what they see in us.*
>
> —James Baldwin

In the United States today, the teaching force remains predominantly White—an institutional feature the American public can no longer afford to overlook. Consider the fact that according to the National Center for Education Statistics (2011a), students who are culturally and linguistically diverse comprise 45% of the nation's K-12 students. Meanwhile, 83% of the teaching force is White (National Center for Education Statistics, 2011b). "This skewed racial representation means that most public school teachers come from significantly different cultures than their students and that as a group, they enjoy unacknowledged privileges denied to many of their students" (Hinchey, 2008, p. 3).

Addressing this racial gap between the teaching and student populations often translates to preparing all teachers, and especially White teachers, to work with diverse students. But is that enough? Consider the following counter-stories.

Jerome peers across a sea of White faces. All of his teachers and most of his classmates happen to be White. "Where are all of the Black teachers? Where are the teachers who look like me?" The only role models who look like him are members of the custodial and lunchroom staff. Nevertheless, Jerome tries to fit in and adopt the White, middle-class norms and values that dominate the curriculum, leaving him to feel like he lives in two different worlds culturally. He has to work extra hard to disprove harsh stereotypes. For instance, once when he lost a homework assignment on the bus, his math teacher refused to believe his story and called him "lazy" (S. Militz-Frielink, personal communication, June 25, 2013).

In a typical suburban high school in America, students of color suffer from boredom as they are unfairly tracked in lower level classes or suspended because of hegemonic policies and practices.

In another classroom, a White teacher gives advice to a student, a Mexican immigrant who was having difficulty finishing his homework: " 'Just go in your room, close the door, shut out all the noise, and focus on your work.' That the student didn't have a room of his own or a door to close apparently never occurred to the teacher" (Michie, 2007, p. 6).

Such counter-stories suggest the need for multiple strategies. Teachers in the White mainstream who have not questioned their assumptions may not realize the impact their own backgrounds and perceptions have on the educational experiences of their students. Currently the majority of teacher education programs require only one diversity course for their teacher candidates (Chang, 2002), and yet professional preparation for teaching diverse students is essential to the success of any teacher who works with students from backgrounds different than his or her own. But even if those who "mirror the national White template" (Hinchey, 2008, p. 3) receive effective professional preparation, the face of the profession itself will not have changed and the racial barriers that maintain a disproportionately White teaching force will not have lessened. Institutional racism continues to shape the teaching profession, and this must be acknowledged and addressed. As Angela Y. Davis (2012) wrote,

> It's true that particular manifestations of racism, such as legal racial segregation, have been eliminated. But we have become so fixated on segregation as constituting the heart of racism that we cannot see the deep structural and institutional life of racism.
>
> (p. 129)

The demographic gap between teachers and students reflects how the institutional life of racism has dominated the profession. Efforts to diversify the teaching force are not new, and this book provides profiles and analyses of innovative programs and initiatives to recruit and retain teachers of color for our nation's K-12 schools. Framed by insights from critical race theory (hereafter, CRT), this volume demonstrates why a diverse teaching force is necessary, how institutional racism continues to produce an overwhelmingly White teaching force, and both historical and contemporary approaches to addressing this problem.

Why Is There a Skewed Racial Representation?

Despite the "separate but equal" ruling in the 1896 *Plessy v. Ferguson* Supreme Court case, which argued that segregated buses and schools were to be equal to those of the Whites, the implementation of this doctrine was never actualized as "Blacks continued to receive 'second-class' facilities and accommodations in public schools" (Milner & Howard, 2004, p. 286). Arguments in favor of integration presented in the 1954 *Brown* case illustrated the harmful psychological effects Black students endured as they observed the superior school conditions of their White counterparts:

> Black elementary children were summarily denied the opportunity to enroll in white schools based upon a criterion of skin color rather than equal protection under the law. In many instances, black children had to travel past nearby schools to attend schools designated for blacks only. Even when these black facilities were substandard (having, for example, no cafeteria or library), boards of education considered them to be equal to those of whites.
> (Neal & Moore, 2004, p. 7)

Prior to the *Brown* ruling—which made desegregation the law of the land—Black students attended these dilapidated schools that were operated mostly by skilled, experienced, and dedicated educators of color who lived in the same communities as their students. Although the buildings and conditions were clearly inferior to those in White schools, teachers of color were able to establish meaningful relationships with their students and families outside of school (Milner & Howard, 2004).

The desegregation era ushered in massive layoffs and demotions for teachers of color: "Approximately 38,000 African Americans teachers and administrators in 17 states lost their positions between 1954 and 1965" (Milner & Howard, 2004, p. 286). When nearly a third of the African American teaching force was laid off, the subsequent quality of African American education came into question. For many students of color, "African American teachers represented surrogate parent figures, acted as disciplinarians, counselors, role models, and most importantly advocates for their academic, social, cultural, emotional, and moral development" (Milner & Howard, 2004, p. 286). According to one study, students of color who were low achieving benefited most from relationships with teachers of color (King, 1993, as cited in Milner & Howard, 2004).

Sixty years after *Brown* attempted to integrate Black and White schools, the population that was supposed to benefit most from the ruling—namely, African Americans—is the group of students whose genius has been sparked the least in U.S. schools. Today, the skewed racial representation of teachers of color continues and is replicated among Latino/as, Native Americans, and Asian Americans, which clearly puts students of color at a disadvantage. Other factors that have perpetuated the skewed racial representation include pejorative public perceptions about the status of teaching, relatively low salaries, and the increase in alternative job prospects, all of which have influenced university students of color to select different careers.

Some students who do choose the teaching profession lack adequate college preparation and guidance navigating the application process while in high school. A study of the disconnection between K-12 and postsecondary education revealed problematic issues with college transition and the adverse effects on students of color:

> [The] poor knowledge students and teachers have of college policies—their lack of clear understanding makes good college preparation difficult. This problem is compounded by the fact that many high school students— especially the most disadvantaged—receive inadequate counseling and opportunities for college preparation.
>
> (Venezia, Kirst, & Antonio, 2003, p. 10)

In addition, the gatekeeper tests (e.g., the SAT and ACT, basic skills tests) that determine who can and cannot enter a teacher preparation program are culturally biased, disproportionally washing out prospective teachers of color (Alberts, 2002). Some university students of color are deterred from finishing their teaching degree by the overwhelming whiteness and irrelevance of teacher education programs that are available to them (Sleeter & Milner, 2011, p. 85). Although most teacher candidates prefer to teach close to home, the available teacher education programs are disproportionately located outside of urban areas (Boyd, Lankford, Loeb, & Wyckoff, 2005).

Clearly, culturally biased gatekeeper tests, the physical location of teacher education programs, public perceptions of teaching as a profession, and the displacement of African American teachers after the *Brown* ruling are among the main historical, structural, and cultural factors that have perpetuated the skewed racial representation of teachers of color. These factors are not isolated but rather come together to reveal a larger system at work to maintain the whiteness of the teaching profession, which CRT makes visible.

Framing the Book With Critical Race Theory

CRT provides a helpful lens for analyzing the skewed racial representation of the teaching force and conceptualizing how it might be addressed. One common conceptualization of racism is that it consists of a set of errant beliefs, false generalizations, and stereotypes about groups of people, such as "Blacks are lazy" or "Chicanos do not value education" (Zamudio, Russell, Rios, & Bridgeman, 2011). Such a conceptualization individualizes racism; that is, racism can be diminished if individuals' beliefs and behaviors change, as with the thinking that if teacher educators approached recruitment and preparation of teachers with less racial bias, the teaching force would be more diverse. However, racism is more than a set of beliefs and individual actions; racism operates not only individually but also culturally, structurally, institutionally, and ideologically. Racism shapes and is shaped by cultural and social norms and by institutional policies and practices—and CRT helps us to see how this is so.

CRT offers conceptual tools for interrogating how race and racism have been institutionalized and are maintained. A core premise of CRT is that "racism is endemic, institutional, and systematic, a regenerative and overarching force maintaining all social constructs" (Valdes et al., 2002 as cited in Aleman & Aleman, 2010, p. 3). Racism is not an aberration but rather a fundamental way of organizing society. The forms it takes today may have shifted from those of the past, but racism continues to be evident in the disproportionate access of Whites to resources such as jobs and education and in the dominant Eurocentric worldview used to explain the disparities. With respect to the teaching force, CRT begins with the premise that this skewed representation is not accidental but rather a product of racist systems designed to meet White needs (Rogers-Ard, Knaus, Epstein, & Mayfield, 2013). Four tenets of CRT are particularly helpful for this analysis.

First is the tenet of interest convergence. In his analysis of who actually benefited from school desegregation and affirmative action policies, Bell (1987) argued that Whites advance interests of people of color only as long as they converge with and advance White interests. This concept is useful for critiquing limited attempts to diversify the teaching force. Milner (2008), for example, argued that teacher education programs often make small changes (such as admitting a few more prospective teachers of color) when White faculty see benefits to other Whites (such as believing White students will benefit from learning from peers of color in their classes). Fasching-Varner (2009) viewed such restrictive conceptions of antidiscrimination as interest convergence. Restrictive conceptions focus on processes used currently, such as adding questions about diversity to admissions screening or adding readings about diversity, asking if they are helpful. However, such incremental changes do not disrupt White dominance. In contrast, expansive conceptions of antidiscrimination focus on outcomes of efforts and on systems that produce those outcomes. An expansive conception—which would disrupt White dominance—means asking why teacher education programs continue to produce predominantly White cohorts of teachers, only some of whom are convinced that racism exists and even fewer equipped to actively challenge it. Taking an expansive conception, chapters in this book offer various program models that substantively and successfully transform the teaching force, critique ways in which such programs are often marginalized, and suggest various forms of pressure that can lead to change. Authors pose an important question: Given the existence of successful efforts to diversify the teaching force, do White teacher educators and policymakers have the political will to act in solidarity and to align their own interests with those of America's richly diverse children and youth?

A second tenet of CRT is its challenge to claims of neutrality, colorblindness, and meritocracy in policies and practices shaped around the dominant ideology (Solorzano & Delgado Bernal, 2001; Stovall, 2013). Policies such as state teacher certification requirements or the federal No Child Left Behind law are presented as impartial and neutral, applied to all individuals equally without regard to race or other demographic identities. The dominant ideology attributes people's widely different levels of success within a system of competitive individualism to talent and effort and racial disparities to those factors plus lingering effects of historical racism. CRT, in contrast, holds that claims of neutrality and colorblindness mask White privilege and power. For example, colorblind conceptions of quality teaching, by failing to account for ways race matters in education, support the continued production of an overwhelmingly White teaching force that is ill prepared for racially diverse students (Milner & Howard, 2013). Tests required for teacher certification, while not necessarily measuring good teaching itself, disproportionately fail prospective teachers of color (Alberts, 2002; Epstein, 2005; Rogers-Ard et al., 2012). Teacher education programs designed for full-time students who do not need to hold jobs make certification more accessible to middle-class Whites than to people of color (Clewell & Villegas, 1999; Rogers-Ard et al., 2012). Urban school districts that import already-certified White teachers rather than preparing local residents as teachers make the job of teaching more accessible to Whites than to people of color (Epstein, 2006). Once hired, racially "neutral" approaches to teacher professional development and support that ignore racial microaggressions that teachers of color routinely experience prompt some to leave the profession (Carrillo, 2010). Chapters in this book expose racism within policies and practices in specific university and school settings, offering alternative ideological frames and practices, such as "culturally efficacious learning communities," that support rather than hindering teacher diversity.

A third tenet of CRT is the centrality of experiential knowledge, expressed through counter-stories by people of color (Solorzano & Yosso, 2002). Because dominant ideologies and knowledge systems, based on White worldviews, deny or mask racism, CRT theorists assume that those who understand racism best are not its perpetrators but rather those who are routinely victimized by it. Experiential knowledge that directly names race and racism can be shared in a variety of forms, such as stories, interviews, family histories, *testimónios*, biographies, and community documents. Such counter-stories not only name how racism works but also usually build solutions. Applied to teacher education, for example, Milner and Howard (2013) used counter-stories to deconstruct myths about teacher education, such as who counts as "best and brightest" and which universities produce such prospective teachers. Several chapters in this book report counter-stories, including those of prospective teachers of color and those of faculty members leading and working in programs to prepare them as teachers. In the process of naming the barriers students and teachers of color encounter, work that deconstructs those barriers is also made visible.

Finally, a fourth tenet of CRT is its commitment to social justice for everyone. Although some theorists see racism as intractable, most hope that deep analyses of it, coupled with rich counter-stories about how people have worked against racism, will ultimately lead to its elimination. This deep hope and tenacious commitment to working toward social justice is visible through all of the chapters in this volume.

As chapters unfold, their counter-stories on race and repression command attention. The experiences of students of color in preservice teacher education programs may determine whether they choose to stay or leave the profession. Instructors and students in teacher preparation programs can create hostile environments for preservice candidates of color. The dominant narrative that permeates the curriculum in U.S. schools today and is reflected in the culture and the politics of schooling can do the same. To that end, we applaud the courage and tenacity of Denise Taliaferro Baszile (2008), an African American teacher who navigated her way through a teacher preparation program on a predominantly White campus. Reflecting on her own traumatic experiences, she wrote about how racism operates through the dominant discourse in preservice teacher education programs. She now does the painful work of confronting racism in her White students and asks difficult questions that probe the deeper more personal issues behind the whitening of the teaching force. She inspires hope for the teachers of color who enter the profession:

> How might a non-European conception of self resituate, re-imagine the purpose and politics of teacher reflection? How might such a shift in one's epistemology of self tackle one's oppressor within, as a path toward inspiring a more revolutionary disposition, one that insists on revolutionary change toward a more just democracy?

> (p. 383)

Why a Diverse Teaching Force Must Thrive

A plethora of reasons justify why a diverse teaching force must thrive in American public schools. Having diverse teachers at the table is paramount for equitable educational policy decisions, student success, and the disruption of degrading assumptions and stereotypes about marginalized groups.

On the basis of an extensive literature review, Villegas and Irvine (2010) identified three research-based arguments for why a diverse teaching force must thrive: teachers of color serve as role models for all students, they are particularly well-suited to teaching students of color because they bring to their work a deep understanding of the cultural experiences of these learners, and they contribute to the education of students of color by reducing the acute shortage of educators for high-minority urban schools. Important here is the recognition that when teachers of color serve as role models, White students, too, benefit as they unlearn racist stereotypes they might have internalized in other settings (Waters, 1989 as cited in Villegas & Irvine, 2010). For students of color, the impact on learning is noticeable as their performance is significantly enhanced when their teachers are of color: "These effects manifest in many different ways in the classroom, including higher graduation rates, higher scores on state assessments, and decreased incidences of absenteeism, suspension and expulsion" (Lodaya, 2013, para. 4). On the contrary, if

> students of color failed to see adults of color in professional roles and instead saw them over-represented in non-professional positions, they implicitly learned that White people are better suited than people of color to hold positions of authority in society.
> (Mercer & Mercer, 1986, as cited in Villegas & Irvine, 2010, p. 177)

That is, as role models, teachers of color convey a strong message about the distribution of power in society.

Perhaps it is not surprising that some teachers of color (both preservice and in-service) self-report that serving as role models for students of color was the primary reason for their desire to enter the profession (Guyton, Saxton, & Wesche, 1996; Jones, Young, & Rodriguez, 1999). They view being a role model as a pivotal building block in their students' overall development, motivating them to increase their academic performance, expand their thoughts about possible career choices, and challenge negative cultural stereotypes (Achinstein & Aguirre, 2008). "Teachers who share cultural, linguistic, racial, and class backgrounds with students provide a source of connection and examples of successful adults for the youth" (Achinstein & Aguirre, 2008, p. 1507).

Although a mass of research justifies the need to diversify the teaching force, many questions still linger, such as the following: How do we more effectively recruit and retain preservice and in-service teachers of color? Can we even speak of building a high-quality teaching force without substantially diversifying who teaches? What kinds of barriers do teachers of color encounter before and after they are hired?

Various barriers exist to diversifying the teaching profession. Some of the barriers involve students of color choosing not to become teachers because of low teacher salaries, lack of prestige afforded to teaching as a profession, and pressure from parents to pursue other careers, which "may be exacerbated in minority communities, especially when the student in question is the first in their family to attend college. If parents had an unsatisfactory or incomplete schooling experience, they might see teaching as a low status profession" (Lodaya, 2013, para. 10).

But some of the barriers involve educational institutions making the path to becoming a teacher less accessible for students of color. Financial barriers, demands on time that take students away from income-generating work and family responsibilities, culturally biased processes for recruitment and admissions, cultural norms within the institution that privilege White students and instructors, Eurocentric curriculum and assessments, inadequate connections to local communities and schools, and lack of role models and mentors are just some of the elements of the educational experience of becoming a teacher that can keep students of color out or push them out after they arrive. Addressing the demographic imperative involves not merely encouraging more students of color to become teachers but also removing the institutional barriers that keep them out in the first place.

Programs That Recruit and Prepare Teachers of Color

Efforts to diversify the teaching population have existed for decades. This is not new work, although it is largely unrecognized work outside local communities being served, mainly because most programs are small, depend on external funding, and are not systematically studied. Sleeter and Milner's (2011) analysis of published information about such programs establishes a context for the specific programs featured in this book. Most programs can be viewed as "grow your own," whether they use that term or not, in that they involve collaborations between communities of color, school districts, and universities to prepare and certify local residents who otherwise lack access to teacher preparation. Sleeter and Milner divided programs into two types: those organized to bring candidates of color into and through existing teacher education programs and those that involve redesign or alternative versions of a teacher education program (some programs draw from both types).

Programs designed to bring candidates of color into and through existing teacher education programs build pipelines and support systems that may start as early as elementary or middle school. For example the Future Teachers Project at Santa Clara University (www.scu.edu/cas/liberalstudies/ftp.cfm) and Project FUTURE at Texas Tech University (Stevens, Agnello, Ramirez, Marbley, & Hamman, 2007) attempt to demystify higher education and support academic preparation of young people while also exposing them to experiences that may attract them into teaching. Pipeline programs for youth include features such as matching youth with a mentor teacher of their same racial or ethnic background, offering academic support workshops, taking youth to university campuses, and involving young people in teaching activities with younger children.

Programs designed to support university students of color going into teaching on predominantly White campuses typically offer financial aid such as scholarships, academic support, and social and cultural support to combat alienation. Examples include Project TEACH, which involved collaboration among a 4-year college, a community-based organization, and a school district (Irizarry, 2007); Grow Kaua'i Teachers (http://growkauaieachers.org), which enables teacher candidates on the island of Kaua'i to compete the University of Hawai'i teacher credential program while remaining on Kaua'i; and Hopi Teachers for Hopi Schools, which grew from collaboration between Northern Arizona University and the Hopi Nation (White, Bedonie, de Groat, Lockard, & Honani, 2007). Call Me Mister, a teacher leadership program adopted by multiple universities, recruits Black men into the elementary teaching profession by offering financial assistance, academic support, a cohort system, and assistance with job placement (www.clemson.edu/hehd/departments/education/research/callmemister).

Programs aimed toward working adults take into account not only ethnic identity and cultural support but also pragmatic concerns associated with adults' need to continue to work and barriers adults may experience in higher education institutions. For example, the Teacher Track Project at California State University at Fullerton, in collaboration with two community colleges and three school districts, recruited and supported instructional aides, most of whom were Latino and some of whom were credentialed teachers from other countries. Support included advisement on course taking, monthly meetings, small financial stipends, and occasional special events such as guest speakers (Yopp, Yopp, & Taylor, 1992).

Implicitly, most teacher preparation programs are designed mainly with traditional-age White students in mind. Ultimately, we believe programs themselves should be transformed to attract, welcome, and prepare diverse teachers. An excellent example is the Multilingual/Multicultural Teacher Preparation Center (M/M Center) in the Bilingual/Multicultural Department at Sacramento State University (Wong et al., 2007). About 75% of its candidates are of color, and most are bilingual, a mix the program attracts because of its focus, its very diverse faculty, and its commitment to working with communities of color and social justice. The M/M Center actively recruits, advises, and mentors undergraduates of color on its campus and over time has developed a network of outreach into schools serving students of color.

Most efforts to redesign university teacher education programs are more limited, mainly consisting of alternative versions of existing traditional programs, reworked to serve adults who wish to become teachers—paraprofessionals, emergency certified teachers, and career changers—but who generally cannot stop working to return to college. In addition, such programs often capitalize on experiences that adults who are already working in classrooms have. The DeWitt Wallace–Reader's Digest Fund launched Pathways into Teaching Careers, the largest cluster of such programs, in 1989; eventually there were 41 sites around the United States. Pathways programs involved partnership between a teacher education institution and local school districts. Partnering districts actively helped to recruit and select participants, using a selection process that included nontraditional criteria such as commitment to teaching in urban schools. Teacher education curricula were modified to meet participants' needs, and programs offered a system of academic support, social support, and financial support (Clewell & Villegas, 1999). For example, the Pathways program at Armstrong Atlantic State University (in collaboration with Savannah State University and Savannah–Chatham County Public Schools) in Georgia, designed mainly for paraprofessionals, successfully certified about 90 African American teachers who lived and worked in the community of students being taught (Lau, Dandy, & Hoffman, 2007).

The Latino Teacher Project (later renamed the Latino and Language Minority Teacher Projects) at the University of Southern California, established through a partnership among four higher education institutions, three school districts, the county office of education, and labor unions representing paraprofessionals, certified bilingual teachers for more than 2 decades. Although its curriculum was similar to the traditional university program, it was made more accessible to participants primarily by scheduling courses during late afternoons and evenings and by allowing participants to student teach in their own classrooms. The project also offered financial, academic, and social support, such as grouping participants into cohorts, assigning on-site faculty mentors, and providing regular seminars (Genzuk & Baca, 1998).

This national context of ongoing efforts not only demonstrates that the teaching force can be diversified but also highlights different viable approaches. Chapters in this book probe deeply into specific current programs that are structured in different ways, illuminating their challenges, their history and structure, and their impact. Ultimately, we challenge teacher educators to conceptualize such programs not as add-ons or temporary supplementary efforts but rather as blueprints for the redesign of teacher education that is truly inclusive and responsive to the students being served in schools today.

Overview of Chapters

This book unpacks the complexities, nuances, and questions surrounding the demographic imperative and provides theoretical and practical guidance on how to recruit, retain, and support a more diverse and effective teaching force. Showcasing the innovative programs and initiatives of education professionals, parents, and community members in cities across the nation, this book aims to inspire policymakers, professors, teachers, administrators, and community members to create stronger partnerships, programs, and plans for this urgent work. From the micro to the macro, the chapters are grouped into four sections that examine professional communities, university-based teacher preparation programs, university–school partnerships, and the broader national context.

Part I focuses on the role of professional communities—communities of practice, professional learning communities, and so on—in supporting the growth and success of teachers of color. Chapter 1, "A Competing Theory of Change: Critical Teacher Development," rejects the deficit-based view dominating current educational discourse that presumes that teachers are failing and need to be reformed through accountability and disciplinary measures. In contrast, Gist, Flores, and Claeys present a theory and a model for teacher professional development that draws on their strengths and positions them as agents of change, and has already demonstrated powerful results in changing the capacity of teachers and schools. Portraits of educators and leaders from the Academy for Teacher Excellence at the University of Texas at San Antonio illustrate the potential of such an approach.

Chapter 2, "Teach Tomorrow in Oakland: History, Teacher Profiles, and Lessons Learned," presents an eye-opening and inspiring history of how this program emerged from grassroots organizing that saw connections between various civil-rights issues, including education. Rogers-Ard and Mayfield Lynch describe the vision and the organizing that led to the creation of this program and illustrate its impact on both individual educators and the schools and communities with profiles of selected participants. Concluding the chapter are lessons learned that can apply to parallel efforts in other cities across the nation.

Chapter 3, "Changing the Field: Teachers of Color Move Into Leadership Positions," reminds us that to succeed, teachers need strong and supportive leaders in their schools; pipelines are needed for people of color to enter both the teaching and the leadership professions. Ross, Watson, and Simmons, through profiles of people who became teachers because of the Woodrow Wilson–Rockefeller Brothers Fund for Aspiring Teachers of Color program and the Newcomer Extended Teacher Education Program in Maine, illustrate the importance and range of leadership that teachers of color can take.

Part II turns to university-based teacher preparation programs to showcase and analyze how some programs have intentionally refashioned themselves to recruit and retain a more culturally diverse teaching force. Chapter 4, "Contextualizing the Demographic Imperative: Teacher Education for Students of Color in a Rural Community," examines the Cortland Urban Recruitment of Educators program at the State University of New York at Cortland campus, a small initiative within a large teacher education program that blends the dual goals of recruiting more teachers of color in a rural area and preparing more teachers for urban schools. Burns Thomas and Ivey-Soto describe the history and components of this program by focusing on its three defining elements: academic achievement, cultural competence, and critical consciousness.

Chapter 5, "The Turning Point of One Teacher Education Program: Recruitment, Preparation, and Retention of Diverse Teacher Candidates," begins where many universities struggle, namely, with a university–community relationship that has not always been positive, particularly regarding accessibility for students of color from the community. Ukpokodu describes this troubled history of the University of Missouri at Kansas City and its "turning point" to intentionally improve its university–school partnerships and strengthen its pipeline for students of color to enroll in the university and in its teacher preparation program that focuses on urban schools, the Institute for Urban Education.

Chapter 6, "Newcomers Entering Teaching: The Possibilities of a Culturally and Linguistically Diverse Teaching Force," expands on a program mentioned in Chapter 3, namely, the Newcomers Extended Teacher Education Program at the University of Southern Maine, which aims to recruit more teachers from immigrant and refugee communities into the teaching profession. Highlighting the unique and significant contributions that recent immigrants can make as teachers in our nation's schools, Ross describes the successes and challenges faced by this program, particularly the challenges any teacher preparation program faces when trying to make the pathway into teaching more accessible to immigrants and new arrivals.

Part III focuses on intentional and impactful partnerships between universities and public schools and districts to recruit and retain more teachers of color. Chapter 7, "Growing Your Own Teachers in Illinois: Promising Practice for Urban and Rural 'High Need' Schools," addresses the growing problem of urban school districts staffing schools with teachers who are not from the communities and who have no intention of staying longer than a few years as teachers. Bartow, Gillette, Hallett, Johnson, Madda, Salazar, and Valle share this history and framework for the Grow Your Own Teachers initiative in Illinois, a partnership of several community organizations and Northeastern Illinois University to develop a pipeline into teaching for paraprofessionals and parents from communities of color who are committed to teaching in their communities' schools. The chapter includes perspectives from a range of leaders of this initiative, and highlights aspects that are spreading across the nation with other initiatives for communities to grow their own teachers.

Chapter 8, "Pathways2Teaching: Being and Becoming a 'Rida,'" focuses on the pipeline that begins even before college with a program that engages high school students in exploring teaching as not only a career path, but also a path for strengthening their communities and broader society. Tandon, Bianco, and Zion describe a program offered in several high schools in which students earn college credit at the University of Colorado at Denver and where they learn about critical theories of education as well as about how teaching can be an act of social justice. The chapter concludes with reflections on challenges that the program grapples with as it continues to grow.

Chapter 9, "Admission System of a Teacher Preparation Program Designed to Allow Access for Diverse Teacher Candidates," describes efforts by Minnesota State University, Mankato to increase the recruitment and retention of teacher candidates of color by implementing two structural changes: creating a new leadership position, the Maverick Teacher Recruitment Coordinator, that would oversee and integrate all recruitment efforts, and creating a new Teachers of Tomorrow initiative that would support candidates from underrepresented groups. Burnett describes aspects of both changes, including the various types of direct support that both changes made possible both inside and outside the university.

Chapter 10, "Tactics and Strategies for Breaking the Barriers to a Diverse Teaching Force," describes five barriers to diversifying the teaching force: recruitment, financing the certification process, high-stakes standardized tests, universities' own (additional) credentialing requirements, and personal support. Ellis and Epstein offer concrete steps that have proven successful in breaking these barriers in the Oakland and San Francisco districts and beyond. The chapter concludes with a push to view these barriers as interconnected with other societal injustices facing communities of color.

Part IV sheds light on broader contexts and trends for teacher education and higher education that have impact on who becomes teachers and how we prepare them to teach. Chapter 11, "Architecting the Change We Want: Applied Critical Race Theory and the Foundation of a Diversity Strategic Plan in a College of Education," describes efforts at Northern Illinois University to go beyond disparate initiatives and instead to develop and implement a college-wide Diversity Strategic Plan that would advance goals related to diversity and social justice across the work of the college. Flynn, Hunt, Wickman, Cohen, and Fox present the history of the development of this plan and focus on the conceptual framework for its goals and objectives, namely, key concepts from CRT: counter-story, intersectionality, and social justice. The chapter concludes with details of sample initiatives from the plan.

Chapter 12, "Diversifying Teacher Education at a Predominantly White Institution: A Public Scholarship Framework," describes efforts by the Collaborative to Diversify Teacher Education at the University of Delaware to increase diversity in the teacher education programs, which are housed in various academic departments across the university. Flynn, Bieler, Kim, Dow, Worden, and Wong conducted a self-study of the experiences of their students and challenges they faced, and through this public scholarship illuminate areas for improvement at their university and beyond, including campus climate, financial support, professional advocacy, and the institutionalization of engaged research.

Chapter 13, "The Potential of Accreditation to Foster Diversity in Teacher Education Programs," provides an overview of accreditation for teacher preparation programs in the United States. Coker-Kolo analyzes the potential of the accreditation process for diversifying the teaching profession, particularly regarding the standard of the National Council for Accreditation of Teacher Education (NCATE) related to diversity, and reflects on the direction that accreditation is heading as the merger of NCATE and the Teacher Education Accreditation Council into Council for the Accreditation of Educator Preparation unfolds.

In conclusion, the overall aim of this book is to scrutinize the skewed racial representation of the teaching profession under a critical lens of possibilities and to inspire policymakers, professors, teachers, administrators, and community members to create stronger partnerships, programs, and plans that address the demographic imperative in culturally efficacious ways. This is the ultimate goal because our journey will not be complete until the demographic imperative has been completely ameliorated. Our journey will not be complete until all students have highly effective, culturally responsive teachers who value diverse cultural heritages and who spark the genius in every child.

References

Achinstein, B., & Aguirre, J. (2008). Cultural match or cultural suspect: How new teachers of color negotiate socio-cultural challenges in the classroom. *Teachers College Record, 110,* 1505–1540.

Alberts, P. (2002). Praxis II and African American teacher candidates (or, "Is everything Black bad?"). *English Education, 34,* 105–125.

Aleman, E., Jr., & Aleman, S. M. (2010). Do Latin@ interests always have to converge with White interests? (Re)claiming racial realism and interest-convergence in critical race theory praxis. *Race Ethnicity and Education, 13,* 1–21.

Baszile, D. (2008). The oppressor within: A counterstory of race, repression, and teacher reflection. *Urban Review, 40,* 371–385.

Bell, D. (1987). *And we are not saved: The elusive quest for racial justice.* New York, NY: Basic Books.

Boyd, D., Lankford, H., Loeb, S., & Wyckoff, J. (2005). The draw of home: How teachers' preferences for proximity disadvantage urban schools. *Journal of Policy Analysis and Management, 24,* 113–132.

Carrillo, J. F. (2010). Teaching that breaks your heart: Reflections on the soul wounds of a first-year Latina teacher. *Harvard Educational Review, 80,* 74–80.

Chang, M. J. (2002). The impact of an undergraduate diversity course requirement on students' racial views and attitudes. *Journal of General Education, 51,* 21–42.

Clewell, B. C., & Villegas, A. M. (1999). Creating a nontraditional pipeline for urban teachers: The Pathways to Teaching Careers Model. *Journal of Negro Education, 68,* 306–317.

Davis, A. Y. (2012). *The meaning of freedom and other difficult dialogues.* San Francisco, CA: City Light Books.

Epstein, K. K. (2005). The whitening of the American teaching force: A problem of recruitment or racism? *Social Justice, 32,* 89–102.

Epstein, K. K. (2006). *A different view of urban schools: Civil rights, critical race theory, and unexplored realities.* New York, NY: Peter Lang.

Fasching-Varner, K. J. (2009). No! The team ain't alright! The institutional and individual problematics of race. *Social Identities, 15,* 811–829.

Genzuk, M., & Baca, R. (1998). The paraeducator-to-teacher pipeline. *Education and Urban Society, 31,* 73–88.

Guyton, E., Saxton, R., & Wesche, M. (1996). Experiences of diverse students in teacher education. *Teaching & Teacher Education, 12,* 643–652.

Hinchey, P. H. (2008). *Becoming a critical educator.* New York, NY: Peter Lang.

Ingersoll, R. M., & May, H. (2011). The minority teacher shortage: Fact or fable? *Kappan, 93,* 62–65.

Irizarry, J. G. (2007). "Home-growing" teachers of color: Lessons learned from a town-gown partnership. *Teacher Education Quarterly, 34*(4), 87–102.

Jones, E. B., Young, R., & Rodriguez, J. L. (1999). Identity and career choice among Mexican American and Euro-American preservice bilingual teachers. *Hispanic Journal of Behavioral Sciences, 21,* 431–446.

Lau, K. F., Dandy, E. B., & Hoffman, L. (2007). The Pathways Program: A model for increasing the number of teachers of color. *Teacher Education Quarterly, 34*(4), 27–40.

Lodaya, H. (2013). The paradox of minority teacher recruitment. *Stemwire.* Retrieved from http://stemwire.org/2013/05/22/the-paradox-of-minority-teacher-recruitment

Michie, G. (2007). Seeing, hearing, and talking race: Lessons for white teachers from four teachers of color. *Multicultural Perspectives, 9,* 3–9.

Milner, H. R., IV. (2008). Critical race theory and interest convergence as analytic tools in teacher education policies and practices. *Journal of Teacher Education, 59,* 332–346.

Milner, H. R., IV, & Howard, T. C. (2004). Black teachers, Black students, Black communities, and *Brown*: Perspectives and insights from experts. *Journal of Negro Education, 73,* 285–297.

Milner, H. R., IV, & Howard, T. C. (2013). Counter-narrative as method: race, policy and research for teacher education. *Race, Ethnicity & Education, 16,* 536–561.

National Center for Education Statistics. (2011a). Public elementary and secondary enrollment, student race/ethnicity, schools, school size, and pupil/teacher ratios, by type of locale: 2008–09 and 2009–10. *Digest of Education Statistics.* Retrieved from http://nces.ed.gov/programs/digest/d11/tables/dt11_094.asp

National Center for Education Statistics. (2011b). Teacher trends. *Fast Facts.* Retrieved from http://nces.ed.gov/fastfacts/display.asp?id=28

Neal, L. I., & Moore, A. L. (2004). Their cries went up together: *Brown et al. v. Board of Education* then and now. *Journal of Curriculum and Supervision, 20,* 5–13.

Rogers-Ard, R., Knaus, C. R., Epstein, K. K., & Mayfield, K. (2013). Racial diversity sounds nice; systems transformation? Not so much: Developing urban teachers of color. *Urban Education, 48,* 451–479.

Sleeter, C. E., & Milner, H. R., IV. (2011). Researching successful efforts in teacher education to diversify teachers. In A. F. Ball & C. A. Tyson (Eds.), *Studying diversity in teacher education.* (pp. 81–104). New York, NY: Rowman & Littlefield.

Solorzano, D. G., & Delgado Bernal, D. (2001). Examining transformational resistance through a critical race and Latcrit theory framework: Chicana and Chicano students in an urban context. *Urban Education, 36,* 308–342.

Solorzano, D. G., & Yosso, T. J. (2002). Critical race methodology: Counter-storytelling as an analytical framework for education research. *Qualitative Inquiry, 8,* 23–44.

Stevens, T., Agnello, M. F., Ramirez, J., Marbley, A., & Hamman, D. (2007). Project FUTURE: Opening the door to West Texas teachers. *Teacher Education Quarterly, 34*(4), 103–120.

Stovall, D. O. (2013). "Fightin' the devil 24/7": Context, community, and critical race praxis in education. In M. Lynn & A. D. Dixson (Eds.), *Handbook of critical race theory in education* (pp. 289–301). New York, NY: Routledge.

Venezia, A., Kirst, M., & Antonio, A. (2003). *Betraying the college dream: How disconnected K-12 post-secondary education systems undermine student aspirations* (Policy Brief). Retrieved from www.stanford.edu/group/bridgeproject/betrayingthecollegedream.pdf

Villegas, A. M., & Irvine, J. J. (2010). Diversifying the teaching force: An examination of major arguments. *Urban Review, 42,* 175–192. doi:10.1007/s11256-010-0150-1

White, C. J., Bedonie, C., de Groat, J., Lockard, L., & Honani, S. (2007). A bridge for our children: Tribal/university partnerships to prepare indigenous teachers. *Teacher Education Quarterly, 34*(4), 71–86.

Wong, P. L., Murai, H., Berta-Ávila, M., William-White, L., Baker, S., Arellano, A., & Echandia, A. (2007). The M/M center: Meeting the demand for multicultural, multilingual teacher preparation. *Teacher Education Quarterly, 34*(4), 9–26.

Yopp, R. H., Yopp, H. K., & Taylor, H. P. (1992). Profiles and viewpoints of minority candidates in a teacher diversity project. *Teacher Education Quarterly, 19*(3), 29–48.

Zamudio, M., Russell, C., Rios, F., & Bridgeman, J. (2011). *Critical race theory matters: Education and ideology.* New York, NY: Routledge.

PART I

Communities of Practice: Supporting Culturally Efficacious Leaders and Teachers

1

A COMPETING THEORY OF CHANGE: CRITICAL TEACHER DEVELOPMENT

Conra D. Gist, Belinda Bustos Flores, and Lorena Claeys

Teachers are agents of change, but are they subjects or objects of reform? The way educational leaders respond to this question has important implications for the teachers of color we develop in the 21st century. Current teacher effectiveness reform positions teachers as individual objects who can be refined using high-stakes evaluation systems to improve student achievement (Rand Education, 2013). This position supposes that if teacher evaluation systems closely monitor and eliminate teachers who contribute to stagnant learning gains and persistent achievement gaps then low student achievement in schools will disappear. However, we challenge reform efforts that attempt to fix teachers as objects of reform; we instead situate teachers as subjects for change. We offer a competing theory of change, critical teacher development theory, positioning teacher development as a socioconstructivist process in which teachers work as change agents in knowledge-centered communities of practice that assess, implement, and refine rigorous and culturally responsive pedagogy to increase achievement for all students.

Teachers of color are important for all students (Epstein & Gist, 2013). Yet, research suggests that rather than becoming change agents, they can be changed by oppressive school systems (Achinstein & Ogawa, 2011). Thus, intentional efforts, anchored within critical social theories of resistance, must guide the recruitment, preparation, and induction of teachers of color. Collins (1998) separated oppressive from liberating uses of theory, explaining that "the difference lies in distinguishing between theory as dogma or closed systems of ideas to be verified and tested, and theory as a story or narrative operating as an open system of ideas that can be retold and reformulated" (p. 200). As educators, we are committed to theorizing social justice for teachers of color and view them as knowledge producers and innovators who create resources and theories that enrich the learning experiences of teachers and students alike (Bernal & Aragon, 2004; Freire, 1970). Collins posed three questions as a way to assess the epistemological criteria of a critical social theory, or in this case, our critical teacher development theory: (a) Does the social theory speak the truth to people about the reality of their lives, (b) does the theory equip people to resist oppression, and (c) does the critical social theory move people to struggle?

We view teachers of color as critical assets for redefining effective teaching for culturally and linguistically diverse students and have drawn from their historical and emerging knowledge systems as well as instructional practices to develop critical teacher development theory. Therefore, this theory challenges teacher education and professional development programs through the intentional inclusion of learning and teaching methods that integrate teachers' cultural, linguistic, and instructional knowledge systems. Thoughtful and targeted focus on nondominant perspectives at each stage of the teacher development continuum (e.g., recruitment, preparation, retention, induction, ongoing professional development) can equip teachers of color to be advocates for social justice in schools. For instance, during teacher preparation, culturally responsive practices can be fostered through instructional opportunities that enable teacher candidates of color to synthesize and apply diverse cultural understandings of learning and teaching. After program completion, teachers continue in *communities of practice* (CofP)—which Lave and Wenger (1991) described as groups who share a common concern regarding a task—and through dialogue, participants learn how to improve performance. The CofP help participants grow as culturally efficacious teachers equipped with the tools to responsively combat schools' hegemonic realities. During their induction phase, mentors are key stakeholders who work to facilitate and foster teachers' construction of knowledge and instruction in meaningful ways in CofP.

Culturally responsive CofP provide spaces for teachers to engage in critical dialogue that serves as a buffer against school contexts saddled with limited economic and human capital resources. Through this process, teachers affirm in community their sociocultural consciousness of the school, geographic community, and classroom context. They become efficacious in their beliefs and practices for successfully raising student achievement in adverse schooling environments. Teachers, as an empowered professional body, can embrace their sociopolitical commitments as lifelong work vested in community.

To illustrate how our critical teacher development theory is evidenced in the real lives of teachers, we feature the Academy for Teacher Excellence (ATE) at the University of Texas at San Antonio to capture the journey visionary leaders and teachers embark on as they grow in evolving culturally responsive CofP.

Stance as Researchers

In order to spotlight the voices of color in our study, we chose portraiture as a method to convey ATE's diverse and rich approach for fostering and sustaining teacher development. As scholars of color, we commit to challenging majoritarian tales of deficit by offering culturally responsive and sociopolitically conscious perspectives on teacher development. Portraitures' search for goodness parallels our commitment to highlight the strengths of teachers of color and can be employed "as a way of reflecting its cross between art and science, its blend of aesthetic sensibilities and empirical rigor, and its humanistic and literary metaphors" (Lawrence-Lightfoot, 2005, p. 6). Therefore, we offer a portrait to cultivate the mind's eye to "see" how ATE's program offers a competing vision of a culturally and linguistically diverse community of educational leaders who are equipped, committed, and empowered with tools to improve students' academic achievement.

ATE's initial program entry interviews, teachers' reflections on their professional development, mentors' classroom observations, and field notes were all used as archival data to develop the program portrait. The beginning of each section opens with reflections from the designers of ATE (authors Flores and Claeys), which are included to paint a coherent and textured picture of the program's development in general, and more specifically as evidence of the critical teacher development theory for which we argue. Although the portrait's opening sections are written in first person, the remainder is structured from a third-person perspective to present a coherent set of findings for the reader.

"Seeing" the ATE's Theory of Change

After analyzing the archival data on ATE's journey toward creating and implementing a theory of change, three key themes emerged: visionary leadership, the work of vision building, and the development of agents of change in CofP. The following portrait describes the reflections, decisions, and commitments the leadership team and teachers made at different points in the program's development.

Visionary Leadership

As a former teacher and counselor, I often witnessed the educational disparities firsthand. When I was an early childhood bilingual education teacher, I focused on providing a learning environment that promoted children's development. After all, that is why I went into teaching, to make a difference, and I personally think that I was successful. I witnessed how children thrived. But early in my career, I began to notice that my way of thinking was not necessarily aligned with some of the other teachers in the building. I was asked, "Why are you wasting so much of your time with those kids and families?" This type of questioning, rather than deterring me, made me dig in my heels and take a stance on my position. Yes, there were other well-intentioned teachers, but some of them were not necessarily equipped with the tools to work with a culturally and linguistically diverse population. What I witnessed was that Latino bilingual teachers and other teachers of color were best equipped, as were some White teachers, but not always. As a school counselor, I saw that the differential treatment of children was even more rampant. Effective teachers had commitment to the community and understood their role as advocates, and their children were successful. Still, there were others who approached teaching from a deficit perspective, with low expectations, and taught content with mediocrity. Later, as a university bilingual teacher-training coordinator, I felt that I was in a position to bring about change. Because of my desire to create greater equitable and responsive schooling practices, this eventually led me to my doctoral program.

Throughout my studies, I copiously read the literature on teacher development. Some nagging questions I had: Why were some teachers responsive to their students' needs, whereas others were oblivious? Why did they not have a sense of commitment? Had the teacher preparation program failed to prepare them adequately? Was the teacher preparation program targeting those with personal commitment to the community? What personal ideas or motives drove these teachers' decisions? Ultimately, these queries led me to my dissertation topic, which examined the epistemological beliefs and practices of bilingual education teachers. But even being a newly minted PhD and new faculty member did not quell my desire to bring about change in teacher preparation. I reached out to several like-minded mentors and colleagues to discuss issues and actively search for funding to set these ideas in motion. (Belinda Bustos Flores, ATE's founder, 2013)

Flores eventually formalized these ideas, drawing from her team's collective experience as teachers, counselors, leaders, and educators to design a comprehensive plan for preparing teachers as effective educators for diverse student populations. A key component of the program's conceptual framework was the idea of the *culturally efficacious teacher*, defined as an individual who demonstrates a strong ethnic–cultural identity, self-determination, critical reflection, positive efficacy, sociocultural competence, and transformative practices (Flores, Clark, Claeys, & Villarreal, 2007). The culturally efficacious teacher has strong interdisciplinary–disciplinary content, has pedagogical knowledge and skills, uses learners' cultural capital to create a supportive learning environment, is confident about his or her capacity to ensure the success of students regardless of the context, and is adaptable to change by engaging in the iterative process of continuous critical reflection and praxis.

ATE's leadership team rejected the notion that there is a finite point that one achieves along this journey; rather, they saw the educator as a perpetual learner. They envisioned becoming a culturally efficacious teacher as a transformative journey commencing during teacher preparation, continuing in the novice years, and enduring throughout the educator's career. Teacher candidates, novices, and career teachers need the assistance of mentors to acclimate to the professional demands of the changing landscape (Flores, Hernández, García, & Claeys, 2011). To actualize this transformative vision, which takes into account that change is constant and that we must be at the forefront of innovation, the team sought to create a support structure that would anchor this vision and actualize a theory of change.

The Work of Building a Vision

> I was fortunate to have institutional support from my dean, Bambi Cardenas, to further develop a proposal. To help us capture our ideas, I sought support from an expert grant writer—Abelardo Villarreal. In fact, he introduced me to the theory of change model (Rogers, 2008) that is used for developing grant proposals as well as transforming and evaluating organizations. We were eventually awarded a Title V for Hispanic Serving Institutions grant to establish ATE. The next step was to recruit the right personnel to ensure that the vision would come to fruition. (Belinda Bustos Flores, ATE's founder, 2013)
>
> When I came on board, I knew I had joined a dynamic visionary duo with passion and commitment to education specifically for ethnically diverse students and teachers. ATE would allow me not only to coordinate the implementation of the project but also to engage in critical reflection, innovation, and leadership undertakings. After 10 years, I am proud to say that ATE continues to be at the vanguard in pioneering compelling approaches for preparing and mentoring culturally efficacious educators for the 21st century. (Lorena Claeys, ATE's executive director, 2013)

In developing the support structures to prepare culturally efficacious teachers, ATE's team wanted to go beyond efforts already in existence while keeping in mind the vision. For instance, there was a demand for teachers in critical teaching areas while at the same time there was a need for greater diverse representation in the teacher corps. From these collective understandings, Flores and the team designed ATE to support teacher candidates in their holistic development to become culturally efficacious teachers by recruiting from the Latino population as well as targeting other students of color and students from low-income or first-generation populations. To support these teachers' development and success, ATE's leadership committed to creating an infrastructure and to recruiting experienced educators as mentors. Through professional development, the mentors' knowledge and skills were augmented to assist teacher candidates, interns, and novices through their professional journey.

Although providing well-trained induction mentors is vital as a support mechanism (Flores et al., 2011), ATE's team considered the notion of self-care to be a missing component in teacher preparation and induction. In an effort to support candidates' and teachers' life and career transitions, one of the team members,

Norma Guerra, utilized her LIBRE Model (Guerra, Flores, & Claeys, 2009), a strengths-based problem-solving and coping-strategies approach, as the basis for developing Career Transitioning Guidance. ATE leadership believed that the Teacher Academy Learning Community, in conjunction with critical elements such as Career Transitioning Guidance, would provide a safe environment for teacher candidates to support each other as they transitioned and navigated institutional systems first as learners and then as teachers.

As candidates transitioned from the teacher preparation program to the classroom, the leadership team noticed that their initial induction activities were prototypical in that campus mentors were assigned at the beginning of internship–novice year. Even when pairing teachers and mentors based on instructional assignments, the lack of time during and after school prevented an effective mentoring experience (Flores et al., 2011). Subsequently, the induction support model was refined to include experienced educators and create the Teacher Academy Induction Community of Practice, which was initially based on Lave and Wenger's (1991) community of practice notion and subsequently supported by research as an effective means for supporting teacher development (Jimenez-Silva & Olson, 2012).

To address ATE teachers' commitment and retention in the classroom, in addition to the face-to-face induction support, an online community of practice was developed as a collaborative platform that connects teacher candidates, novices, and career teachers "whenever and wherever" to facilitate peer mentoring, networking, and other professional development activities. This platform serves as a repository for resources that could be ubiquitously accessed for support while providing synchronous forums for critical dialogue. As a result, ATE has a comprehensive induction program, which works to support teachers as change agents in schools.

ATE's Change Agents

Elena, Monica, and Kennu are first-generation college students who participated in the ATE program. Elena, an elementary 5th-year bilingual teacher, is the daughter of Mexican immigrant parents. Monica, a 7th-year high school science teacher, initially pursued a career in medicine before seeking a graduate degree with teacher certification. As the third child of a Puerto Rican military family, Monica experienced diverse cultural and linguistic experiences both abroad and in the United States. Kennu, a 5th-year science teacher, was born and raised in West Africa. After obtaining a PhD in Tennessee and experiencing a successful career as a scientist, Kennu pursued a teaching certificate to become an ambassador for the sciences among students of color. These teachers' motivation to teach is driven by their passion to serve, to promote a college-going culture, and to make a difference in the lives of Latino and other marginalized students.

Specifically, these teachers were prepared to not simply have a sociopolitical consciousness with a strong ethnic/racial identity but to be culturally efficacious practitioners. As an evolving teacher in the ATE program, Kennu reflected on the support provided to him and his colleagues:

> One of the first things that helped keep me on track and supported my growth as a teacher was being a member of a group. My cohort members were a great help to me. I was able to take my classes along with them and do my professional development activities. I have made some wonderful friends through this journey we shared together. This group of peers was a major factor for aiding my success as a student and teacher.

Although this teacher's reflection affirms ATE's efforts, the initial transition from teacher preparation to the classroom aroused mixed emotions and challenged their commitments. Elena's experience suggests that to be a culturally efficacious teacher who can design and implement culturally responsive teaching requires learning how to overcome obstacles, as described in the following narrative.

I wish I had known the difference between theory and reality. You come into the profession thinking you are going to be able to do all of this, but in reality it does not work that way. What you hope to accomplish is difficult to attain. For example, at School A, I think the school was quite liberal in its approach to the curriculum; however, for a novice, it is tough because if you are not helped, how do you know where to find the materials and how to do things the certain way that this school expects? Over time you struggle along (too often on your own) and you learn; you even learn to respect the curricular approach because of the creativity it affords you. On the other hand, you go to School B, and here the approach to curriculum is restrictive. What I mean by restrictive is they give you a book and they tell you to follow it and have fidelity to the program by following the guide. The guide tells you what to say, when to teach, how to teach, and so on. So in liberal School A, my theory-versus-reality bubble burst because although I could be creative and apply theory to practice, I thought I could do one thousand plus things, but then. . . . [I had] assessments, and meetings, and professional development, and so many more things that I always seemed to run out of time. In School B, I disagree with what we are asked to do, and I cannot even begin to apply my good theory into practice. So I have learned that it is better to be in a School A, but you also have to learn to do it with the proper balance.

These teachers were also surprised to encounter environments where collegiality and expertise were almost nonexistent. For example, Kennu recalled a school-based mentor who did not have the content expertise to support him: "The

mentor they assigned me had her hands full; she was busy running around . . . .
So, again it's difficult [for the mentor] to be helpful." Instead of experiencing an
environment where collegiality was the norm and where more knowledgeable
others were readily available to help novice teachers, Monica and Kennu found
themselves in a high school similar to the "liberal context" as Elena described. As
novices, they were expected to develop science curriculum with little or no guidance. Despite these challenges, they remained committed to their students. Elena
shared as follows:

> I had to remind myself, "Why are you here?" If you believe that you are
> there to help kids believe in themselves, and you constantly remind them
> that they can do it, then it helps you believe the same thing. Always shut
> the door on anyone who says the kids cannot do it; start with believing in
> yourself and pass that on to your students.
>
> (2013)

Similarly, Monica has high expectations and as a role model gets students
excited about college and career opportunities:

> Just [treat] your students as mature adults, as future professionals, because
> that is what they all are. . . . I believe every teacher should have the energy
> and the passion for their students to make sure that their students are going
> to be successful in their class.
>
> (2010)

Taking a different angle, during a reflective interview after his first few years
of teaching, Kennu described his personal commitment and high expectations,
noting,

> Teaching has been my way of giving back in a way, and also to let students
> know that there's more than one option, that there's several options, but for
> you to jump at it you have to know, you have to know what the options are.
>
> (2010)

To illustrate this point, he provided an example of his relationship with students:

> One day [a student] came and told me "I wish my other teachers would
> say stuff like that to me, because you always encourage us to do work even
> when we don't know it. We pretend we know it. We strive to do some-
> thing." I said, "That is all. Just give it your best." [Beaming great pride,
> Kennu interjected] He actually passed his TAKS [state exam].
>
> (2010)

Although these teachers already had a strong content and knowledge base, these experiences affirmed the importance of embodying their care and commitment to their students.

Becoming a Change Agent in CofP

As members of ATE's CofP, Elena, Kennu, and Monica have developed a shared belief and vision that supports their commitment. Monica reflected,

> When I have been to workshops through my district or outside of ATE and fellow CofP members are there, we often get interesting looks because we share our thoughts or the things we learned. We make these our priorities and we strive to be the best teacher to all of our students. I like the districts we partner with; they need us even though others may not see them as a desirable place to work.
>
> (2013)

Believing in and maintaining a commitment despite challenges is a critical attribute of a change agent. Monica shared, "I am trying to bring professionalism back to teaching. Unfortunately, there are teachers experiencing burnout or who may not have the passion" (2010).

One of the ways Monica, Elena, and Kennu are able to cope with the challenges encountered at their schools is through active participation in CofP. They would seek their ATE mentors or peer mentors in the CofP to process the challenges at hand, explore possible solutions, and develop action plans. We see a lifelong journey of teacher transformation that commences early in the teacher preparation when they are designated a mentor and inducted into a community of learners. Once in the schools, they continue receiving support within the CofP:

> I can say I am incredibly thankful and blessed to have experienced this journey with the ATE program [learning communities]. I have grown as a student, teacher, and person. I would not have been able to survive without the support of the staff [mentors], ATE buddies, or learning opportunities I was privileged to have because 3 years ago I made the decision to take a different route rather than a "fast track" certification option. My students have a better teacher because of this. I know that I will only improve as I continue in my career.
>
> (Monica, 2009)

Within the CofP, teachers had the freedom to capitalize on their content knowledge, passion, and commitment to their students to become culturally efficacious. Once teachers began to feel secure about their capacity and see positive outcomes of their culturally responsive practices, they moved beyond advocacy and began enacting as change agents. For example, having observed institutional inequities, Elena did not hesitate to coach a new teacher:

> She was a novice teacher . . . scheduled for her first ARD [Admission, Review, and Dismissal]. . . . It appeared they wanted to put a child into special education. She was not sure what happened at ARDs and what role she would play. . . . I cried and begged her, "Please do not let them put that child into special education—he is quite capable." I also told her that kids generally do not exit special education, and at this young age, you are already predicting what lies ahead for the rest of the child's life. We believed in that child, and he is not in special education, and he is going to be okay!
> (2013)

Rather than acculturating to a school culture that operated from a deficit perspective, Elena was assertive as she challenged the status quo:

> I always speak my mind—professionally, and with respect. It is a scary thing, but if you do not speak up, no one will help you. I had a huge class and I had Spanish-speakers mixed in with English-only speakers. I had to persist. . . . I had to advocate for my students. There was a solution and an alternative, and it was the right decision to speak up for them and insist that changes be made.
> (2013)

Having the courage to verbalize and demand changes respectfully and professionally is a common trait among ATE teachers. Monica's in-depth reflection portrays these teachers' transformative thinking as they transition from learning communities and become agents of change in CofP:

> My concept of a teacher was slightly too straightforward, and possibly because of some of my personal experiences. However, my classes and ATE drastically changed and expanded my idea of what teaching really is. I was able to realize what [a] powerful role teachers have, particularly in a population that has diverse or underserved student needs. I initially thought that being culturally efficacious was a much simpler aspect of being a teacher. Many teachers give examples of using "Juan" instead of "John" in a question, story, or problem as using culturally relevant techniques. However, I feel that there is much more to this. You must make a conscious effort to develop approaches and an attitude that addresses the cultural and linguistic needs or knowledge your students bring to your classroom. And you don't do this out of obligation; you do this because your student deserves to get the best possible education!
> (2010)

The path to a teaching career has not been easy for these teachers. They have experienced some tribulations but are thankful for ATE's social justice mission of preparing them as culturally efficacious teachers in CofP.

Discussion

We began by arguing that our critical teacher development theory, as a theory of change, conceptualizes teacher development as a process in which teachers are situated in culturally responsive CofP that continuously assess and refine their pedagogical commitments to ensure student achievement. Then, we provided an illustration of our theory of change in an effort to counter narratives of teacher effectiveness movements that resolutely focus on test-driven measures and characterize teachers as isolated workers. ATE's portrait demonstrates how program leadership can use their collective knowledge as teacher educators of color to design a system that allows teachers to affirm their commitment to culturally responsive pedagogy and become self-empowered in CofP.

Flores's experiences as an educator grounded her belief that the nondominant knowledge systems and practices of teachers of color needed to be linked to the cultural work teachers enact daily if they are to effectively teach all students. CofP in and out of schools, along with the preparation of culturally efficacious educators, are the human and social networks that allowed ATE to prepare and sustain teachers as change agents. The journey traveled by the ATE designers, mentors, and teachers shines light on a path for developing culturally responsive CofP, including three key steps: (a) capitalizing on visionary leadership, (b) engaging in vision building, and (c) supporting teacher change agents to actualize their pedagogical commitments.

For teacher educators, ATE's portraiture illustrates a vision of teacher development that begins in teacher education programs and extends to lifelong teaching and learning. Our critical teacher development theory views teachers as learners and innovators with cultural and linguistic repositories who grow in CofP to challenge and inspire students towards academic achievement. We are particularly committed to efforts that invest in the development of diverse educators who work for academic excellence of students most often marginalized in schools. In contrast to a fixed focus on eliminating ineffective teachers, we focus on investing in teacher knowledge systems and developing teachers as learners in culturally responsive CofP.

The creation of authentic culturally responsive CofP requires educational leaders who are both committed and knowledgeable enough to foster a learning context that recognizes and builds internal human capacity. The core leaders in the culturally responsive CofP must also embody a type of agility to stay focused and resolute regardless of the constantly evolving political landscape. Kumashiro (2012) warned of the power of "fear" to drive teacher evaluation reform and push agendas that may not be in the best collective interest of students, schools, or teachers. Proponents of critical social theories of change, then, must be clear on their primary motivation and goals in order to effectively challenge oppressive reform efforts.

Are teachers subjects or objects of reform? We believe teachers of color are subjects for change. We must be careful, however, not to romanticize the value of teachers of color; such proclamations must be accompanied with strategies that equip them to work and thrive as change agents in school. The cultivation of culturally responsive CofP within and across schools can be a viable model of resistance for teachers of color, who, by iteratively and responsibly assessing and refining their instructional practice, can work collectively to ensure academic achievement for all. Bold and reflexive leadership, such as exhibited by the Academy for Teacher Excellence, is required for models and theories of resistance to truly equip teachers of color for the enduring struggle for social justice.

References

Achinstein, B., & Ogawa, R. T. (2011). *Change(d) agents: New teachers of color in urban schools.* New York, NY: Teachers College Press.

Bernal, C., & Aragon, L. (2004). Critical factors affecting the success of paraprofessionals in the first two years of career ladder projects in Colorado. *Remedial and Special Education, 25,* 205–213.

Collins, P. H. (1998). *Fighting words: Black women and the search for justice.* Minneapolis: University of Minnesota Press.

Epstein, T., & Gist, C. D. (2013). Teaching racial literacy in secondary humanities classrooms: Challenging adolescents' of color concepts of race and racism. *Race, Ethnicity, and Education,* 1–23. doi:10.1080/13613324.2013.792800

Flores, B. B., Clark, E. R., Claeys, L., & Villarreal, A. (2007). Academy for Teacher Excellence: Recruiting, preparing, and retaining Latino teachers through learning communities. *Teacher Education Quarterly, 34,* 53–69.

Flores, B. B., Hernández, A., García, C. T., & Claeys, L. (2011). Teacher Academy Learning Community's induction support: Guiding teachers through their zone of professional development. *Journal of Mentoring and Tutoring: Partnership in Learning, 19,* 365–389. doi:10.1080/13611267.2011.597124

Freire, P. (1970). *Pedagogy of the oppressed.* New York, NY: Continuum International.

Guerra, N., Flores, B. B., & Claeys, L. (2009). Case study of an induction year teacher's problem-solving using the LIBRE model activity. *New Horizons in Education: Journal in Education, 57,* 42–57.

Jimenez-Silva, M., & Olson, K. (2012). A community of practice in teacher education: Insights and perceptions. *International Journal of Sustainability in Higher Education, 24,* 335–348.

Kumashiro, K. (2012). *Bad teacher! How blaming teachers distorts the bigger picture.* New York, NY: Teachers College Press.

Lave, J., & Wenger, E. (1991). *Situated learning: Legitimate peripheral participation.* Cambridge, England: Cambridge University Press.

Lawrence-Lightfoot, S. (2005). Reflections on portraiture: A dialogue between art and science. *Qualitative Inquiry, 11*, 3–15.

Rand Education. (2013). *The Measuring Teacher Effectiveness Fact Sheet Series.* Retrieved from www.rand.org/education/projects/measuring-teacher-effectiveness/faq.html

Rogers, P. J. (2008). Using programme theory to evaluate complicated and complex aspects of interventions. *Evaluation, 14*, 29–48.

2

TEACH TOMORROW IN OAKLAND: HISTORY, TEACHER PROFILES, AND LESSONS LEARNED

Rachelle Rogers-Ard and Kimberly Mayfield Lynch

Roots in a Movement

From the middle of the 20th century to the present day, Oakland, California, has been a site of progressive political activity. In 1946, Oakland citizens staged and participated in a general strike for wage equity for women sales clerks in two department stores. The strike lasted for 54 hours and shut down all of the establishments in downtown Oakland with the exception of grocery stores and pharmacies (Wolman, 1975). In 1966, the founding of the Black Panther Party for Self-Defense in Oakland served as a defining moment in the Black Power movement. The party was organized by a 10-point platform that addressed every aspect of life for African Americans and the oppressed; education and employment were mentioned in three of the points (Seale, 1991). In 2005, Oaklanders mobilized once again. With the mayoral election a year away, a group of progressive citizens devised a strategy to draft a former U.S. congressman and Oakland native for mayor. Frustrated by hopelessness and despair, these citizens felt that Ronald Dellums's leadership and vision would bring back a sense of hope, democracy, and possibility to the city.

As he transitioned into office, Dellums called for the formation of several task forces to address the most pressing issues in the city as determined by the residents. Instead of hiring outside consultants, he called for Oaklanders to create solutions to the problems they identified, much like the Black Panthers did with their 10-point platform. Task force participants attended 2 hours of training led by facilitators who were experts in bringing people from various backgrounds together to work effectively on community issues and concerns. The key elements of the trainings were how to facilitate, participate, and honor the contributions of all members of the task force, whose participants and conveners represented the City of Oakland ethnically, racially, linguistically, and socioeconomically. To preserve the framework set by the trainings, Mayor Dellums assigned the role of task force liaison to one of his staff members who also served as education director. More than 900 people served on 41 community task forces, eight of which were focused on education. Forty years after the dissemination of the 10-point platform by the Black Panthers, education still proved to be an important issue for Oakland.

One of the authors of this chapter served as co-convener of the Effective Teachers for Oakland Task Force, which was created to develop and implement recommendations addressing the teacher shortage in the public schools and to ensure that all Oakland youngsters have effective teachers. This task force was charged with answering two questions: (a) How can Oakland ensure that there are enough teachers for all Oakland youngsters, and (b) what is the impact of high-stakes testing on Oakland youngsters? The group focused more energy on creating solutions to the first question than the second.

This task force was composed of teachers, nonprofit professionals, consultants and students. One mission of the Dellums administration was to have youth and collegians serve along with adults. For example, the co-convener of this task force was a Holy Names University student, illustrating Oakland's historical commitment to progressive leadership: we develop the next generation of leaders as we lead. The hallmark of the task force process was to leverage the good work already being done in Oakland collaboratively across sectors. This spirit of collaboration transcended not only those who participated in the task force process but also the Dellums mayoral administration. Effective Teachers for Oakland Task Force members were energized by what was possible during the Dellums mayoral administration. Long-time residents reengaged in municipal politics, and young people learned by doing and were the beneficiaries of the wisdom of the elders. Large numbers of citizens were mobilized as they had been during the time of the Black Panther Party in Oakland. The 900 task force participants developed networks and new social capital. We permeated the area with our activism and continued to struggle for increased quality of life and equity in hiring practices for teachers.

The task forces met 2 hours per week for 8 weeks; at the end of the 8 weeks each task force presented Mayor Dellums with three to five recommendations. For recommendations to be ratified, two-thirds of the task force members had to vote for them. The Effective Teachers for Oakland Taskforce conducted literature reviews to investigate how other urban communities were addressing the teacher shortage and lack of diversity in the teaching force. Teachers, students, and the president of the teachers' union (Oakland Education Association) provided testimony on the impact of the teacher shortage. Task force members synthesized the information and developed recommendations, all of which were ratified by 100% of the task force members. The mayor's political platform included five recommendations, described in the following sections.

1. Profile Oakland Teachers on City Website

The task force proposed monthly rotating teacher pictures and profiles that reflected elementary, middle and high school levels on the City of Oakland website, including a brief narrative about the teachers and where they worked. This recommendation was implemented. City staff solicited the Effective Teachers for Oakland Task Force for names of teachers to put on the City of Oakland website, members of the task force interviewed teachers to create their profiles, and teachers submitted pictures to be uploaded. The goal of this recommendation was to recognize and honor Oakland teachers and the teaching profession.

2. Increase Business Community Support for Oakland Teachers

The task force proposed the creation of an Oakland teacher discount card that would allow Oakland teachers to get 10% off purchases or meals at the participating establishments. The focus was to link teaching with the Oakland business community; participating businesses would display a poster that said, "I support Oakland Teachers." This recommendation was not implemented.

3. Town Hall Meeting: High-Stakes Testing

The task force proposed that the Mayor's office hold two town hall meetings to inform the community about the impact of high-stakes testing on Oakland students and the public school curriculum. We proposed that one meeting be held in the spring before the assessment season began and one in the fall at the beginning of the school year. This recommendation was not implemented.

4. City of Oakland and Oakland Unified School District Teacher Recruitment Summit

The task force proposed that the City of Oakland and Oakland Unified School District (OUSD) sponsor a recruitment summit targeted to college seniors, college graduates, and career changers in Oakland and surrounding cities. On August 17, 2007, our task force held a teacher recruitment summit at City Hall by developing cross-sector relationships and partnerships. More than 250 people came to find out how to teach in the OUSD. The school district allowed principals, human resource professionals, and senior administrative staff to do "on-the-spot" teacher and substitute teacher interviews; Holy Names University sent financial aid officers to discuss securing funding for teacher preparation programs; OUSD credential analysts discussed credentialing requirements; the Learning to Teach Foundation provided six test fee reimbursement vouchers to raffle as prizes; Bake Sale Betty's, a local bakery, donated pastries; and other Oakland-based small businesses donated items.

Mayor Dellums and one of the authors of this chapter addressed the attendees to encourage them to become teachers, stressing the importance of Oakland needing teachers from its own community. The use of City Hall was essential in communicating Oakland's commitment to recruiting teachers from the local community. OUSD hired more than 60 teachers and substitutes that day. However, for those who weren't eligible at that time but were still interested, we realized the importance of having the Oakland Teacher Center in place, described in the next section.

5. Oakland Teacher Center

The task force proposed that an Oakland Teacher Center be created on behalf of Oakland youngsters to recruit and retain teachers and to guide any Oakland resident on her or his path to becoming a teacher. Our proposal indicated that the center would operate the following departments: Recruitment, Test Preparation, Test Fee Assistance, and Retention. Although the explicit focus of the center was to solve the teacher shortage in Oakland Public Schools, citizens who wanted work in parochial and independent schools would also have access.

The teacher shortage is defined by the lack of permanent teachers and a string of long-term and day-to-day substitute teachers, which negatively impacts student achievement. Our solution was to create a local permanent diverse teaching force for Oakland schools. We recognized that in the OUSD, 56% of the teachers were from European American monolingual, monocultural backgrounds, whereas 91% of the students were from racially, ethnically, and linguistically diverse backgrounds (Ed-Data, n.d.). We were also aware that because of No Child Left Behind federal legislation, school districts had to have "highly qualified" teachers in every classroom on the first day of school.

To adhere to this mandate and as a result of the state takeover in 2003, OUSD outsourced all of its teaching recruitment to two national partners: Teach for America (TFA) and the New Teacher Project. However, many of the teachers placed by these programs leave the classroom after they have fulfilled their 2-year commitment; they are not from the area and often leave to be near their families. Although both recruiting partners helped ensure that OUSD was fully staffed, it also created a revolving door of teachers who were not committed to Oakland's community and children (Epstein, 2006; Rogers-Ard, Knaus, Epstein, & Mayfield, 2013). These types of programs are based on the belief that the districts for which they recruit have vacancies because the students are hard to teach and hard to reach. TFA's theory of action is to recruit interns from the nation's elite colleges to "serve" in impoverished communities. This framing of urban schools could lead to a bias in the hiring process where hiring managers respond more favorably to young, energetic, mostly White applicants than to other applicants.

The Effective Teachers for Oakland Task Force chose to frame this issue differently. We knew that there were local citizens who reflect the diversity of the student population, who wanted to become teachers, and who would be effective. As a result, the task force examined the structural barriers to becoming a teacher in California. We noticed that the requirements were prohibitive to local racially, linguistically, and socioeconomically diverse citizens. Like other urban school districts in California and the nation, OUSD has struggled to find a "highly qualified" racially and linguistically diverse stable teaching force that is representative of the local community (Sunderman & Kim, 2005). To leverage the collaborative leadership style of Mayor Dellums and the power of his office to engage a cross-section of stakeholders in creating the center, we took specific actions to move the idea forward. This fifth recommendation was ultimately implemented through the development of the Teach Tomorrow in Oakland (TTO) program. In January 2008, one of the authors of this chapter, an Oakland native, former teacher, and product of Oakland Public Schools, was hired as the manager of TTO.

The Program

TTO is not simply a recruitment program; it was developed to stop the revolving door of teachers as described earlier. To that end, TTO's goal is to recruit local citizens who reflect the diversity of Oakland's students and will make a commitment to remain in the classroom for at least 5 years.

TTO is placed within the Talent Acquisition Team, part of Oakland's Human Resource Services and Support department. In this way, TTO is aware of internal district openings and can send candidates to hiring managers right away. TTO's success is due in part to its placement within an urban school district; most teacher recruitment programs are within university education departments.

TTO is not a credentialing agency; partnerships with local universities allow candidates to streamline their application process, but the university recommends candidates to the state for their credentials. Therefore, open communication between the district hiring manager, TTO, and university credential programs are imperative to ensure that appropriate support is provided for each person. Applicants interested in TTO attend a recruiting session, apply to the program, and are interviewed individually. On receiving a conditional acceptance, applicants receive tutoring, reimbursements, and other support services. Applicants apply to the district and TTO simultaneously and receive support in applying to one of the TTO partner credential programs that provide all coursework needed to gain a preliminary credential. In addition, partnerships with local universities ensure that training is aligned between district-sponsored professional development, university coursework, and site-based instruction.

TTO developed partnerships with local after school programs, Boys & Girls' clubs, the Oakland Educator's Association, Dellums's education task force, community members, district personnel, and parents to create a comprehensive screening process for teacher candidates. Multiple-subject and single-subject[1] candidates teach a lesson to students who represent the ages of their credentialing area.

Everyone completes a rubric, and candidates' scores are tallied and ranked. Data and feedback indicate children and adults enjoy being part of this process because it makes them feel important; values their voices; and for many, is the first time they have been asked to evaluate a teaching professional.

Profiles of TTO Teachers

After selection and placement, the work of supporting teachers of color continues. To demonstrate, and to better understand teachers' journeys, we present three profiles of teachers in our program.

Profile 1

Kirk, a 40-year-old African American male long-term substitute in OUSD, was referred to TTO at the request of his White male principal. He was a career changer; familiar with Oakland, having lived there for several years; and his own experiences allowed for a unique understanding of the children he would teach. The principal sent a glowing letter of recommendation, indicating that Kirk's "talents as a teacher and leader are evident, and his ability to teach students complex concepts is a product of his strong classroom management skills, his growing understanding of child development, and his unwavering insistence that all children can and will succeed." As a result of the principal's recommendation, Kirk was placed at the school where he had been a substitute, thus making him an intern and probationary teacher.

In November 2009, Kirk indicated that he was "having some trouble" with a few of the younger White teachers on campus. "They talk to me like I'm less than they are," he said in an e-mail. The TTO manager contacted the principal three times via e-mail to follow up on Kirk's situation. In January 2010, the principal wrote a response, indicating that they had been working with Kirk, who would "benefit from some new planning and support structures that we're putting in place for him. Already the change in the rigor of his class is evident."

In March 2010, TTO was made aware that Kirk's principal had decided to non-reelect him. In California, this process happens each year in March for probationary teachers who can be released from the district without cause; having this on a teacher's record makes him or her ineligible to be rehired within the district. Several people came to Kirk's defense: parents, students, university supervisors, and TTO staff advocated for Kirk to have the non-reelect rescinded. Kirk himself was surprised:

> I really thought I was making good progress. I am the only African American male on campus, and all of the black boys come to hang out in my class. I have brought in my instruments and worked on being a good role model for my students. I was given the hardest students in the school; the kids no

one else wanted, yet I know I've made a change in these kids' lives. And now, after the Principal referred me, he now thinks I'm not a good fit to teach in Oakland FOREVER? I'm trying to remain positive but sometimes it's really hard.

Finally, after months of debate and discussion, OUSD's superintendent Tony Smith rescinded Kirk's non-reelect, suggesting that he take a year to finish his teaching credential and reapply to the district the following year. Because TTO recruits Oakland community members who are resilient and who love Oakland and its children, Kirk chose to take a year off and completed his credential through student teaching. TTO kept in contact with him during that year, inviting him to participate in professional development and other events.

Once Kirk completed his credential, he willingly reapplied to TTO. Kirk was concerned about finding a placement in Oakland because his former principal was still in the district. However, when a position opened in the fall of 2011 at a school with an African American female principal who believed in the TTO program, Kirk was hired despite his previous experience at another school. When asked about his current placement, Kirk wrote,

I am going for the gusto and giving my all. I look forward every day to apply my urban education, professional development resources each day. It makes SUCH a huge difference to have a principal who believes in you, cares about you, and wants you to succeed. Thanks for helping me get placed here!

Kirk's principal indicated that he had the "correct blend of care and rigor that we value at this school." Once again, Kirk was the only African American male on campus, but unlike at his former placement, he felt valued and accepted at this new school. Ultimately, TTO chose him as "Teacher of the Year" for 2012. During the presentation his principal said, "We understand the implications of institutionalized racism run deep within educational settings, but delayed does not mean denied." By 2013, Kirk was the teacher leader at his school site when his principal attends off-campus meetings. He mentors first-grade TTO teachers and has completed his master's degree in urban education.

Profile 2

Yessica, a Latina single parent whose first language is Spanish, was teaching social studies and language arts at an Oakland charter school when she was recruited by TTO. After successfully applying to TTO in the fall of 2009, Yessica enrolled in a credential program, passed the mandatory teacher tests, and was placed at one of Oakland's elementary schools with a large Spanish-speaking population. At the end of the year, because of decreased enrollment at her school, Yessica was placed at another elementary school. Although the students at the new school were 90.1% Latino (Ed-Data, n.d.), Yessica was the only Latina staff member on campus.

The principal contacted TTO in October 2010 to indicate that Yessica needed "intensive support" with lesson plan design. TTO immediately assigned an instructional coach. One month later, the principal indicated that she was not seeing "significant improvements" in Yessica's instruction. The TTO manager, her coach, and the principal met to set up a rigorous coaching schedule that would begin in December.

In December, TTO's coach wrote, "As a result of our coaching session [Yessica] got excited and felt hopeful. She is a person who wants and needs encouragement and to feel that we believe in her, especially her principal. The kids do seem to love her and she loves them." However, as December continued, the increased level of support was overwhelming for Yessica. Soon, Yessica sent an e-mail to the TTO program manager stating, "I honestly don't feel comfortable . . . I have received negative and demoralizing comments that make me feel like no one believes in me."

In January 2011, the TTO program manager met with Yessica's principal, who indicated that she would begin the process for her to be non-reelected. The TTO program manager wrote,

> At issue is that Yessica is a native Spanish speaker from Oakland who was educated in the district where she works and has the same challenges as the students she is currently teaching. Because Yessica does not have Internet access at home, and is a single parent taking intern credential classes during the evening, she is working as hard as possible to respond to her principal's recommendations. Her coaches all applaud Yessica's classroom management, due in large part to the fact that she speaks the children's language and comes from Oakland. However, we must have supports in place for early career teachers who are under-represented in the teaching workforce. I spoke with Yessica's principal; she is moving forward with the probationary release because she is unwilling to allow Yessica to teach elsewhere in the district.

In April 2011, Yessica decided to fight the non-reelect notice. She contacted her union representative; met with several Latino community organizations and board members; received more than 50 letters of support from parents, children, and members of the school community; and took her students to speak on her behalf at a school board meeting. However, the district decided to abide by the principal's decision.

One year later, the TTO program manager saw Yessica at a local grocery store. She had completed her preliminary credential, was teaching in a neighboring district, and was working on her master's degree.

Profile 3

Charlotte, a young African American woman, applied to TTO after attending a recruitment fair. A graduate of Oakland schools, Charlotte went away to college and came back to Oakland to become a teacher. Charlotte scored extremely well with our all of our interviewers, adult observers, and children during the selection process. However, one colleague was concerned about her ability to teach given her tiny stature, soft demeanor, and non-European physical features.

Charlotte passed the mandatory teacher tests, enrolled in a credential program, and was sent on several interviews. Although she was well qualified, she did not have the look that principals wanted and was not hired at first. However, given that OUSD often has last-minute openings, Charlotte was placed as a long-term sub until a class opened.

Three weeks into the 2009–2010 school year and at the direction of the district, Charlotte was placed in a third/fourth-grade combination class in one of the city's poorest neighborhoods with a brand-new African American female principal. Because Charlotte had been placed on the district's overhire list, the principal was unable to actually choose someone; she had to take whoever was available. The second day Charlotte was in class, the principal called her regional officer demanding to know who "told this girl she could teach?" The principal wanted another candidate, but there was no replacement at that time. The TTO manager decided to send in a coach right away.

In addition to the TTO coach, Charlotte's university responded by sending in their intern supervisor to meet not only with Charlotte but also with the principal to hear her concerns. The intern supervisor noted several structural challenges within the school that certainly didn't help Charlotte toward success:

> Charlotte finally got an overhead, but no transparencies. She does not have math manuals. She noticed last week other teachers were getting benchmark tests; when she asked about hers, she was told her name wasn't on the list so research didn't send any. She has a non-English speaking boy who only speaks Mandarin and is not receiving any support. Charlotte does not know what to do. A Student Success Team meeting was held with one of Charlotte's children and she was not included. She was asked to take a class that one teacher had left after having an altercation; she didn't know the children and they were visibly upset. It was that class that the principal observed and asked to have Charlotte removed as a result of that visit. I'm trying to be as positive as possible.

The TTO manager visited Charlotte's class to offer some support. As they talked, she asked if Charlotte would be able to handle teaching in an environment where her principal was non-supportive. Charlotte said, "I'm not going to let her win. I'm going to prove her wrong."

Charlotte's principal submitted a non-reelect in February 2010. However, by March the principal wrote, "I would like to rescind my request to have Charlotte dismissed. She has improved tremendously."

Because of her amazing resilience, Charlotte was awarded TTO's first Teacher of the Year award in June of 2010. In the fall of 2013, entering her 5th year at the same school with the same principal, Charlotte had become the math lead teacher, had presented to her colleagues in the district around math at the elementary level, and had spoken extensively about race and equity at local conferences. Charlotte had cleared her teaching credential, was mentoring second- and third-grade TTO teachers, and was pursuing a master's degree in math education.

At the very core of the TTO program is its connection to the community as evidenced by its advocacy board, whose members are composed of task force conveners, school district board members, current and retired teachers, university faculty, nonprofit organization representatives, local business owners, and California assembly staff members. In fact, the TTO steering committee and the program manager cowrote the Transition to Teach grant that was funded for $2.3 million over 5 years, enabling an increase in staffing from one to two.

Lessons Learned

As of fall 2013, TTO had placed a total of 112 teachers; 25 of those left or received a probationary release. With a 78% retention rate overall, and 86% of those retained being teachers of color, we understand that this work is complex. In order to properly address the demographic imperative of recruiting and retaining a diverse and highly effective teaching workforce, programs must do more than host frequent recruitment sessions; programs must have the resources to prepare underrepresented teacher candidates as well as provide support for the teacher's first few years.

Diversifying the teaching workforce is a major imperative for all students. There is an unspoken assumption that students in predominantly White schools don't need teachers of color, but the reverse is actually true: White students also need to see people of color as holders of knowledge. With people of color in this country becoming a larger portion of the population (Yen, 2013), educators must send the correct message to all children: We can no longer accept that those who hold and deliver knowledge are predominantly young White women. As the profiles above indicate, diversifying the teaching workforce is not simply a recruitment issue. After several years doing this work, we have learned four valuable lessons:

1. Target recruitment for specific audiences.
2. Partnerships with universities are beneficial.
3. Support for candidates navigating the educational system is crucial.
4. Retention requires many layers.

Targeted Recruitment

In order to attract more people of color, it is necessary to use recruiters who reflect the cultural, linguistic, and racial diversity of the target group as well as to utilize networks that people of color already access. For example, both authors are African American with extensive networks in the African American community. When TTO wanted to increase the number of Latino applicants, it reached out to numerous community organizations that serve Latino communities. Using shared resources, TTO contracted with several people who had insider knowledge about the Latino community, local meeting places, and media outlets.

TTO's theory of action is that local teachers will remain in the classroom, thus improving their own skills and student outcomes. To that end, TTO asks for a 5-year commitment from participants. We also believe that teaching is a practice that requires time and diligence to perfect. Because TTO recruits locally, applicants make this commitment because they already live in the area, they are familiar with the children and the community, and many attended Oakland schools growing up. When a teacher sees his or her student at the neighborhood supermarket or local Target, that teacher becomes more than just the person at the front of the class; he or she becomes part of the child's community.

Partnerships With Universities

TTO has three university partners that participate in all aspects of the program. University personnel educate and supervise, but they also partner in ensuring retention and long-term success. As seen in Kirk and Charlotte's profiles, university supervisors, chairs, and credential analysts were deeply involved in advocating for them at the site and district level. The universities selected for partnership met a certain criteria; all have a history of supporting applicants of color and understanding the barriers these teachers face. Our collaboration is evidenced by TTO staff teaching credential courses; partnership meetings where support is triangulated between the site, TTO, and the university; TTO's streamlined university application process (in some cases, removing barriers to admission); and university participation in TTO's recruitment, interview, and selection process.

Supports for Navigating Barriers

TTO provides reimbursements for all expenses incurred on the journey to becoming a teacher; the average amount is more than $750 per person. In addition, TTO helps fast-track the process of applying and being enrolled in our partner university credential programs, provides free tutoring toward passage of mandatory teacher tests, provides resume and bio development, practices interviewing skills, and provides placement assistance within the district. Because there are no guaranteed placements for TTO candidates, TTO develops relationships with hiring managers, uses personal referrals, and acts as a liaison to the principals to ensure candidates are hired. As of June 2012, TTO has been placed within the Talent Acquisition Team, the recruiting arm of Oakland's Human Resources Services and Support department.

Retention Activities to Negate the Isolation Teachers of Color Will Ultimately Face

Even more than recruitment, the notion of retaining teachers, particularly those of color within urban districts, is multilayered. TTO's requirement of a 5-year commitment messages the importance of remaining in the classroom, and data indicate that making such a commitment is at least 50% of the reason why TTO teachers do remain in the classroom.

However, even those who want to remain in the classroom for 5 years have some challenges, as indicated by our profiles. Granted, not every person of color who wants to be a teacher is effective within the classroom; despite our best efforts, some teachers are encouraged to seek other ways to work with children outside of classroom of the profession. But those who do desire to remain teaching must learn to handle all of the challenges associated with teaching in a large urban district, one of which is the isolation associated with being a teacher of color.

Most TTO teachers face four challenging issues: (a) the assumption that they are less qualified than TFA candidates; (b) they don't meet the stereotype of what traditional teachers look like because they tend to be career changers and people of color; (c) many find themselves desegregating the site faculty; and (d) they must learn how to navigate their school structures, advocate for themselves, and keep the kinds of data that can change their principal's narrative if necessary.

To the district's credit, OUSD no longer partners with the New Teacher Project and has decreased its reliance on TFA over the past 5 years. What remains, however, is the assumption that TFA candidates are better prepared to teach in urban environments because they come from elite universities, are young, and are willing to work much harder. TTO helps to resolve this issue by developing relationships with hiring managers, demonstrating our commitment to supporting our candidates, and touching base with principals frequently. We have seen some growth; once a principal has hired an effective TTO teacher, he or she is much more likely to hire another, and we have some schools where TTO teachers are one-third of the faculty.

Although much has been written about teacher perceptions and race within teacher preparation programs (Joseph & Burnaford, 1994; Jussim, Eccles, & Madon, 1996; Solorzano & Yosso, 2001), there is little discussion around stereotypical notions of how teachers physically look (Weber & Mitchell, 1995). Seventy-one percent of teachers in America are White women (Feistritzer, 2011), so it may be difficult for some hiring managers to see teachers who look physically different as hirable.

The issue of isolation is at the heart of the retention issue. As evidenced in our profiles, many teachers of color find themselves the only one of their race and/or gender on campus. For Kirk's first placement, he was the only African American male, and one of few people of color. Yessica was the only Latina staff member.

To combat isolation, TTO provides several supports. First, teachers are brought into TTO as a cohort and encouraged to work with each other and share best practices. It is imperative that teachers of color reach out to each other and have the opportunity to share resources and support each other in their journey.

Second, TTO hosts monthly professional development sessions, led by TTO's senior teachers, as a vehicle for professional learning communities by subject matter and/or grade level. In this way, teacher–facilitators are developing leadership skills while also being recognized for their own pedagogy. Similarly, newer teachers understand and appreciate skill development around lesson planning, transitions, data management, and so on, from classroom teachers who are teaching in similar environments.

Third, TTO provides leadership sessions for third-year to fifth-year teachers in which they commiserate, share best practices, hold each other accountable for setting and working toward goals, and look intently at their own practice. These sessions are an invaluable way to ensure that TTO teachers' concerns are heard and shared in a way that doesn't usually happen for most teachers.

Fourth, research indicates that some hiring managers have perceptions of African American teachers as primarily classroom managers instead of curriculum specialists (Knaus, 2013; Milner, 2012). Some White hiring managers give professional development opportunities around content instruction to young White teachers while giving opportunities to demonstrate management techniques to African American teachers. To combat this racial bias, TTO supports teachers of color in keeping their own data, advocating for professional development opportunities, and marketing their successes to help provide a counterperspective for principals and other stakeholders.

We are now seeing the results of work begun by the Black Panthers in 1966, the Dellums administration's call for education task forces in 2007, and the development of TTO in 2008. We are proud of what has been accomplished but are constantly aware of the great amount of work that still needs to be done as highlighted through Charlotte's reflection:

> First, I was the youngest person on that campus. Second, I don't look like what people think of when they think "Teacher." Third, I started off really rough. But my University Supervisor and TTO kept me moving forward. Fourth, I spent a lot of time in prayer. But most of all, I knew I could do this. And not just do it, but do it well. I have always wanted to be a teacher in Oakland because our young people need someone they can relate to and know that this person has their best interest in mind. Too many of our

students fall between cracks and refuse to be a part of the continuum; a good education for me is power and falls on the responsibility of the family, the students, but most especially, the teacher.

Note

1 Although many states certify teachers as elementary or secondary, some states, such as California, distinguish between whether a teacher specializes in one subject area (usually high school teachers but may also include specialists such as art teachers) or multiple subject areas (usually elementary teachers, may also include middle school teachers).

References

Ed-Data. (n.d.). Retrieved from www.ed-data.k12.ca.us

Epstein, K. K. (2006). *A different view of urban schools: Civil rights, critical race theory, and unexplored realities* (Vol. 291). New York, NY: Peter Lang.

Feistritzer, C. E. (2011). *Profile of teachers in the US, 2011*. Washington, DC: National Center for Education Information.

Joseph, P. B., & Burnaford, G. E. (1994). *Images of schoolteachers in twentieth-century America: Paragons, polarities, complexities.* New York, NY: St. Martin's Press.

Jussim, L., Eccles, J., & Madon, S. (1996). Social perception, social stereotypes, and teacher expectations: Accuracy and the quest for the powerful self-fulfilling prophecy. *Advances in Experimental Social Psychology, 28,* 281–388.

Knaus, C. B. (2013). *Seeing what they want to see: leadership development in urban schools.* Unpublished manuscript.

Milner, H. R. (2012). Beyond a test score: Explaining opportunity gaps in educational practice. *Journal of Black Studies, 43,* 693–718.

Rogers-Ard, R., Knaus, C. B., Epstein, K. K., & Mayfield, K. (2013). Racial diversity sounds nice; systems transformation? Not so much! Developing urban teachers of color. *Urban Education, 48,* 451–479.

Seale, B. (1991). *Seize the time: The story of the Black Panther party and Huey P. Newton.* Baltimore, MD: Black Classic Press.

Solorzano, D. G., & Yosso, T. J. (2001). From racial stereotyping and deficit discourse toward a critical race theory in teacher education. *Multicultural Education, 9,* 2–8.

Sunderman, G. L., & Kim, J. (2005). *Teacher quality: Equalizing educational opportunities and outcomes.* Cambridge, MA: Civil Rights Project, Harvard University.

Weber, S. J., & Mitchell, C. (1995). *That's funny, you don't look like a teacher! Interrogating images and identity in popular culture.* Abingdon, Oxon, England: RoutledgeFalmer.

Wolman, P. J. (1975). The Oakland general strike of 1946. *Southern California Quarterly, 57,* 147–178.

Yen, H. (2013, June 13). TPMDayBreaker. *Talking Points Memo.* Retrieved from www.huffingtonpost.com/2013/06/13/minorities-in-america-census_n_3432369.html

3

CHANGING THE FIELD: TEACHERS OF COLOR MOVE INTO LEADERSHIP POSITIONS

Flynn Ross, Audra M. Watson, and Robert W. Simmons III

What difference can it make to have persons of color in teaching and leadership positions in schools? The presence of individuals who bring perspectives from different communities to our graduate classrooms, our faculty meetings, and our leadership team meetings changes the conversations, the narratives, and therefore the action plans. Identifying and supporting high quality teacher candidates who come from non-White racial and ethnic communities is essential and can take various forms. This chapter highlights the leadership of graduates from two programs that demonstrate a commitment to increasing the number of teachers of color in K-12.

United by a common vision of increasing the number of teachers of color in the United States, the Woodrow Wilson–Rockefeller Brothers Fund for Aspiring Teachers of Color program (WW-RBF) and the Newcomer Extended Teacher Education Program (NETEP) have worked in different ways. WW-RBF has significantly impacted the number of African American and Hispanic teachers in communities throughout the United States, while the NETEP has targeted recent immigrants representative of the immigrant populations in a federally designated immigrant and refugee resettlement community. Alumni of these programs have now been teaching for many years and are moving into leadership positions. This chapter tells a few of their stories and the ripple effects their presence has had in their communities.

In 1992, the Rockefeller Brothers Fund (RBF) created a fellowship for aspiring teachers of color. The fellowship, transferred to the Woodrow Wilson National Fellowship Foundation (WWNFF) in 2009, has supported 450 fellows as of 2012. The WW-RBF is a nationally competitive fellowship that is awarded to high-achieving individuals from 59 colleges or universities across the country. On their acceptance into the WW-RBF, they choose one of 29 graduate teacher preparation programs to attend, one of which is NETEP at the University of Southern Maine beginning in 2010. As they matriculate through their programs and their early years of teaching, the WW-RBF program brings fellows together twice a year as a cohort for support and networking.

While WW-RBF is a nationally focused effort, the NETEP is a localized effort that came about through a school–university partnership (see Chapter 6, this volume). The program has targeted culturally and linguistically diverse teaching candidates from the local immigrant communities since 2000. The WW-RBF supported four of the NETEP students between 2010 and 2014. The authors of this chapter, connected through their work in nominating, selecting, and preparing WW-RBF fellows, were moved to collaborate because of their mutual interests in advocating for the importance of teachers of color in our school systems and capturing how their presence as leaders has influenced their communities.

Alumni of NETEP

NETEP emerged from a long-standing school–university partnership in 2000. As a "grow your own" model (Haselkorn & Fideler, 1996; Skinner, Garreton, & Schultz, 2011) of teacher preparation, NETEP has been very successful, as described in Chapter 6.

Alumni of NETEP—immigrant teachers of color—have served as "gate openers" (Koerner & Hulsebosch, 1995; Ross, 2004), role models, advocates, and change agents. They have also experienced the frustrations of ignorance, bias, and discrimination as well as the supports of advocacy and affirmative action in various ways from the public school institutions in predominantly White communities where they work. Several were employed as paraeducators—language facilitators and community liaisons—prior to being certified teachers. These positions were explicitly designed so that these educators could serve as advocates, cultural brokers, and linguistic translators. As teachers, these immigrant teachers of color have opened gates by serving as community role models for their own children and the children within their religious and cultural communities. For example one high school physical science teacher, who also served as the director of the Saturday Koranic schools and as a past president of the local Islamic Society, made his classroom available for Muslim prayers at the school where nearly 15% of the student population was Muslim. He has shared how his very presence in department meetings has influenced some colleagues' comments about students as he quietly will question an assumption, contribute information about a family background, or inform about a cultural practice. He also regularly serves as a linguistic translator and cultural broker between school administration and immigrant families to address students' behavioral and academic needs.

The leadership that culturally and linguistically diverse teachers have provided in the schools is both explicit with leadership positions as well as subtle with the often unknown influence on students and colleagues. In Maine, the Whitest state in the nation, the NETEP and WW-RBF alumni were sometimes the first teachers of color in their school districts. One alumna shared, after her district's opening assembly, that the superintendent had announced that the district had "gone international." She was surprised to learn that the superintendent was talking about her as the new Spanish teacher from Brazil. Many of the alumni in Maine were inducted into schools with low social capital with regard to global education. At best, the schools did not facilitate teacher collaboration to capitalize on the multicultural knowledge of the new teachers. At worst, the new teachers experienced prejudice, negative attitudes from some colleagues, challenges in relating to White parents, and a sense of professional isolation (Basit & McNamara, 2004, cited in Achinstein & Ogawa, 2011, p. 25). The challenges to persisting as a new teacher of color are numerous, even beyond the testing hurdles, financial barriers for tuition, and workload as a profession (Ross, 2001). Barriers also include the racial stigma and biases that remain in our society, including multiple denied attempts to obtain administrator positions for several alumni. Yet the leadership within their teacher positions has influenced students, colleagues, parents, teacher educators, and even public policy.

Profiles of NETEP Teachers

Abdullahi fled Somalia in 1991 with the outbreak of civil war after having graduated from high school as a top-scoring public school student. He earned a bachelor of science degree in mining engineering from the University of Engineering and Technology in Peshawar, Pakistan, in 1999. He immigrated to the United States to Maine in 2000. In the fall of 2002, while working in the Portland Public Schools as a language facilitator, he began in NETEP. He completed the program in the spring of 2004 and was hired to teach physical science and math in middle school and later high school. He has been a very valuable teacher in the school, piloting Internet-based instructional supports to reach a wide variety of students and offering his classroom as a safe place in which Muslim students can pray. He completed his master's degree and is now a doctoral candidate at University of Maine, Orono, in educational leadership, where he is completing his dissertation on refugee parental involvement in schools. As of fall 2013, Abdullahi is the first certified teacher of Arabic in public schools in Maine. His students are an interesting mix of Somali students who have Koranic schooling and can recite Arabic, Iraqi students who can write in Arabic, and American-born students who are unfamiliar with the Arabic alphabet and pronunciations. These classes offer a unique democratic setting in which adolescents from across the globe work together to better understand each other.

In September 2013, the importance of well-educated, articulate leaders from all of our ethnic communities was again made apparent during the tragic mall siege in Kenya by members of al-Shabab. When American media reported on a tweet that identified one of the gunmen as coming from Maine, Abdullahi met with media and U.S. representatives to explain to the public that the Somali immigrants emigrated to escape violence and warn their children of al-Shabab. He also sought to assure the public that members of the Maine Somali community were not involved in recruiting members nor were they involved in the violence. Later the press confirmed what Abdullahi had said.

Elena, a NETEP alumna from 2010, was hired as the English Language Learner Coordinator for a consolidated rural district of eight towns. Elena emigrated from Russia and came to the United States to raise her sister after the early death of her parents. She was certified to teach middle and high school English and endorsed to teach English as a second language (ESL). She wrote the *Lau* Plan, the legal document delineating how to provide services for English language learners, in the newly formed district in her first few months on the job. Elena also created a global language awareness curriculum and presented workshops to mostly monolingual, White, rural students about the origins of the English language and language families. In addition, she worked to build bridges of unified heritage between the Spanish-speaking migrant students and students from both Asian and Slavic communities whose parents were medical professionals at the rural military base in their district.

Ina Demers taught for 2 years after graduating from NETEP but was not renewed as a full-time classroom teacher. Instead, she has continued on as an educational technician, volunteer ESL coordinator for adult education, and founder of a nonprofit organization providing conversational English classes in the community. Ina collaborates with university faculty to have college students volunteer in the conversational English classes and earn service-learning credit in their undergraduate programs. She has also been an active member of the Maine Educational Association and the Teachers of Color subgroup, an affiliate group created to support teachers and paraeducators of color and to advocate for families and children of color in a predominantly White state. She has been encouraged to look for teaching jobs in other districts due to the perception that she has been "Blacklisted" in the district in which she was not renewed. She says that she persists in this district because of her work as a cultural broker and translator for the Asian immigrant community and because of the parents who say, "What would we do without you?" Ina was raised and schooled in Indonesia where she was a cultural minority as the child of Chinese parents. She was not allowed to teach in the public schools in Indonesia because of her Chinese cultural heritage. The feelings of cultural discrimination have become a common fact throughout her life, as has the struggle against such discrimination.

Pamela Otunuu Porensky, the most recent NETEP graduate, has connections to both NETEP and WW-RBF. She and her family emigrated from Uganda when she was 5 to escape violence. Pamela attended Portland Public Schools and then the University of Southern Maine where she earned a bachelor's degree in business administration. Pamela became involved in schools through a National Association for the Advancement of Colored People (NAACP) research project in which she ran focus groups with students in a middle school. She learned about the WW-RBF program and eagerly applied. The fellowship provided her financial resources for graduate school that she would not have had otherwise as the mother of three young children. On graduation, Pamela was a highly sought-after candidate in a job market in which there are often 100 applicants for each teaching position. With a few job offers in hand, she chose a school district in a town with a recently closed military base that has a reputation for supporting the success of its teachers.

The WW-RBF Program

The WW-RBF is one of the few programs in the United States solely committed to recruiting and supporting people of color as teaching professionals. The program serves an important purpose as the nation's educational policy focus has been steadily trained on education reform policies over the course of multiple decades. Although there has been increasing emphasis on student achievement, teacher quality, and most recently on curriculum redesign, too little substantive discussion has been generated regarding the troubling homogeneity of the nation's teacher workforce. The WW-RBF program seeks to address the challenge of diversifying the teaching force.

In 2009 the RBF transferred its Aspiring Teachers of Color program to the WWNFF, widely known for recruiting and funding talented scholars in selected disciplines to address the nation's challenges. The resulting $5 million 6-year grant had an expectation that three new cohorts of fellows would be recruited, prepared, and mentored during their early years. Remarkably, four cohorts were possible, adding 82 new WW-RBF teaching fellows to the approximately 450 RBF fellows recruited nationally between 1992 and 2008. In addition to the 82 WW-RBF fellows, 88 fellows still in the process of completing their educational coursework were also transferred to the WWNFF from RBF in 2010.

An analysis of archival program data in 2013 reveals that among the fellows named between 1992 and 2009, slightly more than half were teaching in K-12 public school classrooms, and the other half held various administrative positions in public and private schools or school systems. Additionally, a small fraction of RBF fellows were employed in higher education as professors or were pursuing doctoral degrees in education. In its current iteration the program has continued to recruit the most talented students of color but is now aligned with the WWNFF and its other teaching fellowship programs. In accord with the guiding principles established in other WWNFF programs, fellows receive a $30,000 stipend to support a master's degree, teaching certification, and mentoring support during each of their first 3 years teaching in a high-need urban or rural school. Moreover, WW-RBF fellows are part of the foundation's commitment to not only transform teacher preparation but to increase the number of teachers of color.

In an effort to change teacher preparation, an RFP was issued to teacher education programs to nominate potential candidates and/or receive WW-RBF fellows. The 29 schools ultimately selected as receiving institutions offer intensive clinical experiences, are committed to diversifying their teacher candidate population, and are focused on preparing teachers to both thrive and impact achievement in high-need urban and rural K-12 schools. Program liaisons at the 59 nominating campuses are expected to identify academically gifted undergraduates for fellowship consideration. These faculty liaisons also mentor and shepherd students, if selected, through the graduate school application process.

Because the growing racial and ethnic diversity of the U.S. student population does not mirror the demographics of our nation's public school teachers, fellows associated with WW-RBF fill a needed gap in the teacher supply pipeline on a national scale. In stark contrast to the more localized approach of NETEP and other programs described in this book, WW-RBF fellows are engaged nationally in various educational enterprises. This certainly is not meant to suggest that this national effort supersedes local approaches, such as those described in several chapters of this book, or previous efforts in places like Detroit (Griot Program) or South Carolina (Call Me Mister), but simply that both approaches have an impact. Although there is widespread interest in increasing the number of teachers of color in American classrooms, the national discourse on teaching has largely consisted of a fixation on standards, test scores, and other elements tightly linked to the myopic neoliberal agenda, giving minimal attention and funding to efforts to diversify the teaching force.

In contrast, the WW-RBF teaching fellowship challenges the false dichotomy between diversity and teacher quality. Our experiences with four cohorts of WW-RBF teaching fellows, RBF transfer fellows, and RBF alumni reveal that when provided with financial and mentoring supports, smart and passionate students of color more readily enter the profession and stay. Although the newer cohorts of fellows have had fewer years in the classroom, what has been consistent about those selected both by RBF and Woodrow Wilson is that all fellows are playing important formal and informal leadership roles in classrooms, schools, and school districts. Aside from their leadership in a variety of contexts, Fellows also provide a sense of hope that other highly talented young people of color might enter teaching with the express purpose of grappling with the multiple structural inequities faced by economically disadvantaged students and students of color in urban public school systems. WW-RBF fellows offer the prospect of minimizing the opportunity gap and challenging educational inequities such as the overrepresentation of African American males in special education classes, the disproportionate rate of suspensions and expulsions for youth of color, and the increasingly robust school-to-prison pipeline.

What has become evident over the years of the WW-RBF program, from informal conversations and focus group data, is that numerous fellows have suggested that their own unequal educational experiences are the primary drivers of their sense of urgency about the needs and challenges of students of color in urban classrooms specifically. Although their presence in classrooms provides an opportunity for students of color to see themselves in their teachers, a significant number of fellows have spoken passionately about their attempts to ensure academic achievement (literacy, numeracy, and critical thinking skills) while simultaneously attending to the critical social issues that affect students' lives and communities. Despite much of the current education reform rhetoric, which speaks to an era of hyperaccountability and hyperstandardization, fellows view their positionality as something more than a test score and a narrowly focused curriculum—they see themselves as positive role models; knowledgeable conduits between the school community and communities of color; surrogate parents; and overall advocates for the social, moral, and academic development of children of color (Lewis, 2006; McCullough-Garrett, 1993; Milner & Howard, 2004). Running contrary to Charles Barkley's assertion that he "isn't a role model," these fellows understand that the role model mantle, desired or not, carries an obligation to open doors for their students while also being mindful of their actions in and outside of school. Certainly their presence provides role models for students of color, but a critical race theory perspective would suggest that their presence also serves to undermine the dominant narrative whereby White teachers constantly ride to the rescue of African American, Native American, and Latino youth in urban schools as portrayed in such films as *Dangerous Minds*, *Freedom Writers*, and *The Ron Clark Story* (Simmons, 2012).

In August of 2013, while participating in a convening, 13 WW-RBF fellows and RBF alumni who preceded them gathered to discuss teaching and their views on education. During our time together, several themes emerged. Fellows indicated that their missions revolve around an intense desire for students of color to believe, despite pervasive depictions to the contrary, that they are worthy and capable of intellectual pursuits. To accomplish this, WW-RBF fellows take on multiple identities and employ varied strategies. Specifically, coaching, facilitating, mining for information, and co-creating knowledge are central to their educational identities. They also explicitly teach habits of mind and critical thinking with the deep knowledge that these skills must not be reserved for a limited few. Simultaneously, it is not uncommon for fellows to use the term *activist* to describe the ways in which they interact with students. Some act as surrogate parents, providing food and/or listening as students share the events of their lives. Additionally, they advocate on behalf of what their students need and deserve and serve as cultural translators while helping students accrue social capital and adopt mindsets that will enable them to constructively name challenges and negotiate unfamiliar terrain. Perhaps the most profound and revolutionary aspect of how they view their roles as educators is their embracing of teaching as a political act. Having a deep understanding of the role that education has historically played in the lives of disenfranchised groups worldwide, all of the fellows engaged in this small group discussion viewed their work similarly. Although these abstractions, and the relevant data, provide a brief sketch of the program, a portrait of two successful fellows brings the program into a clearer perspective.

Profiles of WW-RBF Alumni

For fellows who are young men of color, the call to teach seems to have been particularly profound. Travis Bristol provides one example. Like many academically gifted African American male teachers, Travis hadn't initially considered teaching. Aware of the many career possibilities available to him, he intended to study law. It was the offer of funding from the RBF that changed his professional trajectory. Travis is illustrative of the first- and second-generation RBF fellows leading initiatives, which seek to ensure that young males of color have role models and advocates in schools that support both their academic and social development.

A graduate of Stanford University's Stanford Teacher Education Program, Travis began teaching freshman and sophomore English at a selective public school in New York City. Increasingly alarmed by the number of African American and Latino boys who were being referred to the dean, he created Eviscerating Emasculation, a program dedicated to providing a school-based outlet for young men of color. There were a few curious colleagues interested in his work; however, the principal was largely distant, including choosing not to attend a special event for the young men featuring former Mayor David Dinkins. Ultimately, Travis was recruited to teach at the Urban Assembly School of Law and Justice where he directed an even larger young men's initiative with principal support. The program featured a monthly speaker series and a vertical mentoring program partnering well respected seniors with "at-risk" freshman. Travis also understood the need to engage his teaching colleagues in his work and led them in community visits to make them more knowledgeable about the East New York community in which they worked. During his tenure as a teacher in New York City, Travis also worked closely as an advisor to City University of New York's Black Male Initiative, the New York City Department of Education's Young Men of Color Initiative, and interned at the World Bank. Currently, Travis is a clinical teacher educator for secondary English at the Boston Teacher Residency program. He has made it a priority to provide extra support to the teachers of color within the cohort while simultaneously completing his doctoral work on the intersection of race and gender in schools and prisons, at Teachers College.

Unlike Travis, Julian Braxton knew he wanted to teach early in life. Julian was a Pace College political science major and education minor, and an academic advisor for the RBF program nominated him. An unsuccessful endeavor to find a teaching position in the New York City Public Schools during the summer of 1994 led to an unanticipated career in independent schools through the Howard Hines Foundation Fellowship, which was seeking to recruit teachers of color into independent schools. The opportunity became a passion. In 1999, Julian began his graduate studies at the Harvard Graduate School of Education where he was able to channel his interest in policy and politics into coursework at the John F. Kennedy School of Government. Though Julian works with a different population than those he initially prepared to teach, he is emphatic that "these students needed to see me as one of many." He insists that independent schools' largely White student populations need experiences with teachers and educational leaders of color.

For more than a decade, Julian has been committed to engaging students in issues of diversity and equity. Now after more than 12 years as a history teacher and 10 years as the Director of Community and Multicultural Affairs, Julian is the Acting Assistant Head of School at Winsor Academy in Boston, Massachusetts. His leadership at the school has manifested in a multicultural curriculum and various initiatives aimed at community engagement. Finally, and notably, Julian is making a substantial impact regionally and nationally through his membership in Call to Action, a national think tank focused on diversity in independent schools, and as a member of the executive board of the Association of Independent Schools of New England—an organization at the forefront of what independent schools must do to prepare students for the 21st century.

Two Approaches, One Mission

Although these programs are situated in different geographic contexts, and the alumni have arrived at their decisions to become educators for a variety of reasons, one thing is very clear—they all view their work as more than an exercise in testing students, evaluating students, and operating as the sage on the stage. Aligned with bell hooks's (1994) assertion that "teaching was about service, giving back to one's community" (p. 2), our discussion of alumni from both programs shows they have impacted the lives of various communities. What is most significant is their commitment to equity and facilitating conversations and programs focused on diversity and equity-related issues. These efforts, beyond the classroom, provide ample evidence that both programs are not only impacting schools, but broader communities as well. Although we applaud their work and efforts, we acknowledge that there is still much to do.

The profiles in this chapter offer glimpses of the benefits of broader representation of cultural and linguistic diversities in our teaching force and educational leadership, but too often these teachers of color find themselves isolated. Imagine the power of having networks of leadership in schools that are representative of the student populations. The potential for understanding the needs of all students, adapting school structures and policies to be more inclusive, and inspiring all students to participate in a democratic public school system lies in the hands of an empowered teaching profession that is both representative and responsive. The ripple effects of a diverse teaching and leadership force have the potential to strengthen education for all students by fostering diverse, global perspectives to prepare our children for the 21st century.

References

Achinstein, B., & Ogawa, R. (2011). *Change(d) agents: New teachers of color in urban schools.* New York, NY: Teachers College Press.

Basit, T. N., & McNamara, O. (2004). Equal opportunities or affirmative action? The induction of minority ethnic teachers. *Journal of Education for Teaching, 30,* 97–115.

Haselkorn, D., & Fideler, E. (1996). *Breaking the class ceiling: Paraeducator pathways to teaching.* Belmont, MA: Recruiting New Teachers, Inc.

hooks, b. (1994). *Teaching to transgress: Education as the practice of freedom.* New York, NY: Routledge.

Koerner, M., & Hulsebosch, P. (1995, February). *Teaching to give students voice in the college classroom.* Paper presented at the annual meeting of the Association of Teacher Educators, Detroit, MI.

Lewis, C. (2006). African American male teachers in public schools: An examination of three urban school districts. *Teachers College Record, 108,* 224–245.

McCullough-Garrett, A. (1993). Reclaiming the African American vision for teaching: Toward an educational conversation. *Journal of Negro Education, 62,* 433–440.

Milner, H. R., & Howard, T. C. (2004). Black teachers, Black students, Black communities, and *Brown:* Perspectives and insights from experts. *Journal of Negro Education, 73,* 285–297.

Ross, F. (2001). Helping immigrants become teachers. *Educational Leadership, 58,* 68–71.

Ross, F. (2004). Teaching in a democracy: Learning from immigrants and refugees. *Maine Journal of Education, 20,* 29–32.

Simmons, R. (2012). Don't just talk about it be about it: The role of narrative and activism as a Critical Race Theorist. *PowerPlay: A Journal of Educational Justice, 4,* 217–224.

Skinner, E., Garreton, M., & Schultz, B. (Eds.). (2011). *Grow your own teachers.* New York, NY: Teachers College Press.

PART II

Teacher Education Programs: The Promise and Possibilities of Preparing a Culturally Diverse Teaching Force

4

CONTEXTUALIZING THE DEMOGRAPHIC IMPERATIVE: TEACHER EDUCATION FOR STUDENTS OF COLOR IN A RURAL COMMUNITY

Anne Burns Thomas and Mona Ivey-Soto

As chapters in this book demonstrate, teacher education programs designed to recruit and prepare teachers of color remain contested sites, often operating in isolation and lacking associated longitudinal research. One critical, but often overlooked, aspect of such programs is their context, specifically the impact of the university context and geographical location on the nature of recruitment and preparation programs for teachers of color. For the past 15 years, the State University of New York (SUNY) College at Cortland, a comprehensive college with a large teacher education program located in a rural area in central New York State, has operated a scholarship program designed to recruit and prepare students of color to become teachers in urban areas. The Cortland Urban Recruitment of Educators (C.U.R.E.) Program illustrates the importance of context for design and implementation of programs that aim to recruit and prepare higher numbers of teachers of color.

Much of the growing body of research about such programs focuses on those that operate at larger universities, particularly those located in urban areas. As problematic as it is to conflate recruiting high quality teachers for urban teaching and the lack of teachers of color, well-publicized and researched examples do exist (Achinstein & Ogawa, 2011; Ladson-Billings, 1999; Quartz, 2009; Villegas & Lucas, 2004). By comparison, research about programs to increase the number of teachers of color on rural college campuses and rural communities is scarce (Ayalon, 2004). In practice, the dual foci of the C.U.R.E. Program—to recruit students of color for teaching careers and to improve the preparation of prospective teachers for urban teaching—is seen as a single focus because of the nature of diversity and teacher education in this context. C.U.R.E. becomes the location for urban education at SUNY Cortland and also the perceived location for all teacher education students of color. This practice may be rooted in reality because, as

Achinstein and Ogawa (2011) reported, "53.6% of new teachers of color (in their first three years) were concentrated in urban schools as compared to just 27% of their White peers" (p. 24). The context of this small program makes both goals easier to segregate from the broader college. Important questions emerge from the lack of research about such programs: What is the value placed on a diverse teaching force in the midst of a university embedded in a rural, homogenous community? What is the relevance of a desire to increase the number of teachers of color in this setting? How is it understood, articulated, and supported?

To introduce the context of the C.U.R.E. Program, a brief description of SUNY Cortland is necessary. SUNY Cortland is located a 45-minute drive south of Syracuse, the closest urban center. Cortland is a rural area with a largely homogeneous, White population. Recent data from the Cortland County Community Action Program (2013) indicate that 95.1% of the county identifies as White. SUNY Cortland boasts the largest teacher education program in New York State, with 933 graduating students poised to become certified teachers each year. Student diversity at SUNY Cortland is low; figures from 2012 indicate that 3.4% of the student population identifies as Black/African American, 7.8% as Hispanic, and 0.2% as American Indian (SUNY Cortland Institutional Research and Analysis, 2012). Although tuition and housing costs have risen significantly in the past 10 years, Cortland remains an affordable option for many students and has a strong reputation for teacher education in the state. Another dimension to consider is faculty. Demographic data from 2012 indicate that SUNY Cortland has 13.8% faculty of color across campus. Within the School of Education where the C.U.R.E. Program resides and where the majority of teacher education students take courses, faculty of color make up only 6% of the total teaching faculty (see www2.cortland.edu/offices/hr/index.dot).

Within this context, the C.U.R.E. Program has been in operation since 1998. The program is small, offering 10 scholarships each year to students who are interested in teaching in urban areas; priority is given to students from groups underrepresented in teaching (defined as African American, Latino, and Native American) and students who meet limited income requirements. Students are eligible for the program once accepted to Cortland and enrolled in any program leading to teacher certification. Students are admitted following an application and interview process. C.U.R.E. scholarships cover more than 80% of tuition costs and are funded from a combination of sources: a private foundation, college funds, and individually funded scholarships. Since 2006, the college has funded a dedicated faculty line assigned as C.U.R.E. Program Administrator (three course releases per academic year) and one faculty assigned as C.U.R.E. Research and Follow-Up Coordinator (two course releases per academic year). On campus and in the broader community, the C.U.R.E. Program is understood as successfully increasing the number of teachers of color working in urban schools. Most recent data suggest that 92% of C.U.R.E. graduates have completed at least 2 years of teaching in urban districts, and more than 70% remain in urban teaching positions after 4 years. The data are striking when compared with national averages that describe a "revolving door" of teachers entering and leaving each year and about 20% of minority teachers leaving the profession each year (Ingersoll & May, 2011).

Given the relative success of the C.U.R.E. Program in recruiting, preparing, and supporting teachers of color for the complexities faced in their teaching placements, the program remains small and relatively unknown. Context here is critical. What does it mean to have a teacher education program for students of color that is such a small part of an institution that certifies close to 1,000 teachers every year? In part, it means that numerically speaking, the C.U.R.E. Program's impact on increasing the numbers of teachers of color is difficult to measure and even more difficult to use as a platform for growth. Equally important to understand are the theoretical and practical justifications for a program like C.U.R.E. In the next section, theories that underlie efforts to increase the number of students of color are examined, particularly in relation to the urban context.

Framing the Conversation

The theoretical framework guiding this chapter is critical race theory (CRT; Ladson-Billings & Tate, 1995), which maintains the salience of race as a factor in understanding inequity in education. From the foundation of the continued importance of race, Ladson-Billings and Tate (1995) argued that CRT is "a radical critique both of the status quo and the purported reforms" (p. 62). This framework requires the continued examination of practices and policies, even and especially those that are intended to remedy inequity. This book's introductory chapter elaborates on how, seen through the lens of CRT, the democratic imperative becomes a critical extension of efforts to recruit more teachers of color.

Critical examinations of traditional teacher preparation programs abound, particularly those that call attention to the ways in which programs fail to address preparation for urban schools or preparation for students of color (Irizarry, 2009; Ladson-Billings, 1999; Sleeter, 2008; Villegas & Lucas, 2004). Acknowledging the impact of these analyses that used anthropological, sociological, and race-based approaches, this analysis relies on CRT in order to, as Ladson-Billings (1999) argued, "move beyond both superficial, essentialized treatments of various cultural groups and liberal guilt and angst" (p. 241). This is especially important when researching programs that are seen as an effective response to the lack of diversity in the teaching force. If not for CRT's insistence on the futility of incrementalism to create real change, as explained in the introductory chapter, programs such as C.U.R.E. might seem sufficient, rather than as an opportunity for growth and more lasting changes.

Since the inception of the longitudinal research study in 2006, C.U.R.E. Program faculty have been presenting to conferences of teacher educators and teachers in an attempt to improve the program through continued inquiry. The most common response to presentations about the troubling issues of cultural match and the preparation of future teachers of color through C.U.R.E. has been that the program is fine, better than what most institutions do, and that C.U.R.E. students are, at the very least, thinking about culture. Although that response may be objectively correct, its orientation contributes to the perpetuation of the status quo, which is a lack of concern about the diversity of the teaching force in the vast majority of teacher education programs. As a framework for research, CRT creates space for rejection of this acceptance of the "good enough" program preparing the "good enough" teachers of color for urban schools.

Theories Informing Teacher Education for Students of Color

The demographic imperative rests on several arguments about the need for a racially and ethnically diverse teaching force. The *cultural match* argument holds that if students and teachers share a racial or ethnic background, the teacher may be better able to help students achieve academically (Gay, 2000; Villegas & Lucas, 2004). A collection of studies highlighted by Achinstein and Ogawa (2011) reported that teachers of color, when compared with White teachers, positively impact the following outcomes for students of color: standardized test scores, attendance, retention, advanced-level course enrollment, and college-going rates. The *culturally relevant pedagogy* argument, when connected with the cultural match argument, holds that teachers of color will be better able to implement curriculum and pedagogical approaches related to students from racial or ethnic backgrounds similar to their own (Cornbleth, 2008; Gay, 2000; Ladson-Billings, 1994). Cornbleth (2008) argued that the "credibility" of the arguments in favor of culturally relevant pedagogy "raises questions about why there is so little evidence of their incorporation into teacher education programs in the United States" (p. 147).

Critiques of both the cultural match and culturally relevant teaching arguments hold that a shared cultural background is no guarantee of academic success or relationships between teachers and students (Achinstein & Ogawa, 2011; Au & Blake, 2003). Achinstein and Ogawa (2011) found the reality of cultural match far from ideal in their research with Latino teachers and students; they argued, "Just being a person of color does not guarantee effectiveness in teaching students of color, nor do new teachers of color necessarily have knowledge of pedagogy for diverse students" (p. 15).

The C.U.R.E. Program is informed by ideas of cultural match and culturally relevant teaching, but the program's focus has been challenged by concerns about affirmative action in college programming. In 2004, college administrators were advised that admission criteria based solely on race could be problematic in light of the 2003 U.S. Supreme Court ruling related to race-based admission to colleges and universities. Admission criteria for the C.U.R.E. Program were expanded to include an income-based priority. In practice, this has resulted in the program's original intent being diluted because several White students were admitted since the realignment of admission criteria. The context of the college means that the overwhelming majority of students applying to SUNY Cortland, and therefore eligible for the scholarship, are White. For a program that was designed to increase the number of teachers of color prepared at SUNY Cortland, this decision negatively impacted the already small number of prospective teachers of color who were recruited through the scholarship. The C.U.R.E. Program's ability to prepare new teachers who were a good fit for urban schools on the basis of cultural match or culturally relevant pedagogy was challenged.

When the C.U.R.E. Program was founded, there were serious teacher shortages in most urban districts in New York State. Even though there is no longer a strictly numerical teacher shortage (because of policies and programs such as New York Teaching Fellows and other alternative certification programs), the demographic imperative remains. Cross (2005) argued, "Grounding teacher education reform in multiculturalism, diversity and urban education—frequently accepted as soft, safe code words (contrasted to racism, White privilege, and power)—has led subsequently to only moderate advances in preparing teachers for racially diverse classrooms" (p. 265). In some ways, the C.U.R.E. Program's dual focus on increasing teachers of color and addressing urban teacher shortages allows the two ideas to be conflated. Conversations about the salience of race and the lack of student and faculty diversity on campus are difficult, and focusing on providing high quality teachers for urban schools can provide a screen for other, more difficult decisions.

Reflecting a broader understanding of the need for a more racially and ethnically diverse teaching force, a third argument rests on the *democratic imperative*, articulated by Sleeter and Milner (2011) in this way: "Teachers of color are valuable to the teaching profession, not only because students of color benefit but all students can benefit from what the teachers bring into the learning environment" (p. 83). Although it seems obvious, the need for teachers of color for all schools has not been embraced widely. The democratic imperative calls for a recast of all teacher education programs to recruit and prepare teachers of color for all schools, a daunting but highly necessary and appropriate action.

Program Elements in Context

The C.U.R.E. Program was founded from a desire to address the demographic imperative and recruitment of students of color to the college. Stemming from an interest by a former college president, the program was intended to recruit, prepare, and support new teachers of color to work in urban school districts in New York State. From its inception, it was informed by three key tenets of culturally relevant teaching (Ladson-Billings, 1994): academic achievement, cultural competence, and critical consciousness. In the following sections, we discuss these components of the C.U.R.E. Program, highlighting ways that the rural location and context shape the experience for program participants. Using CRT and theories underlying the demographic imperative, we discuss critical aspects of the program that serve to illustrate the constraints and affordances of a rural, homogeneous campus and community context.

Academic Achievement

Students who are accepted into the C.U.R.E. Program are required to take three courses in issues related to urban education alongside courses that are required by their major for certification. The three courses, Introduction to Urban Education; Race, Class, and Gender in Education; and Exploring Education With an Urban Focus, are intended to support a developmental perspective and understanding of urban education. At Cortland, these courses are required for students of only one major outside of C.U.R.E. and are not widely taken by students from other teacher certification programs, a structure that results in a specific kind of isolation for both the C.U.R.E. students as prospective teachers of color and the urban education issues on campus.

The introductory course, taken during students' first semester enrolled in C.U.R.E., is unique on campus in that it requires a 30-hour field experience in an urban school that the students complete as a cohort. Long recognized by graduates and faculty as a powerful component of the program, this field experience requires special funding for transportation to Syracuse schools and special scheduling for students to complete the block of hours, reflecting the continued commitment of the college to the C.U.R.E. Program. However, the "special" nature of the course calls to mind Nieto's critique of English as a second language programs as housed in school basements (Nieto, 2002). Though the lens of CRT, the C.U.R.E. coursework, as a "purported reform" (Ladson-Billings & Tate, 1995) can be seen as an obstacle that further isolates the teachers of color on campus. An extremely limited number of students each year are involved in a course that echoes many calls for reform in teacher education, with a clinically rich field experience supported by full-time faculty in the school and at the college.

Research about the C.U.R.E. Program has also led to the realization that the coursework required of students is fairly traditional, mirroring in many ways the courses offered to students to fulfill a diversity requirement at other teacher education institutions. Why, when the students of color are understood to bring so many resources to teaching in terms of cultural match and culturally relevant teaching, are they required to take courses that do not build from those strengths? Ladson-Billings (1999) argued that CRT helps to expose the ways that current instructional practices are based in a deficit perspective about students of color. If not a deficit perspective, then the structure of C.U.R.E. courses seems to reflect a blind spot when it comes to curriculum design building from students' strengths.

This blind spot is further exposed when data are analyzed about C.U.R.E. students' initial field experiences in urban schools through this course. Far from a cultural match, most C.U.R.E. students express dismay at the placement and identify very strongly with the teachers (a vast majority of whom are White). A recent C.U.R.E. graduate described this phenomenon in an early reflection paper:

> I look at the kids and I just don't see me. I know I am supposed to because of C.U.R.E., but I don't. I was the good girl who always paid attention and did what I should. I was the one getting annoyed at all the other Black kids and Brown kids around me for doing what they shouldn't.

These sentiments are echoed among many 1st-year C.U.R.E. students, especially those who do not attend urban schools before coming to Cortland. The assumption of cultural match downplays the significance of economic background and prior school experiences, in effect essentializing culture in ways that are not borne out by experience.

Another component of the C.U.R.E. Program's approach to academic excellence that deserves interrogation is the process of providing academic support to students. As a primarily grant-funded program, the academic performance of C.U.R.E. students is an important measure of success. Students who are accepted into the C.U.R.E. Program participate in a competitive scholarship process, including a rigorous interview conducted by several faculty members, and they typically earn a semester grade point average of 3.2, which is much higher than the campus average and above that required for all teacher education programs. Students are required to receive an evaluation from the campus learning support office and to attend weekly meetings with the C.U.R.E. graduate assistant during their 1st year on campus. Although students point to these meetings as beneficial during exit interviews, there are certain deficit perspectives that are evident in this measure. Why are these students assumed to need academic support in order to be successful in college? Again, context is an important factor here because C.U.R.E. students are often the only students of color in many of their courses. C.U.R.E. faculty and staff have numerous interactions with other faculty on campus about the academic performance of students of color. Ironically, some interactions occur when a faculty member approaches C.U.R.E. staff about a student of color, only to be surprised that the student in question is not actually in the program. In the context of this campus, teacher education students of color are assumed to be part of the special program for urban education. Often, there are concerns about students' written and spoken language, which are seen to be substandard. For C.U.R.E. students who speak another primary language, faculty have expressed concerns about how these students will become effective teachers. While expectations for academic achievement are high, the students of color in C.U.R.E. continue to be viewed through a deficit lens, which is a result of the unexamined impact of the context on the program goals and design.

Cultural Competence

Irizzary (2009) pointed to the importance in teacher education of what he called "representin'," or developing a shared sense of responsibility and identity based on membership in a community. At SUNY Cortland, this shared identity is clear in the informal slogan of the Educational Opportunity Program (EOP), "We all we got." In EOP, another location with a high percentage of students of color on a predominantly White campus, shared identity and community are a significant source of student support. In the C.U.R.E. Program, attempts are made to balance the need for students to build cultural competence and the demands of teacher education programs that call for multiple classroom and co-teaching assignments with peers outside of C.U.R.E. Students support each other when diversity, multiculturalism, and urban education are denigrated and when they feel like the sole representatives of diverse points of view. As a C.U.R.E. alumna stated in her exit interview, her cohort "helped me deal with some of the issues that we [as students of color] were going to face at college, at Cortland, and without C.U.R.E., it would have been unbearable." In some ways, though this is the type of support that was envisioned by C.U.R.E. Program founders, reliance on peer comfort and coping strategies keep college administrators in the dark about the difficulties that students of color routinely face.

The isolation and discrimination that students of color experience in college and particularly in teacher education (Milner, 2010) is well documented. *Institutional insensitivity* is defined as "a pattern of collective behavior, which results in negative outcomes for students of color" (Taylor, 2011). A very real and present example of this would include recruiting students of color to a campus but providing limited programming to support their experiences once they have arrived. The standard curriculum present and deeply embedded at predominately White institutions often provides a very general overview of multicultural contributions and does not personalize this research such that the campus community would respond with any urgency. Within teacher education, there is often a stand-alone diversity course that often is not even required for all education students and may not provide a field experience that allows preservice students to engage in the content in a real and meaningful way. Less well understood, though, are the ways in which programs designed to support students of color serve to isolate them while providing a protective cover for the institution. If C.U.R.E. students were not encouraged to develop a strong peer network and if they were not supported by program faculty and staff, more attention might be paid to the issues facing students of color in teacher education at SUNY Cortland. In this context, the ways in which students support one another, build shared identity, and develop responsibility all serve to reinforce the status quo.

Critical Consciousness

The C.U.R.E. Program reflects a strong belief in the importance of teachers as critically conscious activists and has long encouraged student leadership to promote a vision of teaching as actively engaging with issues of social justice. In practice, this results in a requirement that students participate in one campus club or activity that is related to diversity or education. At Cortland, the very low numbers of students of color result in the same students participating in most of the multicultural life clubs and activities. Because C.U.R.E. students are encouraged through coursework, mentoring, and field experiences to develop a critical consciousness about becoming teachers of color, they often become troubled about the isolated nature of the program in this rural community. Although the Conceptual Framework for Teacher Education at SUNY Cortland promotes an understanding of social justice teaching, C.U.R.E. students often find themselves cast as spokespeople for concerns relating to students of color and urban education.

For example, C.U.R.E. students have to advocate for themselves and the goals of the program by securing field experiences in high-needs schools to fulfill the requirements of their major. Students report confronting concerns from other faculty and staff that they will not witness high-quality teaching in urban schools; that the hassle of transportation to and from Syracuse will become a burden; and that their request to be placed in urban schools, where other teacher candidates are not placed, interferes with program co-teaching or cohort models. As has been widely researched, students of color are often seen as representatives of ideals of diversity and social justice in overwhelmingly White teacher education programs (Irizarry, 2009; Villegas & Lucas, 2004). Here, C.U.R.E. students are forced to become advocates for urban field experiences in opposition to a community that often fails to recognize the importance of these placements. Although these experiences do help C.U.R.E. students to develop and practice skills of activism, it remains troubling to require students of color to take on this responsibility.

Directions Forward: Making Context Matter

Achinstein and Ogawa (2011) argued,

> While research suggests that teachers of color may have a particular ability to address the education needs of students of color by performing as role models, teaching in culturally and linguistically responsive ways, and thereby acting as agents of change . . . the presence of teachers of color is not sufficient.

(p. 5)

The C.U.R.E. Program has been successful at increasing the presence of teachers of color within the context of a rural university with a largely homogeneous student, faculty, and community population. The lens afforded by the framework of CRT and the democratic imperative suggest the need for a shift in the orientation of the C.U.R.E. Program that is underscored by the rural university context in which the program exists. Far from isolating efforts to recruit and prepare teachers of color to work with students of color in urban schools, the program should be expanded to increase the potential impact of both program foci. In the following paragraphs, we outline ways in which we can move beyond a mere presence to more fully embrace and enhance the democratic possibilities that can result from a program such as C.U.R.E.

The faculty members involved in the C.U.R.E. Program recognize that students of color bring a unique set of strengths, ideologies, and frameworks to teacher education programs. As Sleeter's (2001) review found and our experience reveals, students of color generally bring richer experiences and perspectives to multicultural teaching than do most White students, who dominate numerically. With this in mind, how can faculty examine the C.U.R.E curriculum and position prospective students of color as content experts and deliverers of critical knowledge? How can faculty step back from positions of power and encourage students to create learning opportunities for C.U.R.E. students and other teacher education students across campus? Although faculty associated with the C.U.R.E. Program can begin to identify these places and spaces in need of change, it is all too common for other teacher education faculty to feel isolated and disconnected from the highly rigid and routinized practice within teacher education programs. Creating space for open dialogue that helps to activate the prior knowledge and rich educational experiences that C.U.R.E. students bring will help to move the teacher education curriculum and the program overall to a more authentic place.

The ways in which the rural context of Cortland's campus impacts the community of students in C.U.R.E. are complex and not yet fully understood. The program's insistence that students preparing to become teachers understand and experience the urban context, while ignoring the local community, is misguided and continues to perpetuate many of the issues articulated here. It is tempting to say that additional research is required, but, in fact, a rethinking of the program's isolation on campus and from the broader community is going to require a more comprehensive, inclusive approach.

By combining the purposes of recruiting students of color for teacher education and urban teacher preparation, a valuable opportunity to promote the democratic imperative (Sleeter & Milner, 2011) for *all* students has been lost. Because of the campus and community context, the C.U.R.E. Program is uniquely positioned to develop closer relationships with nearby rural school districts. C.U.R.E. Program faculty can increase awareness of the need for teachers of color in rural districts while supporting prospective teachers of color through field experience opportunities. This will be a new undertaking for SUNY Cortland faculty and staff because until recently, both increasing the focus on urban education and recruiting teachers of color have been allowed to exist in isolation, as if each could only exist to serve the other.

By being explicit about the context of teacher education at SUNY Cortland, students can be encouraged to advocate for increased emphasis on diversity and diverse field experiences for all prospective teachers. In 2010, a small group of C.U.R.E. students revived the Urban Education Club by appealing to the Student Government Association for reinstatement. The student advocates were disturbed by questions from Student Government Association members about why urban education was important, what kind of students would join such a club, and what good could come from becoming involved in urban schools and with urban students. This was a powerful opportunity for students to practically experience the importance of the homogeneous context of the campus community and to understand that most of the general student population did not understand the importance of equity and social justice in education. The C.U.R.E. Program must continue to support students as we push for the importance of teachers of color in all districts, a concept that will undoubtedly leave some campus and community members uncomfortable.

In the recent past, increasing the number of teachers of color was designated as the work of a small number of teacher education programs and communities, mainly located in urban areas. The rural context was seen as a limitation of our program, rather than what we now come to see as a remarkable strength. We approach the work to come in truly embracing the democratic imperative with many more questions than answers, but we believe that intentional interrogation of the impact of the college context on preparing teachers of color has the potential to lead to real and lasting improvements.

References

Achinstein, B., & Ogawa, R. (2011). *Change(d) agents: New teachers of color in urban schools.* New York, NY: Teachers College Press.

Au, K., & Blake, K. (2003). Cultural identity and learning to teach in a diverse community. *Journal of Teacher Education, 54,* 192–205.

Ayalon, A. (2004). A model for recruitment and retention of minority students to teaching: Lessons from a school–university partnership. *Teacher Education Quarterly, 31,* 7–23.

Cornbleth, C. (2008). *Diversity and the new teacher: Learning from experience in urban schools.* New York, NY: Teachers College Press.

Cortland County Community Action Program. (2013). *2013 community assessment.* Retrieved from www.capco.org/images/stories/pdfs/CAPCO%20community%20assessment%20 2013.pdf

Cross, B. E. (2005). New racism, reformed teacher education and the same ole' oppression. *Educational Studies, 38,* 263–274.

Gay, G. (2000). *Culturally responsive teaching: Theory, research, and prac*tice. New York, NY: Teachers College Press.

Ingersoll, R., & May, H. (2011). *Recruitment, retention, and the minority teacher shortage.* Philadelphia and Santa Cruz: Consortium for Policy Research in Education, University of Pennsylvania, and Center for Educational Research in the Interest of Underserved Students, University of California, Santa Cruz.

Irizarry, J. (2009). Representin': Drawing from hip-hop and urban youth culture to inform teacher education. *Education and Urban Society, 41,* 489–515.

Ladson-Billings, G. (1994). *The dreamkeepers: Successful teachers of African American children.* San Francisco, CA: Jossey-Bass.

Ladson-Billings, G. (1999). Preparing teachers for diverse student populations: A critical race theory perspective. In A. Iran-Nejad & D. P. Pearson (Eds.), *Review of research in education: Vol. 24. Toward a new science of education* (pp. 211–247). Washington, DC: American Educational Research Association. doi:10.3102/0091732X024001211

Ladson-Billings, G., & Tate, W. F. (1995). Toward a critical race theory of education. *Teachers College Record, 97,* 47–68.

Milner, H. R., IV. (2010). *Start where you are, but don't stay there: Understanding diversity, opportunity gaps, and teaching in today's classroom.* Cambridge, MA: Harvard Education Press.

Nieto, S. (2002). *Language, culture, and teaching: Critical perspectives for a new century.* Mahwah, NJ: Erlbaum.

Quartz, K. H. (2009). The careers of urban teachers: A synthesis of findings from UCLA's longitudinal study of urban educators. In M. Bayer, U. Brinkkjær, H. Plauborg, & S. Rolls (Eds.), *Teachers' career trajectories and worklives: An anthology.* Philadelphia, PA: Springer.

Sleeter, C. (2001). Preparing teachers for culturally diverse schools: Research and the overwhelming presence of Whiteness. *Journal of Teacher Education, 52,* 94–106.

Sleeter, C. E. (2008). An invitation to support diverse students through teacher education. *Journal of Teacher Education 59,* 212–219.

Sleeter, C., & Milner, H. R., IV. (2011). Researching successful efforts in teacher education to diversify teachers. In A. F. Ball & C. A. Tyson (Eds.), *Studying diversity in teacher education* (pp. 81–104). New York, NY: Rowman & Littlefield.

SUNY Cortland Institutional Research and Analysis. (2012). *Enrollment facts.* Retrieved from www2.cortland.edu/about/facts-figures/enrollment-facts.dot

Taylor, C. (2011). *Ten problems that students of color face on predominately White campuses.* Retrieved from www.diversitybenefitseveryone.com/tenproblemsthatstudentsofcolor-faceoncampus.html

Villegas, A. M., & Lucas, T. (2004, April). Diversifying the teacher workforce: A retrospective and prospective analysis. *Yearbook of the National Society for the Study of Education, 103,* 70–104.

5

THE TURNING POINT OF ONE TEACHER EDUCATION PROGRAM: RECRUITMENT, PREPARATION, AND RETENTION OF DIVERSE TEACHER CANDIDATES

Omiunota N. Ukpokodu

As a multicultural teacher educator in an urban institution, my priority and commitment have been toward preparing a cadre of teachers who are highly competent to foster effective educational experiences for diverse students. About 8 years ago, I had the privilege of becoming a part of a historic and defining experience in the institution of a one-of-a-kind urban teacher education program. In this chapter, I examine the historic turning point of my institution's bold effort—an out-of-the-mold intervention—to evolve an urban-focused teacher education that recruits, prepares, and retains diverse teacher candidates for successful teaching in urban schools.

Historically, universities were designed to serve the people of their communities. In their traditional role, universities prepare students for economic and political engagement in their communities and society in general. Besides this, a desired but rarely recognized or acted-upon role of universities is their responsiveness to local communities and especially their ability to link their resources and support for the community's K-12 public schools where the young are educated. Many universities are located within urban communities, and so they share space with school districts. This begs many questions: How good is a university in an urban community whose schools graduate only 40% of its students and where fewer than 15% of students perform at the "Proficient" level and none perform at the "Advanced" level? How good is a university whose major school district is stripped of its accreditation because of failure to meet acceptable standards? What happens when that university becomes a major driver in reforming the community's public school education? What happens when it commits to fully engage and partner with the community to reform its ailing schools and prepare a cadre of teachers who can teach in urban schools? This is the story I unpack in this chapter. The chapter is written in hopes that it will inspire and encourage other universities, especially those in urban communities, to engage in similar transformational endeavors.

The chapter discusses the complex historical and sociopolitical forces that shaped the racialized, hegemonic, and acrimonious relationships between the university and the urban community, including its public schools. Specifically, it focuses on (a) the historical and transformative context of the University of Missouri–Kansas City's (UMKC) urban-focused teacher education; (b) the university's campuswide collaborative "interdisciplinary institute" that birthed the urban-focused teacher education; (c) the strategies used to recruit, prepare, and retain diverse urban teacher candidates and the effectiveness of those strategies; (d) the program's structure; and (e) the lessons learned and the implications for teacher education and for nurturing a diverse and high-quality teacher preparation. The chapter is significant in that it highlights the critical role the university, not just the school of education, plays in leading revolutionary reforms for teacher education and K-12 public school transformation. Specifically, it conceptualizes a collaborative partnership model that engages the university's chancellor, provost, and various academic units; the city mayor; community leaders; and communities of color.

Historical Perspective

In 2005, UMKC made a historic shift when it launched its urban-focused teacher education, commonly known as the Institute for Urban Education (IUE) that is located within the UMKC School of Education (SOE). Initially established as the University of Kansas City in 1933, UMKC today is a comprehensive research university with an enrollment of approximately 16,000 students as of the fall semester of 2013, located in a large diverse urban community. Historically, relations between UMKC and the metropolitan urban community were not cordial, especially with marginalized minority groups. The university was "segregated and exclusionary—literarily closed off to the minority populations" (Ukpokodu, 2010, p. 30). This situation had its roots as far back as the era of racial segregation, where strict race-based housing and school segregation were lived realities. The city was known for its redlining of neighborhoods and racialized spaces whereby racial minorities, particularly African Americans, were restricted to the east side and Whites to the west side of the city. As a result, Troost Avenue was redlined as "the racially identifiable school attendance boundary" (Gotham, 2002b, p. 25) and became known as the "Troost wall" or Troost line" (Gotham, 2002a, p. 18). African American students attended substandard schools east of Troost where educational opportunities were limited, while White students attended high-quality schools west of Troost. In fact, Massey and Denton (1993) identified Kansas City as one of the most "hypersegregated metropolitan areas in the nation" (p. 75). Even after race-based school segregation was declared unconstitutional following the *Brown vs. Topeka Board of Education* court case, the Kansas City, Missouri, school district continued to maintain de facto segregation that limited educational opportunities for African American children.

As a reflection of the era, UMKC, a predominantly White institution, was not immune from racial segregation and social stratification. Until recently, UMKC did not engage in efforts to challenge educational inequalities in the urban community, including the school district and its struggling schools. The prevailing belief among the minority community was that UMKC, including its SOE, engaged in racist and segregative practices. Admission and enrollment of students of color were rare. In the late 1990s, through a grant opportunity, the SOE was briefly able to offer a program known as Paraprofessional Evolving Into Teaching, which provided for the recruitment and preparation of one cohort of teacher candidates of color who were paraprofessionals in the urban school district. With that exception, however, for the most part, like many other schools and colleges of education, the UMKC teacher education program has been demographically homogeneous.

For decades, the Kansas City community and the Kansas City, Missouri, school district criticized UMKC for lack of responsiveness to the needs of the community and the crisis in its schools. The school district, with its large population of low-income students and students of color who are predominantly African American and Latino American, has consistently underperformed academically. Low graduation rates, among other unsatisfactory outcomes, resulted in the state department of education stripping the school district of its accreditation in the early 1990s. In 1995, the graduation rate of high school students in the district was 33% (Swanson, 2009). In 2002, fewer than 2% of sophomores scored at Advanced or Proficient levels in math. In 2010, 80% of the students (26,078 in public and charter schools) did not meet the state's standard of academic performance (Kauffman Foundation, 2010). The district has also been disturbingly unpopular for its high teacher and administrator turnover. Within 4 decades, more than two dozen of the school district's superintendents went through a phenomenon that Ingersoll (2001) called the "revolving door." This begs the question: How can a university with a supposedly urban mission assess its worth given the dismal achievement realities of this school district?

UMKC and the Turning Point

By 1998, the negative relations between UMKC and the local community had intensified. The interim chancellor and the university community knew they had to change and that the change had to happen quickly. In 1999, the university established the Urban Mission Task Force that comprised several committees, including the community education committee. The education committee recommended and called for the creation of "an interdisciplinary campus institute," with its central mission to address the educational issues of children and youth in the urban community. In 2000, the university appointed a new chancellor who embraced the transformative mission the university had begun. The chancellor encouraged a series of transformation activities, including focus-group conversations with faculty and staff and with the Kansas City community that included the mayor, the Urban League, and communities of color (especially the African American and Latino American communities), which resulted in what was known as the "chancellor's blueprint for the future." The chancellor's blueprint had as its primary goal redefining the university's institutional mission: to develop a professional workforce that serves the community and collaborates with the community to solve its problems, including the local school districts' educational needs.

In 2002, following the chancellor's lead, the dean of the UMKC SOE and its faculty also engaged in series of focus-group conversations with the African American and Latino American communities and three urban school district superintendents. The dean issued a statement to underline working collaboratively: "The School of Education will work together with the urban community to eliminate the achievement gap between black and white, poor and affluent, urban and suburban" (Waddell & Ukpokodu, 2012, p. 16). By 2003, the chancellor had set up steering and advisory committees composed of internal and external groups to begin work on the urban education project. By 2004, the idea of the IUE, a collaborative-based interdisciplinary campus institute, was born. Processes for operationalizing the institute were put in place, including the appointment of the institute's staff and the establishment of the Writing and Design Teams. As an SOE faculty member with a focus on diversity and multicultural education, I served on both teams.

Given that the traditional SOE teacher education had not boldly focused on urban teacher preparation, the Writing Team specifically evolved both vision and mission themes that were urban focused, adopting the theme "to prepare exemplary teachers for urban education" and the following vision statement: "UMKC will be nationally recognized for preparing exemplary educators who are successful change agents in urban settings." These helped in the creation of the mission statement: "The IUE will partner with the community to prepare exemplary educators for urban school settings; exemplary educators who are change agents with demonstrable cultural, pedagogical, subject matter, and interpersonal competencies" (SOE Writing Team Report, 2004). By the end of 2004, the program had been embraced and supported by the university at large. A chancellor's national advisory board was constituted and composed of well-known national educators and scholars, the university trustees, local philanthropic groups, and community agency and leaders from the communities of color—local chapters of the National Association for the Advancement of Colored People and La Raza—that provided moral or financial support.

The primary focus of the IUE was to recruit, prepare, and retain diverse teacher candidates who possess knowledge and understanding of the realities of the local community—"funds of knowledge" (Moll, Amanti, Neff, & González, 1992). The IUE reasoned that the best hope of placing highly competent teachers in urban classrooms was to recruit and train those who understand the needs and realities of the community—teacher leaders who are willing to give back to the community and who will be "dreamkeepers" (Ladson-Billings, 2009) and "star teachers" (Haberman, 1995).

The IUE: An Overview

The IUE is a 4-year cohort-based undergraduate degree program in elementary and middle school education with a focus on math, science, and literacy. The program began in fall 2005. At its conception, the program was approached boldly, strategically, and collaboratively. Partnerships were forged with several businesses and partner school districts within the metropolitan urban community. Interdisciplinary curricula and rigorous courses were developed collaboratively between faculty of the SOE and the College of Arts and Sciences. Given the urban focus and mission, the program's conceptual framework was grounded on a sociocultural and sociopolitical construct with a focus on multicultural education and culturally responsive and social justice pedagogy. Participating faculty members of the design and writing teams developed and teach program courses.

Recruitment

From the outset, the program's target population is teacher candidates from underrepresented groups, particularly high school students of color from urban schools, first-generation college students, and others with an urban life and schooling experience (Haberman, 2005; Weiner, 2000). Although teacher candidates are recruited from across the nation (candidates have come from as far as North Carolina and Florida), a significant proportion of the recruitment comes from the local urban communities—high school graduates from the three Kansas City urban school districts—who are mostly racial minorities and first-generation college students. Teacher candidate recruitment is deliberate, systematic, intentional, and innovative. The program works closely with the urban partner school districts. Applicants are carefully selected through a rigorous, competitive process that involves essay writing and on-campus interview using the Haberman "Star Teacher Pre-Screener" (Haberman, 2006). Over the years, the selection requirement has been broadened to include a video response to the prompt, "Why do you want to become a teacher in an urban school?" (Waddell & Ukpokodu, 2012, p. 17)

Realizing the difficulty in recruiting teacher candidates of color into teaching and the need to attract highly qualified candidates, the IUE task force committee recommended the provision of substantive scholarship support for successful applicants. Initially, teacher candidates received full funding—tuition, housing, and supplies—through their years of matriculation. Successful teacher candidates sign a contract to teach in the local partner urban school district for at least 4 years after graduation. Between the program's inception in 2005 and 2012, four cohorts with a total of 52 students have been successfully prepared. Ninety-four percent of students from the first three cohorts obtained teaching positions, and 88% have remained teaching in urban schools. Of the 52 graduates, 49% are of color, and 12% are men of color. A majority of the teacher candidates of color are African American and Latino American. As of 2012, 62% of the teacher candidates who have not yet graduated are of color—45% women and 17% men (Waddell & Ukpokodu, 2010, p. 20).

Preparation

Recruitment of diverse teacher candidates is extremely important, but preparing and retaining them is equally and significantly vital. Given the focus on recruiting, preparing, and retaining teacher candidates from underrepresented backgrounds, the IUE designers envisioned a rigorous program with an emphasis on literacy, mathematics, science, and multicultural education and social justice. Students are expected to maintain a minimum cumulative grade point average of 3.0. High expectation is a hallmark of the program. Program courses are rigorous, extensive, and challenging. From the start, IUE teacher candidates are oriented to the high standards of expectation but are provided a strong mentoring and supportive network. Each teacher candidate is supported by nurturing faculty and mentors who regularly monitor their academic and personal activities through weekly meetings and midsemester conferences and evaluations. As a cohort model, the program provides opportunities for the teacher candidates to develop close and supportive kinship relationships with each other. The success of the cohort model was particularly enhanced when the teacher candidates had full scholarships that offered them opportunities to enroll in similar classes, room together in the university residence halls, study together, scaffold each other's learning and success, and attend community events together.

The IUE Design Team deliberately and explicitly created well-focused, innovative curricular experiences with appropriate scaffolding to build the teacher candidates' knowledge base, skills, and professional dispositions. Prior to the commencement of the program, and given its collaborative, interdisciplinary framework, participating SOE and College of Arts and Sciences faculty were engaged in professional development, where they learned to work together and develop the knowledge base on multicultural education, urban education, and culturally responsive and social justice pedagogy. The program design required that all IUE courses, including noneducation courses, integrate cultural and social justice perspectives with an emphasis on experiential learning. Given the interdisciplinary collaborative nature of the program, special class sections both in general education and in SOE courses were exclusively created for the IUE teacher candidates and taught by selected IUE faculty. A signature piece of the IUE program is the extensive–intensive field experiences teacher candidates are provided throughout the program years. Field experiences start in the first semester with the community immersion experience in which teacher candidates "spend three to four days per week immersed in experiential learning and reflection on the complexity of the urban community . . . and [gain] access to community resources" (Waddell & Ukpokodu, 2012, p. 19). They culminate in a yearlong internship in a partner school. On graduation and transition into full-time teaching classrooms, the teacher graduates are provided yearlong "structured induction" experiences—a mentorship and teacher assistantship structure in which experienced teachers are specifically appointed to work with the IUE teachers for 2 to 3 hours per week on matters related to instructional preparation, urban school culture, and building relationships, among other things.

Teacher candidates also have the opportunity to experience best practices in the form of culturally responsive teaching. Participating faculty are expected to teach in ways that model culturally responsive and social justice pedagogy in their courses. In some cases, courses are team-taught to model interdisciplinary, integrated instruction. For instance, I co-taught the integrated social studies and language arts course with another colleague where we modeled interdisciplinary planning and instruction, integrated curricular units, and lessons. A recent innovation to the program involves faculty teaching off campus in partner schools.

Impact and Challenges

The UMKC IUE is a unique program that has had and continues to exert tremendous impact on UMKC as a whole, the SOE, the urban partner school districts, and the urban community. The goal of UMKC and SOE to partner with the community to address the educational challenges of the urban school district has become a reality. For the past 5 years, the IUE program has provided the urban community with well-prepared teachers who are committed to urban teaching. A majority of these teachers have been retained in the urban schools where they have been hired, although the lasting effect will be determined once they fulfill their contractual agreement. Regardless, the IUE graduates are in high demand by urban schools. Today, UMKC SOE has forged partnerships with nine urban school districts that eagerly hire the IUE graduates. I remember a superintendent once said at a meeting, referring to IUE graduates, "I want them all." In 2011, one of the IUE graduates received the Teacher of the Year award at her school (Waddell & Ukpokodu, 2012, p. 21) and the Teacher of the Year award by the Missouri Association of Colleges for Teacher Education. The IUE has provided UMKC SOE a small but steady pool of teacher candidates of color, which has been a positive experience for faculty and White teacher candidates.

In 2010, I conducted a large qualitative study with SOE and UMKC College of Arts and Sciences participating faculty about their experience and engagement with the IUE program. Their perspectives shed insights into the impact and challenges of the IUE program relative to recruitment, preparation, and retention of the teacher candidates. The study involved in-depth interviews with faculty members who had developed at least one course and taught the IUE teacher candidates for at least 2 consecutive years. Through inductive analysis (Patton, 2002), I identified themes that revealed the impact of the program.

First, all participants viewed the IUE teacher candidates as valued asset to the SOE and in their classes. Participants expressed value for the diverse background that teacher candidates, especially those of color, brought to their classroom. As indicated earlier, although UMKC SOE is in an urban community, it had previously not been successful in attracting teacher candidates of color into the teacher education program. Participating faculty valued the commitment of IUE teacher candidates toward urban teaching, appreciated their disposition toward the discourse on diversity and social justice, and particularly valued their openness and responsiveness. Because of the small number of the IUE teacher candidates, it was necessary to enroll them in some courses serving traditional teacher candidates. There, they were often strong advocates of diversity and social justice. All participating faculty commented that the teacher candidates had a great attitude toward diversity and that their desire to serve urban children was infectious. One participant noted, "They bring liveliness, engagement, and high levels of confidence to the room."

All participants shared that they were confident that the teacher candidates were well prepared for enacting culturally responsive and social justice pedagogy in their classrooms and that they would be successful urban teachers. One participant made this comment:

> The IUE teacher candidates are getting a good preparation for urban teaching. You know—the standards are high and there is high expectation for them. Sometimes I feel sorry for them. We challenge them to do rigorous work. These are 17- and 18-year-olds. We make them read books like Ladson-Billings's *The Dreamkeepers,* Bill Ayers's *To Teach: The Journey of a Teacher,* Linda Christensen's articles, and lots of children's books.

A majority of the participants noted the impact on their own personal and professional development. They pointed out how they were challenged to develop their own journey of culturally responsive and social justice teaching in order to model such practices for the students.

One of the goals of the IUE at its conception was that it would be recognized as a national model. Today, the UMKC SOE teacher education program is known and recognized nationally. As such, the IUE attracts members of both local and national institutions who visit to benchmark the program.

Finally, the most profound impact of the IUE is evident in the transformation of the entire SOE programming, curriculum, and faculty pedagogy. It is important to note that the IUE initially existed side by side with the traditional teacher education but with different curricula pathways. Today, all teacher education curricular experiences are modeled after the IUE. Its success has benefited SOE in ways unimagined, including providing leverage for seeking highly competitive grants. In 2009, SOE received a large grant ($8 million) from the U.S. Department of Education Teacher Quality Partnership. This grant has made it possible to recruit many instructors of color who teach courses and supervise clinical experiences and serve as role models and mentors for the IUE teacher candidates.

Like every new initiative, the IUE has had some challenges. The most notable one is resources. As previously mentioned, one of the program goals was to provide teacher candidates full scholarships for the duration of their program—tuition, books and supplies, housing, and food. In the proposal to establish the IUE, it was recognized that in order to attract highly qualified and underrepresented teacher candidates, it was vital that UMKC aggressively seek and provide financial support. Today, because of the economic and budget challenges that the state and the university are experiencing, IUE teacher candidates no longer receive full scholarships. Although the university still supports the IUE, the current economic downturn has deeply affected the potential and sustainability of the IUE endowed scholarships. The impact of this limited resource is evident in the dwindling number of teacher candidates of color now interested and entering the program.

Another challenge relates to the lack of college readiness of recruited teacher candidates. As noted earlier, a majority of the teacher candidates are recruited from high school, and many of them are between the ages of 17 and 18. My study participants expressed challenges faced in preparing this age group for responsibilities in high-needs and highly marginalized school communities. Although all study participants valued the IUE teacher candidates for their positive attitude toward diversity and teaching in urban schools and for their desire to be successful urban teachers, they nonetheless expressed serious challenges teaching them, specifically their academic and study skills such as writing and math and their self-regulatory skills. Most IUE teacher candidates of color are from marginalized communities and are graduates of urban school communities that have been well documented for their "savage inequalities" (Kozol, 1991) and "pedagogy of poverty" (Haberman, 1995). Although the IUE teacher candidates are supposedly the cream of the crop (high grade point averages and great reference letters) from their respective high schools when they are selected, participants noted they lacked the academic and social capital needed for college engagement and success. One participant's comment illuminates this experience: "The students come from the urban core where the educational system and curricular experiences have not been rigorous. So you have students who have tremendous potential but have been poorly prepared for college education." Although the participants expressed feeling empathetic toward the teacher candidates and recognized that they were shortchanged by the school system, they nonetheless felt challenged teaching them. As one participant commented, "I really learned to be patient and resisted the temptation of blaming the victim. It was not their fault, still it was hard."

Another major challenge relates to the lasting impact and retention of the IUE teacher graduates once they transition into full-time teaching. Although my study participants expressed feeling confident that the teacher candidates were empowered and well prepared for urban teaching, they also painfully lamented the impact of the toxic culture in urban schools on the IUE graduates. In describing how well prepared the teacher candidates are, one participant commented,

> They are definitely well prepared. We have planned and provided a rigorous program, modeled for them, and they have demonstrated their learning so well. But the only sad thing is that, I am afraid the [urban school] system will beat them down.

This prophetic comment is becoming a reality as some of the teacher graduates have begun to pursue other programs that will take them out of the classrooms. I recently met a few of the IUE teacher graduates who are pursing master's degrees in related and specialized programs such as administration, counseling, and teaching of English as a second language. In my conversations with some of them, especially those seeking to become principals, they painfully lamented the difficulty of teaching in urban schools and the thought of leaving the classroom. Some of the reasons they gave include the pressure and demand of high-stakes testing and mandated curriculum and scripted instruction that limit their abilities to teach in ways that are culturally responsive and engaging. Most important, they mentioned that they feel inefficacious as classroom teachers and that as administrators, they believe they will be able to make more meaningful impact—change the lives of many more students than the 20 in their classrooms—by working with teachers and transforming the schools. Although these teachers expressed a commitment to remain in urban schools and still make an impact, it is sad and disappointing that they will not be in the classroom as regular teachers. This compromises the goal of the IUE and at worst jeopardizes the best hope of putting a highly competent teacher in an urban classroom.

Lessons

In this chapter, I have provided the historical and contextual factors of IUE and the turning point leading to its evolvement. As I indicated earlier, although the purpose of universities is, among other things, to prepare students for economic and political engagement in their communities and society in general, their mission is also to engage with the immediate community and work to solve its problems. Oftentimes, although this purpose may be espoused in the university's mission statement, it is rarely accomplished, especially in urban communities with serious educational crisis. This was the case with UMKC before its turning point.

Perry and Mendez (2011) contended that urban universities should be "anchors for urban and metropolitan development" (p. 4) and so must form partnerships with the urban communities in order to leverage resources for solving problems such as the educational crisis in urban schools. Today the IUE is one of UMKC's prized accomplishments. It models the collaboration between universities and community and how this collaboration can disrupt the "savage inequalities" in marginalized school communities and provide opportunities to recruit and prepare teachers who will teach, become efficacious, and be retained in urban schools. So what lessons can be learned from the UMKC IUE project?

Central Administration Leadership

Recruiting diverse teacher candidates for preparation for teaching requires a bold, aggressive, collaborative, and out-of-the-mold action, which in turn requires bold intervention and leadership from the university's upper administration. The IUE project models for universities the leadership needed to create programs that meet the needs and challenges of diversifying the teaching force and putting highly competent teachers in urban schools. Although schools and colleges of education may have the vision and, in some cases, the will to engage with public schools, especially those in marginalized communities, they may lack the social capital as well as the leadership needed to execute such endeavors.

The UMKC SOE would not have been able to establish the IUE program without the university's top administration leadership. The chancellor and the provost provided the driving force and made the recruitment of diverse teacher candidates front and center of the mission of the university. In the proposal to establish the IUE, "the UMKC Urban Mission Taskforce had as its defining top element the imprimatur of the Chancellor and the Provost" (UMKC, 2003, p. 10). Both the chancellor and provost were deeply committed and invested in the program, which made it possible for the entire university to embrace or at least accept and commit to the IUE program. Simply, the IUE teacher preparation program was more or less the chancellor's project. The project management office was located in the chancellor's office, and all activities were reported directly to the chancellor and the provost.

Collaborative Partnership

An out-of-the-mold approach to creating programs for recruiting, preparing, and retaining diverse teacher candidates requires forging collaborative partnerships with internal and external communities. The success of the IUE program rested on collaboration among the major university schools and units—College of Arts and Sciences, SOE, the Block School of Business, and the School of Biological Sciences—and external communities, especially agencies such as the Urban League, the African American and Latino American communities, the urban partner school districts, and the business community. It is this form of partnership that organizations such as the Coalition of Urban Serving Universities and the Coalition of Urban and Metropolitan Universities have called for in order to address the pressing problems of urban schools and the achievement gaps between students of color and their White peers.

Culturally Responsive Faculty

Recruitment of diverse teacher candidates is only one piece of the puzzle. As Ingersoll (2001) proposed, efforts to recruit teachers should focus not only on recruitment but also on retention. Recruitment must be accompanied by bold efforts to prepare and retain teacher candidates of diverse backgrounds. Given that a majority of the IUE teacher candidates come from marginalized urban school communities that are notorious for the "pedagogy of poverty" (Haberman, 1995) and "savage inequalities" (Kozol, 1991), and that in some cases, they are first-generation college students who may not have had the opportunities to develop the academic skills and social capital (Bourdieu, 1986) needed for college success, bold efforts must be taken to provide both academic and social support (Hill & Gillette, 2005; Sleeter & Thao, 2007; Villegas & Davis, 2007). Faculty working with adolescent teacher candidates who are first-generation college students and from marginalized school communities must be culturally responsive (Sheets & Chew, 2002) and capable of demonstrating a genuine ethic of care (Gay, 2010) and commitment to their success.

For the IUE program, it was made clear that all participating faculty would engage in culturally responsive pedagogy (Gay, 2010; Ladson-Billings, 2009). As a result, they were encouraged to participate in professional development that fostered their development of sociocultural consciousness (Villegas & Lucas, 2001). The IUE faculty learned to engage in practices that involved (a) cultivating respectful relationships and interactions with the teacher candidates, (b) establishing learning communities, (c) holding high expectations and being "warm demanders" (Gay, 2010), (d) scaffolding and experiential learning, and (e) adjusting dispositions. This is critically important if the teacher candidates are to be retained and successfully graduate. In particular, faculty disposition is critical. Teaching young adults from minoritized school communities requires faculty patience, nurturing, compassion, empathy, and pedagogical flexibility. One participant in my study commented,

> For the most part, I think that, you know, teaching in this program has been an asset to the overall quality of college teaching. For me, as a faculty, I appreciate the program. It is a huge responsibility and the desire to fulfill it is great so you adjust your philosophy, disposition, and pedagogy. I really had to adjust my attitude and pedagogy. I learned to be patient, compassionate, caring, and flexible.

Conclusion

Today, the IUE has evolved and remains the signature piece of UMKC. Although the challenges noted above are debilitating, the IUE is the best gift the university and its urban community could have ever given to children in marginalized communities. UMKC continues to work to improve the program and to live its mission of urban engagement. If every university and college located in urban communities will commit to genuine community engagement like that of the IUE that recruits, prepares, and retains diverse teacher candidates, especially those of color, the problem of homogeneity in the teaching force, the mismatch between teachers and their diverse student population, and the persistent achievement gap phenomenon will be minimized if not eliminated (Haycock, 2002). The need to diversify the teaching force and improve the quality of teachers for minority and low-income students is a moral and social justice imperative. Duncan (2009) powerfully summed it up when he said,

> If we want to close achievement gaps, if we want to make sure that many more African-American and Latino male students are graduating rather than dropping out . . ., having those teachers [of color], having those role models, having those [teachers as] coaches is going to make a huge difference in their lives.

Villegas & Davis (2007) concurred, saying that diversifying the teacher workforce is the best chance to make schools in the United States more democratic and just. To this end, universities, especially those in marginalized communities, must become the community university!

References

Bourdieu, P. (1986). The forms of capital. In J. G. Richardson (Ed.), *Handbook of theory and research for the sociology of education* (pp. 241–258). New York, NY: Greenwood.

Duncan, A. (2009, October 22). *Teacher preparation: Reforming the uncertain profession* (Address presented at Teachers College, Columbia University). Retrieved from www2.ed.gov/news/pressreleases/2009/10/10222009a.html

Gay, G. (2010). *Culturally responsive teaching: Theory, research, and practice.* New York, NY: Teachers College Press.

Gotham, K. F. (2002a). Missed opportunities, enduring legacies: School segregation and desegregation in Kansas City, Missouri. *American Studies, 42,* 5–42.

Gotham, K. F. (2002b). *Race, real estate, and uneven development: The Kansas City experience* (1900–2000). Albany: State University of New York Press.

Haberman, M. (1995). *Star teachers of children in poverty.* West Lafayette, IN: Kappa Delta Pi.

Haberman, M. (2005). *Selecting and preparing urban teachers.* Retrieved from www.habermanfoundation.org/Articles/Default.aspx?id=32

Haberman, M. (2006). *The Star Teacher Pre-Screener.* Retrieved from www.habermanfoundation.org/starteacherprescreener.aspx

Haycock, K. (2002). Toward a fair distribution of teacher talent. *Educational Leadership, 60,* 11–15.

Hill, D., & Gillette, M. (2005). Teachers of tomorrow in urban schools: Recruiting and supporting the pipeline. *Multicultural Perspectives, 7,* 42–50.

Ingersoll, R. (2001). Teacher turnover and teacher shortages: An organizational analysis. *American Educational Research Journal, 38,* 499–534.

Kauffman Foundation. (2010). *Putting performance on the map: Locating quality schools in the Kansas City, Missouri school district.* Retrieved from www.kauffman.org/~/media/kauff man_org/research%20reports%20and%20covers/2010/10/quality_schools_report.pdf

Kozol, J. (1991). *Savage inequalities: Children in America's schools.* New York, NY: Harper Perennial.

Ladson-Billings, G. (2009). *The dreamkeepers: Successful teachers of African American children* (2nd ed.). San Francisco, CA: Jossey-Bass.

Massey, D. S., & Denton, N. A. (1993). *American apartheid: Segregation and the making of the underclass.* Cambridge, MA: Harvard University Press.

Moll, L. C., Amanti, C., Neff, D., & González, N. (1992). Funds of knowledge for teaching: Using a qualitative approach to connect homes and classrooms. *Theory Into Practice, 31,* 132–141.

Patton, M. (2002). *Qualitative evaluation and research methods* (3rd ed.). Thousand Oaks, CA: Sage.

Perry, D., & Mendez, C. (2011). *The impact of institutions of higher education on urban and metropolitan areas: Assessment of the coalition of urban and metropolitan universities.* Retrieved from www.cumuonline.org/downloads/impactSurveyComplete.pdf

Sheets, R. H., & Chew, L. (2002) Absent from the research, present in our classrooms: Preparing culturally responsive Chinese American teachers, *Journal of Teacher Education, 53,* 127–141.

Sleeter, C., & Thao, Y. (2007). Guest editors' introduction: Diversifying the teaching force. *Teacher Education Quarterly, 34,* 3–8.

SOE Writing Team Report. (2004). *Urban Teacher Preparation Program Narrative.* (Unpublished document). Kansas City, MO: University of Missouri–Kansas City.

Swanson, C. B. (2009). *Cities in crisis 2009: Closing the graduation gap.* Retrieved from www.edweek.org/mmedia/cities in crisis 2009.pdf

Ukpokodu, O. N. (2010). How a sustainable campus-wide diversity curriculum fosters academic success. *Multicultural Education, 17,* 27–36.

University of Missouri–Kansas City. (2003). *IUE proposal draft.* Kansas City: Author.

Villegas, A., & Davis, D. (2007). Approaches to diversifying the teaching force: Attending to issues of recruitment, preparation and retention. *Teacher Education Quarterly, 34,* 137–147.

Villegas, A. M., & Lucas, T. (2001). *Educating culturally responsive teachers: A coherent approach.* Albany, NY: State University of New York Press.

Waddell, J., & Ukpokodu, O. N. (2012). Recruiting & preparing diverse urban teachers: One urban-focused teacher education program breaks ground. *Multicultural Education, 20,* 15–22.

Weiner, L. (2000). Research in the 90s: Implications for urban teacher preparation program. *Review of Educational Research, 70,* 369–406.

6

NEWCOMERS ENTERING TEACHING: THE POSSIBILITIES OF A CULTURALLY AND LINGUISTICALLY DIVERSE TEACHING FORCE

Flynn Ross

In a traditional, aspiring college preparation high school chemistry class of predominantly White, monolingual students with professional parents, the teacher explained that although the name of each element on the periodic table was called by a different name in various languages, the symbols are universal. The teacher, Constant Bamani, proceeded to name several of the elements in three different languages—English, Arabic, and French—to illustrate his point. Bamani, originally from Congo, has been a culturally and linguistically diverse high school physical science teacher for more than 10 years in an old mill town with Francophone roots in coastal Maine.

The call to prepare students to be global citizens who are multilingual and cross-culturally aware has been made by diverse groups, including Standards for 21st Century Learning, Asia Society's International School Study Network, and International Baccalaureate. Many of our local communities have an untapped human resource: culturally and linguistically diverse potential teachers living in our local immigrant communities. Some have bachelor degrees and teaching experience in their home countries. As teachers, they offer all of our students firsthand experiences working with professionals from different cultural traditions and languages.

The ability to work in an increasingly diverse, heterogeneous, and complex society was determined to be a compelling state interest by the U.S. Supreme Court in 2003 with *Grutter v. Bollinger*, in which the courts allowed law schools to consider race as one factor in admissions. The Supreme Court majority opinion stated that student body diversity is a compelling interest for colleges and universities because it "better prepares students for an increasingly diverse workforce and society, and better prepares them as professionals" (U.S. Supreme Court, 2003). The evidence was further updated with the amicus brief filed in September 2012 by the American Educational Research Association, along with others, regarding the U.S. Supreme Court case *Fisher v. University of Texas, Austin* (Levine & Ancheta, 2013). In large-scale statistical research studies, Gurin, Dey, Hurtado, and Gurin (2002) argued that if participation in a democratic society is a key educational outcome, "students educated in diverse institutions will be more motivated and better able to participate in an increasingly heterogeneous and complex society" (p. 9). The same holds true for our K-12 student body and teaching force.

This chapter reports on a teacher preparation program in a northern New England city that is targeting recent immigrants and refugees to become certified teachers. The city is experiencing rapid demographic changes as a federally designated immigrant and refugee resettlement community. The Newcomer Extended Teacher Education Program (ETEP) program is an adaptation of the existing graduate-level ETEP. Both programs were built through school and university partnerships and are based on the core principles of professional development schools (Holmes Group, 1990).

Design of the Newcomer ETEP Program

The Newcomer ETEP is a 5th-year postbaccalaureate program (Ross, 2001, 2004) resulting in teacher certification and 33 credits toward a 45-credit master's degree. The program was designed explicitly as a way to develop a teaching force that was demographically more representative of the rapidly changing student population in Portland, Maine. As a federal immigrant and refugee resettlement community, the Portland Public Schools saw a 158% growth in the number of English language learners between 2000 and 2010 (Portland Public Schools, n.d.). It is a slightly modified version of the nationally recognized graduate-level ETEP (Darling-Hammond, 2006). Such 5th-year programs represent a mere 6% of teachers' professional preparation pathways, according to the Schools and Staffing Survey of 2003–2004 (Achinstein & Ogawa, 2011).

The ETEP program was modified for culturally and linguistically diverse teachers by extending the time needed to complete it. This made the program longer but less intense, allowing more time for learning. The admissions process was also mediated to provide additional supports. Admissions comprises two stages. First, a candidate applies to the Newcomer program, which allows the student to take two entry graduate courses in the program on special instructor permission, gain experience in public school classrooms, and work toward passing the Praxis I entry exams. Next, the candidate formally applies to the graduate ETEP program to be a matriculated master's degree candidate. This two-stage process was developed in response to the identified needs of many candidates. The standardized Praxis I exam required for full admission has been shown consistently to be a barrier for many culturally and linguistically diverse candidates as well as for many minority candidates (Ross, 2005). This two-stage admissions allowed for supports to be provided and for the candidate to feel as if progress was being made. This worked well when the program had grant funding to help pay tuition for the first two entry-level courses because students are not eligible for financial aid until they are fully matriculated, making finances a barrier.

ETEP is historically a 9-month teacher certification program. The extended Newcomer program usually consists of 2 academic years, which allows students to continue to work in the public schools as language facilitators and educational technicians (paraprofessionals) while taking courses with the ETEP cohort after school. The Newcomer ETEP students take two to three university courses along with the internship for three semesters and must leave their employment for a full-time internship in mainstream classrooms for the fourth semester (see Table 6.1). The full-time, 12-week internship is combined with six to nine credits of university coursework.

Program Leadership and Funding

The development and daily operation of the Newcomer ETEP program was historically guided by a steering committee consisting of university faculty and administrators, school district teachers and administrators, and representatives of the ethnic communities who contributed graduates of the program. The steering committee helped secure local grant money to pilot the program, which later leveraged a federal professional development grant for 5 years (2002–2007), which was then extended with some state grants to recruit minority teachers. The funding was essential for paying tuition and fees for students and hiring a program coordinator.

The program coordinator had several responsibilities including recruitment, pre-admissions advising, testing supports, and securing grant funding. Grant funding paid for analysis of international transcripts, prerequisite content courses for the area of certification, and testing fees. Tutoring for PRAXIS I and English as a second language college writing courses were also paid for by the program when it had grant funding.

With the loss of grant funding in 2011, the coordinator position was discontinued, but some elements of the program continue with institutionalized capacity, faculty support, and other resources for student tuition, including a trustees' tuition waiver and the Woodrow Wilson–Rockefeller Brothers Foundation Fellowship for Aspiring Teachers of Color (see Chapter 3).

Design of Programs for Culturally and Linguistically Diverse Teachers

The nationally recognized ETEP program was designed around several core commitments that are essential to quality teacher preparation programs: school–university partnerships that link theory and practice, extended mentored internship, embedded assessment system, and a cohort structure (Canniff,

TABLE 6.1 Teacher Certification Newcomer ETEP 2-Year Program Coursework

	Fall Term	Spring Term	Fall Term	Spring Term
Requirements				
			K-8 certification	
Coursework	Understanding Diverse Learners Exceptionality	Science Methods	Seminar I Math Methods Writing Methods Reading Methods	Seminar II Social Studies Methods Internship in Elementary Education
Assessments	Student Learning Profile Praxis I exam		Philosophy Statement Video-taped lessons	Curriculum Unit Portfolio Video-taped lessons Praxis II exam
			7–12 certification	
Coursework	Understanding Diverse Learners Exceptionality	Literacy in the Content Areas	Seminar I Instructional Strategies Content Methods (math, science, English, social studies, or world languages)	Seminar II Curriculum Design Internship in Secondary Education
Assessments	Student Learning Profile Praxis I test		Philosophy Statement Video-taped lessons	Curriculum Unit Portfolio Video-taped lessons Praxis II exam

Fallona, & Shank, 2004). A cohort structure and mentoring are strategies that have been reported to be particularly important for minority teacher candidates to "persist, minimize burnout, overcome feelings of isolation, and minimize feelings of being overwhelmed" (Quiocho & Rios, 2000, p. 503). The cohort structure supports the "dialogic conversation" that is part of the sociotransformative constructivism (Rodriguez, 2002, p. 1020). It allows students to know each other as individuals, build trust, have conversations reflecting on their school experiences, and be able to speak and listen as individuals situated in their social contexts. The cohort structure also creates a sense of critical mass even when actual numbers and percentages of minority students compared with majority students are very small throughout the entire program.

Identifying high-quality, veteran teachers to serve as mentors is another issue widely considered vital to the success of teacher education students (Holloway, 2002; Meyers & Smith, 1999; Torres-Guzman & Goodwin, 1995). However, the research cautions that the relationship between minority teacher candidates and their mentors is especially sensitive to the cross-cultural communication and expectations that are inherent in our diverse society. The challenges of cross-cultural communication and clarifying cultural expectations of authority relationships in mentor-teacher and student-teacher pairs are discussed later in this chapter.

Student Profiles and Identity

Research has found that many teachers of color intentionally choose to enter teaching to serve as role models and change agents in schools who might contribute to transforming education (Achinstein & Ogawa, 2011, p. 14). Many of the Newcomer ETEP students who were immigrants and refugees identified as teachers and were selected by others to work as teachers in their home countries prior to coming to the United States. Constant Bamani responded to the question, "Why did you want to be a teacher?" by stating, "I am a teacher. It's all I've ever done. My goal was to return to my profession." Ina Demers recounted that her mother identified her as a teacher when she was a child prior to her teacher training in Indonesia. Ljubica Forkapic was the daughter of a teacher and grew up in schools in Serbia.

The Newcomer ETEP teachers speak about becoming teachers as a career choice and a logical way to financially support their families. Abdullahi Ahmed stated that he and his wife set a goal of "becoming incorporated in the mainstream within 7 years" of their arrival in Maine from Somalia. He became a teacher, she became a nurse, and they bought a condominium within their targeted time frame. In contrast, Newcomer students who were schooled in the United States as immigrant children or adopted children or those who were Native American articulated an explicit social justice mission in their choice to pursue teaching as a career, similar to the teachers in the research by Achinstein and Ogawa (2011). There does appear to be a difference in self-identity and purpose for teaching between immigrant teachers and teachers schooled in the United States.

Program Successes

The Newcomer ETEP program has a strong record of program completion, employment, and retention, along with benefits to the classroom and community.

Retention and Graduation

The Newcomer ETEP program supported 39 candidates as of 2013 to pursue teacher certification. Of these, 28 were fully admitted as graduate students, 21 entered the program, and 100% of those who were admitted and entered graduated. The 2-year admissions process allowed for the early recruitment and support of potential candidates, some of whom decided they did not want to teach in American public schools; three were not able to get through the required standardized tests for full admission.

Seventeen of the 21 who graduated were employed as teachers (13) or paraeducators (four); 100% remain in their positions as many as 10 years later. Two of the 21 just graduated, and the other two returned to their positions as community liaisons with social service agencies.

The seven who were fully admitted but chose not to attend the program did so for a variety of reasons. One started his own business, another became an information technology specialist for the school district, one remained home with children, and another could not attend because of her need to work full time to support her children. The remaining three were employed as conditionally certified teachers, not having completed a teacher preparation program but rather pursuing alternative certification directly through the state department of education. Two of the three conditionally certified teachers were not successful, and their contracts were not renewed after the 1st year, so they left teaching. Their experience supports the need for high-quality teacher preparation as opposed to short alternative routes or quick recruitment of teachers of color without quality preparation.

The exceptional retention rate of those who became teachers is characteristic of grow-your-own programs in which strong teaching candidates from the local community are identified and supported (Haselkorn & Fideler, 1996; Skinner et al., 2011; see also Chapters 2, 7, and 8). The Newcomer ETEP alumni were embedded community members prior to entering the graduate teacher education program, and many of them were paraeducators—educational technicians, language facilitators, community specialists—as well as parents of children in the school district. Like graduates of other grow-your-own programs, their retention rates are excellent by any standard.

Benefits to the K-12 Classroom

In interviews and e-mail questionnaires, mentor teachers identified numerous benefits and challenges to having Newcomer ETEP students in their classrooms. The benefits included connections with individual students, enrichment of curriculum, and education of veteran teachers about cross-cultural communication and student needs. Mentor teachers identified a number of strengths of the Newcomer ETEP students, including their high motivation, sophistication, awareness of world issues, and literacy in three to five languages. From interviews, fellow teachers expressed that

> the greatest benefits have been the stories they [Newcomer students] bring with them. They have been able to shed light on some of the difficult issues we may be facing when interacting with students from other countries. Their stories and knowledge about their cultures have helped us to understand why a child may be acting the way they do; perhaps they have brought their "culture" to school with them.

In another example, during an immigration unit, children in a middle school classroom were able to compare history with the present-day experiences of their Newcomer intern who was himself a recent immigrant. When schools and teachers are open to learning from others and honor the cultural capital that culturally and linguistically diverse teachers bring, the experience has been positive for everyone.

Benefits to the Graduate Level Classrooms

Course instructors reported that the Newcomer ETEP students brought a richness of understanding to the graduate-level classroom discussions. For example, in an interview one said, "We wouldn't be able to have the discussions we do without the Newcomer ETEP students. It gives us a deeper understanding of our own system as we reinvent American education" (July 30, 2002). In the integrated seminar, graduate students raised in the United States brought up questions about working with English language learner children and their parents. Graduate students reported informally that it was a tremendous asset for them as beginning teachers to turn to their Newcomer ETEP classmates who were themselves English language learners and parents of children in the school system. The open dialogue in a trusting environment allowed these beginning teachers to ask questions about discipline expectations, communication with parents, cultural expectations for gender roles, religious differences, and other often unexamined issues. Having peers in the graduate classroom who were members of cultural and linguistic minority groups changed the discussion. The graduate students would not talk about culturally and linguistically students as "them" or "those students" when in the presence of culturally and linguistically diverse peers.

Program Challenges

A number of challenges have been identified over the years, both formally at steering committee meetings as well as informally through observations and conversations. Recurring challenges include passing standardized tests; meeting the academic writing demands of university coursework; cultural differences in educational philosophy; preparation of mentor teachers for working with non-traditional teaching candidates; and employment, interviewing, and education of hiring boards.

Standardized Tests

Passing standardized tests, including Praxis I, is well documented as a recurring challenge for minority teaching candidates (Gay, Dingus, & Jackson, 2003; Memory, Coleman, & Watkins, 2003; Quiocho & Rios, 2000; Sleeter & Milner, 2011). High passing scores set by the state board of education were creating such an obstacle for admissions to the graduate program and subsequent certification as a teacher that a coalition of educational leaders and legislators lobbied the state board of education with case studies and research on the validity of test scores for predicting teacher quality. The coalition was successful, and a more flexible composite test score was allowed that recognized the strengths of several teacher applicants in their math scores and permitted them to "borrow" points from a high score in one area to compensate for the challenges on the writing portion of the test, particularly for those for whom English was not their native language (Ross, 2005).

Along with the changes in the state cut scores on the test, students were supported with test preparation, targeted tutoring one on one and in small groups, and the development of an online resource tailored specifically for nonnative English speakers, Free Praxis Prep (www.freepraxisprep.com/).

Educational Philosophies—Cultural Differences

Mentor teachers, program coordinator, and course instructors identified several issues related to cultural differences as in other programs (Weintroub, 1996). Cultural differences in educational philosophies played out in the classroom. For example, gender roles are culturally conditioned in different ways across various cultures. There were often different cultural expectations regarding children's behavior in classrooms, with the Newcomer ETEP students expecting much more obedience from children and more authoritarian teacher behaviors. Student-led cooperative learning and inquiry-based project learning were very foreign arrangements for most of the Newcomer ETEP students.

In the graduate classrooms, several immigrant students tended to be uncomfortable with having a "voice" and representing their opinions orally and in writing in a program that emphasized reflective practice. Many mentor teachers expected interns to "take initiative" in the internship, which some Newcomers were reluctant to do because they perceived such boldness as disrespectful of the perceived hierarchical relationship of intern and mentor. Rather, the Newcomers were waiting for direction and invitations from the mentor teacher as their superior. Over time, faculty have learned to anticipate some of these cultural differences and be explicit about the potential differences in supervision meetings with Newcomer ETEP interns and their mentor teachers.

University Teacher Educators—Coursework

Instructors consistently identified challenges for Newcomer ETEP students with academic writing in English, comprehension of extensive reading assignments, and use of technology. Suggested solutions included more preparation with technology, more preparation for academic writing, more time for reading the texts, and possibly identifying translators for difficult concepts.

There were also more subtle challenges that are culturally based. One instructor said that Newcomer ETEP students "aren't familiar with the give and take of discussion. I'm not sure how they felt in small group discussions." The structures of the constructivist classroom in a program designed to prepare "reflective practitioners" was very different from the delivery model of teacher training that some of the Newcomer ETEP students experienced in their home nations. Previous research has shown that this adaptation to a new cultural philosophy may be very difficult (Carter & Doyle, 1996; Hollingsworth, 1989; Richardson, 1996; Zeichner & Gore, 1990). However, strategies such as reflective journaling and discussion, along with firsthand experience in progressive classrooms, appeared to have had an influence on preparing progressive, constructivist teachers, at least intellectually.

Preparation of Mentor Teachers for Working with Nontraditional Teaching Candidates

In interviews and e-mail surveys, three of the mentor teachers identified the following challenges working with Newcomer ETEP interns: language, educational philosophy, classroom management, and balancing coursework and teaching.

Mentor teachers reported that "it is more work having a Newcomer ETEP intern because their first language is not English." As one explained, "Some students reported difficulty understanding the interns" because of their accents. Some teachers raised the concern that it is important to have a native English speaker for students, especially in the primary grades where students are learning letter–sound relationships like various consonant blends. This is an area in which more research is needed, and even then it may be a very individualized situation depending on the degree of accent of the teacher and on the receptive language skills of the students.

With respect to educational philosophy, the mentor teachers reported that

> sometimes it can be frustrating because they [Newcomer ETEP interns] don't see it the same way as American educated teachers. I see education as a process, while the intern was more concerned with product; we help each other to understand another way of thinking and doing, but it takes time.

Many of the Newcomer ETEP students experienced traditional, didactic, drill, and skill education in their own K-12 schooling. Many studies document the strong, persistent influence of pretraining experiences on beginning teachers (Carter & Doyle, 1996; Hollingsworth, 1989; Richardson, 1996; Zeichner & Gore, 1990). Prior beliefs and attitudes provide the schemata through which prospective teachers experience their teacher preparation programs (Achinstein & Ogawa, 2011; Calderhead & Robson, 1991; Weinstein, 1990). Intellectually, the Newcomer ETEP interns could talk and write about the benefits of a constructivist curriculum in which students have freedom to think and question; however, the influence of their own schooling still appeared to be strong.

Most beginning teachers struggle with classroom management. However, the Newcomer ETEP interns, as a group, have had a greater challenge with the democratic classroom management style than the ETEP interns who were educated in similar classrooms. Mentor teachers who have mentored both Newcomer ETEP and ETEP interns have reported that Newcomer ETEP interns "experience some difficulty with classroom management." This also varied by individual personality, gender, and cultural background.

Employment, Interviewing, and Hiring Boards

In 2000, finding employment as full-time classroom teachers was a challenge for graduates of the Newcomer ETEP program. The two graduates from 1999–2000 worked for a year as paraprofessionals and then received lead teaching positions in English language learner classrooms. Until 2005, none of the graduates found teaching jobs in the mainstream classrooms for which they were prepared immediately after program completion in part because of their challenges with meeting the high standardized test score requirement prior to the institution of the more flexible composite score in 2004. However, this situation has improved in the past few years, with all of the graduates since 2010 securing employment as teachers in mainstream classrooms following program completion.

The challenge of minority candidates being hired is well documented in the research (Kearney-Gissendaner, 2012; Quiocho & Rios, 2000). Preparation for interviewing included the understanding that graduates needed to learn "flagrant self-promotion," which is culturally distinctive to the interview expectations for schools in the United States. Another need identified by the steering committee was for review of the hiring process for sources of bias in the questions asked and the scoring of candidates. It was suggested that workshops be provided for hiring boards to broaden the perspective of what quality teaching to reach all students might include and to be aware of possible biases in the interview process.

Conclusion

Our democracy is enriched by the multitude of languages, cultures, and skills of immigrant and native populations. Our public schools are the laboratory for refining and rebuilding our future by shaping the next generation. School, community, and university partnerships have the potential to recruit, prepare, and retain high-quality teachers of color who are culturally and linguistically diverse from our local immigrant communities to prepare all of our children for a global 21st century. The legacy of this program and ripple effects of its alumni can be seen in the portraits in Chapter 3.

References

Achinstein, B., & Ogawa, R. (2011). *Change(d) agents: New teachers of color in urban schools.* New York, NY: Teachers College Press.

Calderhead, J., & Robson, M. (1991). Images of teaching: Student teachers' early conceptions of classroom practice. *Teachers and Teacher Education, 7,* 1–8.

Canniff, J., Fallona, C., & Shank, M. (2004). *Strengthening and sustaining teachers, Portland, Maine. Project Report 2002–2003.* Gorham: University of Southern Maine.

Carter, K., & Doyle, W. (1996). Personal narrative and life history in learning to teach. In J. Sikula, T. Buttery, & E. Guyton (Eds.). *Handbook of research on teacher education* (2nd ed.). New York, NY: Macmillan.

Darling-Hammond, L. (2006). *Powerful teacher education: Lessons from exemplary programs.* San Francisco, CA: Jossey-Bass.

Gay, G., Dingus, J. E., & Jackson, C. W. (2003). *The presence and performance of teachers of color in the profession.* Washington, DC: Community Teachers Institute.

Gurin, P., Dey, E. L., Hurtado, S., & Gurin, G. (2002). Diversity and higher education: Theory and impact on educational outcomes. *Harvard Educational Review, 72,* 330–366.

Haselkorn, D., & Fideler, E. (1996). *Breaking the class ceiling: Paraeducator pathways to teaching.* Belmont, MA: Recruiting New Teachers, Inc.

Hollingsworth, S. (1989). Prior beliefs and cognitive change in learning to teach. *American Educational Research Journal, 26,* 160–189.

Holloway, J. H. (2002). Mentoring for diversity. *Educational Leadership, 59,* 88–89.

Holmes Group. (1990). *Tomorrow's schools of education.* East Lansing, MI: Author.

Kearney-Gissendaner, J. E. (2012). *Minority teacher recruitment and retention strategies.* Larchmont, NY: Eye on Education.

Levine, F., & Ancheta, A. (2013). The AERA et al. amicus brief in *Fisher v. University of Texas at Austin*: Scientific organizations serving society. *Educational Researcher, 42,* 166–171.

Memory, D. M., Coleman, C. L., & Watkins, S. D. (2003). Possible tradeoffs in raising basic skills cutoff scores for teacher licensure: A study with implications for participation of African Americans in teaching. *Journal of Teacher Education, 54,* 217–227.

Meyers, H. W., & Smith, S. (1999). Coming home—Mentoring new teachers: A school–university partnership to support the development of teachers from diverse ethnic backgrounds. *Peabody Journal of Education, 74,* 75–89.

Portland Public Schools (n.d.) *Demographic data: Twelve-year ELL enrollment.* Retrieved from www.portlandschools.org/schools/multilingual/about/demographics.html

Quiocho, A., & Rios, F. (2000). The power of their presence: Minority group teachers and schooling. *Review of Educational Research, 70,* 485–528.

Richardson, V. (1996). The role of attitudes and beliefs in learning to teach. In J. Sikula, T. Buttery, & E. Guyton (Eds.), *Handbook of research on teacher education* (2nd ed., pp. 102–119). New York, NY: Simon & Schuster Macmillan.

Rodriguez, A. J. (2002). Using sociotransformative constructivism to teach for understanding in diverse classrooms: A beginning teacher's journey. *American Educational Research Journal, 39*, 1017–1045.

Ross, F. (2001). Helping immigrants become teachers. *Educational Leadership, 58,* 68–71.

Ross, F. (2004). Teaching in a democracy: Learning from immigrants and refugees. *Maine Journal of Education, 20,* 29–32.

Ross, F. (2005). Creating flexibility in teacher certification to ensure quality and equity. *Maine Policy Review, 14,* 56–63.

Skinner, E., Garreton, M., & Schultz, B. (Eds.). (2011). *Grow your own teachers.* New York, NY: Teachers College Press.

Sleeter, C. E., & Milner, H. R., IV. (2011). Researching successful efforts in teacher education to diversify teachers. In A. F. Ball & C. A. Tyson (Eds.), *Studying diversity in teacher education* (pp. 81–104). New York, NY: Rowman & Littlefield.

Torres-Guzman, M., & Goodwin, A. (1995). Urban bilingual teachers and mentoring for the future. *Education and Urban Society, 28,* 48–66.

U.S. Supreme Court. Majority opinion, *Grutter v Bollinger,* 539 U.S. 306, July, 2003. Retrieved from http://supreme.justia.com/cases/federal/us/539/306/case.html

Weinstein, C. S. (1990). Prospective elementary teachers' beliefs about teaching: Implications for teacher education. *Teaching and Teacher Education, 6,* 279–290.

Weintroub, E. (1996). Breaking down barriers: The adjustment of immigrant teachers to new educational frameworks. *Teacher Trainer, 10,* 20–22.

Zeichner, K., & Gore, J. (1990). Teacher socialization. In W. R. Houston (Ed.), *Handbook of research on teacher education* (pp. 329–348). New York, NY: Macmillan.

PART III

Recruiting and Retaining Teacher Candidates of Color: University Partnerships With Public Schools

7

GROWING YOUR OWN TEACHERS IN ILLINOIS: PROMISING PRACTICE FOR URBAN AND RURAL HIGH-NEED SCHOOLS

Jeff Bartow, Maureen Gillette, Anne Hallett, Katelyn Johnson, Christina L. Madda, Imelda Salazar, and Victor Manuel Valle

The Grow Your Own Teachers (GYO) initiative in Illinois, as state law with state funding, invests in low-income paraprofessionals, parents, and community leaders who want to be teachers but cannot afford college. Developed through an unusual partnership between community organizers and university teacher educators, GYO creates a pipeline of highly effective, community-based teachers of color for schools in low-income, high-need areas. GYO is an organizing solution to developing great teachers who look like and share the culture of students they will teach in their neighborhood's low-income schools.

In this chapter, we provide an overview of the GYO initiative. We examine one GYO community–university network that represents collaboration among six Chicago community-based organizations and the College of Education (COE) at Northeastern Illinois University. This network links organizers and educators who jointly invest in teacher candidates, on campus and in the community, to prepare them to be teachers and community leaders. This dual approach suggests a promising policy direction for significantly strengthening teacher education for low-income students.

GYO provides a solution to growing national crises. Most large, urban school districts such as Chicago experience what Ingersoll (2003, p. 11) and Miner (2010) have called the "revolving door" phenomenon, where the constant transition of "inadequately prepared teachers" disrupts the organizational structure of schools and student achievement. Roughly half of Chicago teachers leave the 100 most troubled schools every 3 years. As Allensworth, Ponisciak, and Mazzeo (2009) noted, teacher turnover in Chicago's highest poverty African American schools averaged 53% for a 3-year period. This situation is exacerbated by the teacher–student cultural mismatch. Illinois has been cited as the nation's third worst state with respect to the demographic gap between the number of students of color and teachers of color (Boser, 2011). In many cases, the students most in need of experienced teachers with content, pedagogical, and cultural expertise are often taught by the least experienced teachers, who lack community ties and cultural compatibility.

GYO: A Short History

The initiative that was to become GYO was started by Logan Square Neighborhood Association (LSNA), a community organizing group working in a low-income Latino neighborhood. In the late 1990s, LSNA launched their first parent mentor program aimed at transforming a group of roughly 30 neighborhood parents into community leaders. While working alongside teachers in their neighborhood schools, many participating parents realized that they wanted to become teachers but could not afford college. Recognizing this as an opportunity to further develop community–parent–school relations, LSNA partnered with a faculty member from Chicago State University and was awarded a federal Teacher Quality Enhancement grant to launch Nueva Generación, the precursor to GYO.[1]

During the same period, Action Now, a community group organizing in several of Chicago's African American neighborhoods, had been struggling with teacher quality and retention at their local schools. They learned about LSNA's program and realized that "growing their own" teachers from paraprofessionals and parents could reduce teacher turnover while also creating a much-needed pipeline of African American teachers. Action Now brought together other community organizations[2] to work on what would become the GYO initiative. In 2004, this group of organizers wrote and successfully advocated for a state law, the Grow Your Own Teacher Education Act, putting the concepts of LSNA's program into statute. In 2005, the group won state funding for the GYO initiative (Mediratta, Shah, & McAlister, 2009).

The GYO law spells out criteria for GYO teacher candidates and specifies key supports to be provided. Candidates must have a high school diploma or GED but cannot already have earned a bachelor's degree. Moreover, they must be eligible for federal financial aid, which means candidates must be U.S. citizens or permanent legal residents. Target candidate populations are parents, paraprofessionals, and community leaders who are active school volunteers or engage in other community activities. Once accepted into GYO, candidates receive forgivable loans (forgiven after teaching for 5 years in a low-income school) for college tuition, books, and fees. Other financial support includes stipends for student teaching, child care, and transportation. Candidates also receive academic support such as individualized tutoring and test preparation for the Illinois state licensure exams.

Once GYO was funded, the Chicago community-based organizations formed Grow Your Own Illinois (GYO IL), a not-for-profit organization. GYO IL, selected by the Illinois State Board of Education to develop the initiative statewide, researched and sought out high-need communities and key stakeholders interested in developing their own GYO consortia. GYO IL assisted them by brokering partnerships among community organizations, local school districts, and 4-year degree-granting universities. When GYO IL finished organizing statewide, there were 16 consortia: eight in Chicago and eight in other high-need Illinois communities. Today, there are 12: six in Chicago and six downstate.[3]

The GYO Structure

Each GYO consortium is a partnership among a community-based organization, a COE, one or more local school district(s), and often a community college. The community organizations recruit candidates from their membership and from among paraprofessionals at local schools. In a typical candidate selection process, representatives from the partner organizations work together to review application materials (including a written essay) and any prior college transcripts. The next step is to interview potential candidates and discuss with them the commitment they would be making to academic excellence and community involvement. If the consortium partners and the potential candidate agree regarding program fit, the candidate is admitted into GYO, whereupon she or he signs a contract committing to the terms of the program and a Family Educational Rights and Privacy Act waiver so that his or her academic progress can be shared between the university and the community organization.

After several years of implementation, GYO coordinators and academic advisors recognized that many candidates were facing challenges. Because the majority of GYO candidates are parents, employed full-time with family responsibilities, and beginning or returning to college after many years out of school, personal and academic issues could be overwhelming. In response to the need to strengthen recruitment and ensure student success, a Pre-GYO program was developed. In Pre-GYO, a potential candidate applies for federal financial aid (required of all GYO candidates) and uses only those funds to take one or two college-level courses. At the same time, the potential candidate joins a GYO cohort and is expected to play an active role. This provides the potential candidate a glimpse at both the rigors and supports of GYO. If the potential candidate succeeds academically and shows a high level of participation in the cohort, he or she is invited to join GYO and receive the full range of GYO social, academic, and financial supports.

The Essential Features: Focusing on Success

Despite some differences in operation, GYO consortia are characterized by common components that have been recognized as keys to success. The most important is the financial support that GYO grants provide for candidates (i.e., forgivable loans for tuition, fees, and books plus funds for tutoring, child care, transportation, and student teaching stipends). Without this financial support, current candidates would be unable to pursue teacher certification.

Academic and social supports are the second key element. Each community organization has a part-time GYO coordinator and each university has a GYO academic liaison. These individuals work together to ensure candidate success from recruitment to graduation and into the classroom. Because many candidates are entering college after years out of school, the GYO coordinator and academic liaison play key roles in helping candidates navigate the bureaucratic inner workings of the university. Moreover, the coordinator and academic liaison track the academic progress of candidates in order to connect them with other resources needed for success (e.g., tutoring, test preparation, help with financial aid paperwork). The coordinator and liaison encourage candidates and organize meetings and celebrations so candidates stay connected with and help each other. The community organization coordinator also trains candidates to be community leaders and involves them in local organizing campaigns and initiatives around issues such as education, immigration, foreclosures, and violence prevention. When GYO candidates become teachers, they understand from these firsthand experiences the issues faced by their students and families.

Relationships are a third key element of success. Consortium members build strong, trusting relationships with each other and with candidates through regular and ongoing communication. These relationships keep candidates from falling through the cracks when they need help. To complement the relationships within individual consortia, GYO IL has also created a Statewide Learning Network that facilitates communication and the sharing of expertise among the different consortia across the state. This practice has been key to developing successful practices and to exchanging strategies that help candidates succeed.

The GYO@NEIU Case Study

An unusual feature of GYO is the partnership between a community organization and a COE. Northeastern Illinois University's (NEIU) COE and the six Chicago community organizations that form the GYO@NEIU network have developed deep partnerships with ground-breaking results. Their work together to prepare community-based teachers of color has policy implications in Illinois and nationally.

NEIU and the six community organizations support almost 100 GYO candidates and more than 50 potential candidates in Pre-GYO and on waiting lists. As of June 2013, GYO@NEIU had 45 graduates, 90% of whom were teaching or seeking teaching positions in low-income neighborhood schools. Faculty and community organizers who work in the GYO@NEIU network have published a book (Skinner, Garreton, & Schultz, 2011) and have written several articles about the philosophical framework, key features, and the growth and development of the network. Perspectives from the university and the community follow.

Doing It Better Together: The University Perspective

Perhaps the most significant change resulting from our GYO network is the degree to which the NEIU COE faculty are involved in the GYO communities and the community organization members are involved in COE work. For example, one COE faculty member has taught a civics class for 2 years in a neighborhood convent to 50 immigrant mothers, giving them the literacy skills they need to talk to legislators about housing, safety, and a successful campaign that allows undocumented immigrants to get driver's licenses. These parents feel honored to meet a Latino professor who speaks their language and who has helped them learn how to navigate their new country.

Several faculty members mentor GYO alumni who are teaching in Chicago schools; others have partnered with community organization coordinators to lead "Saturday Sessions," helping candidates analyze educational trends and issues. In 2010, the COE began sponsoring "community study" days in our partner communities, and more significant curricular and pedagogical changes resulted, as the vignette that follows suggests.

VIGNETTE: CHANGING FACULTY THROUGH COMMUNITY INVOLVEMENT

When faculty member Jim Crawford rose to speak at a collegewide retreat on diversity issues, no one expected the heartfelt testimony that he was about to give. Jim was a regular participant in the COE's community study days, and he often complained about colleagues who did not attend. His brief remarks were designed to motivate his peers, but he also acknowledged what often happens when university professors spend time in local communities. Here are his remarks:

> As I drove to the Southwest Organizing Project neighborhood on that Friday morning, I was so full of myself. I kept thinking about what I could "do" for the people in our partner schools. It never occurred to me that they were about to teach me so much more than I could ever teach them. I have started to help one of the elementary schools and have done a few parent workshops on how special education should be working in the schools. I am humbled by the resiliency and resourcefulness of the parents and continue to learn from them every time I am in the community. We have to do more to prepare all of our students to understand and want to work in our partner communities. I'm sorry if I sound like I'm preaching, but you really need to go on a study day and we really need to do a better job of helping our students build commitment to our partner communities.

The benefits of working alongside community-based organizations extend well beyond the university's support of its GYO candidates. This unique partnership has begun to impact and strengthen the preparation of *all* preservice teachers and other school professionals (i.e., principals, school counselors, and reading specialists) at NEIU.

One area in which we see evidence is within COE coursework. As faculty increase their knowledge of the school and community contexts for which they are preparing teachers, they are better equipped to address the community challenges within the courses they teach. For example, faculty have begun to rethink and redesign assignments, materials, and methods of engaging students because they have a better understanding of issues such as foreclosure rates, neighborhood violence, and Chicago's system of tax increment financing. They no longer view exploration of such topics as ancillary but rather as integral to developing highly effective practitioners capable of reaching and teaching all students.

In one instance, within a course focused on teaching methods for supporting literacy in the content areas, a tenured faculty member redesigned a lesson on instructing adolescent students in note taking to include the topic of the growing number of homeless students. Students watched and took notes on a short Public Broadcasting Service video on homeless children in schools, allowing them to reflect on their own thinking and practices on note-taking skills and to apply new learning from course readings. Then the class discussed students' comprehension of text through note-taking practices as well as the implications of homelessness in schools. The faculty member attributed her visit to the Southwest Organizing Project neighborhood as the impetus for incorporating the topic of homeless students in her courses.

In another significant instance, the Special Education department created a new course entitled "Community Engagement and Advocacy," required of all initial certification candidates, in which candidates complete an action research project based on their work in a community organization. Further, two COE faculty have begun working with community partners and other groups to help preservice teachers learn to construct student-centered, community-based curriculum units. They now sponsor an annual Grassroots Curriculum Conference for candidates covering topics such as emancipatory curriculum and pedagogy, grassroots school reform, and equity issues. GYO teachers and principals from partner P-12 schools facilitate discussions to help candidates develop sensibilities for working within a P-12 environment that often pushes prescribed curriculum and an overemphasis on standardized testing as the sole means to measure student progress.

In 2007, the COE began regularly placing non-GYO candidates in schools in our partner communities for pre–student teaching and student teaching experiences. When this occurs, the GYO candidates are the community "experts" for their peers, helping them navigate the school and the community for more in-depth clinical experiences. Additionally, increased numbers of non-GYO teacher candidates are seeking jobs in low-income neighborhoods as a result of these school experiences. GYO is increasing the likelihood that all of the COE's graduates are prepared for and committed to strengthening schools in high-need neighborhoods.

These illustrations of the impact that the GYO partnership has had on teacher preparation at NEIU point toward increased faculty awareness of the need to address the broader challenges affecting teaching and learning in underserved neighborhoods. Impressively, the commitment shown to the GYO concept, to GYO candidates, and to the community partners has grown in the 7 years that NEIU has been involved in GYO. As a result, all of NEIU's candidates are better prepared to be activist teacher leaders.

Doing It Better Together: The Community Perspective

At a statewide GYO meeting several years ago, Jeff Bartow, Executive Director of the Southwest Organizing Project, made an important and unexpected connection.

VIGNETTE: GOOD TEACHING, GOOD ORGANIZING

I was struck by the deep connections between strong teaching and strong organizing as I listened to Dr. Charles Payne share the results of a study about the key qualities of an effective teacher in an urban classroom (Payne, 2008). He named three things: strong social supports (students sense their teachers are actively committed to their learning and well being and they receive the help they need to succeed); a high level of demand (teachers hold high levels of expectations of their students, both in light of the strong social supports provided and because they believe their students can do the work); and most important, excellent diagnostic skills (teachers understand how to respond to "breakdowns" in students' learning processes, which require less attention to the answers and more to the process by which they arrived at them. Strong teachers strive to identify the point where students have gone amiss).

Where Dr. Payne referred to strong social supports, high level of demand, and strong diagnostic skills, the community organizer would speak of "building trust," "accountability" in the context of that trust, and a strong understanding of the "power" dynamics (the ability to "diagnose" the intricacies of a problem) at play in the issues addressed by the leaders with whom they work.

Good teaching and good organizing are both rooted in building excellent relational skills, along with content knowledge, whether the content is algebra or the foreclosure crisis in Chicago. Good teaching and good organizing effectively prepare students in schools and leaders in public life to negotiate these challenges. This is the essence and strength of GYO, something that cannot be replicated in a type of teacher education that does not embed the work of preparing teachers in the community.

From the perspective of the community organizations, GYO is not a "program"; it has always been an organizing tool. The community organizations see GYO as a way both to prepare excellent teachers for their neighborhood schools and to develop them as leaders, advocating for strong and equitable public schools and other community issues that their students-to-be face. Organizers formally train GYO candidates in leadership that helps them define a leader, understand power and conduct a power analysis, understand public versus private relationships, and learn how to create an agenda and conduct effective meetings. These and other skills are also developed in the candidates' regular cohort meetings. They have time to practice developing relational skills by spending 15 minutes at the meeting talking to someone they might not know. They practice power analyses—discussing who makes decisions about education in the school, in the district, and at the state level. They also discuss and analyze issues important in the community, such as immigration or foreclosure.

Candidates put their leadership skills to work long before they reach the classroom. GYO candidates are active in the annual fight for GYO's state funding, enabling them to learn the link between budget and school policy and to practice public speaking. Many candidates participated in protests against Chicago's 2013 closings of 50 schools, many of which were in their neighborhoods. During the Chicago teachers' strike in fall 2012, candidates ran social justice "freedom schools" for neighborhood children and often joined teachers on the picket line, and faculty members worked with organizers to create a youth justice retreat on campus for students from GYO neighborhood schools. In an example of personal leadership, one candidate challenged her professor who used negative stereotypes about African American students. She felt comfortable doing so, because of her leadership training and the trusting relationships she enjoyed within the College of Education. Another candidate, in addition to providing math tutoring in Spanish to young men in his community, started a math study group at the university. He developed close friendships with faculty and other students who all came to his house to celebrate his birthday, resulting in a wonderfully diverse neighborhood party.

The community groups recruit as GYO candidates leaders who bring to teaching their life experiences and their community-based understanding of education. They believe that the potential for education is enhanced when the social knowledge of teacher candidates combines with the content knowledge provided by the university. Community organizers work to build a common voice and a common vision based on shared community values because they are building power for families.

Community organizers reflect on neighborhood power dynamics that include schools as part of the larger context of community life. Many low-income neighborhoods in Chicago have been devastated by the foreclosure crisis. Housing issues are directly connected to schools, which require stable housing for families and a safe environment for students. Community organizers build power and political will to address these issues, all interrelated, and share lessons learned with their faculty partners.

GYO works for genuine reciprocity between the community and the university—ensuring that there is substantive consultation on academic work, that the realities in the neighborhood are integrated with the academics, and that the university and the community are accountable to each other. The community organizations have enjoyed many benefits from their university relationships. The dean of the COE serves on the board of directors of Organizing Neighborhoods for Equality (ONE): Northside, the GYO organization that serves the neighborhood near NEIU where she lives. The COE is an institutional member of ONE and contributes to their power, their reach, and their work. The dean is a member of Southwest Organizing Project's Community Education Team, working with local schools, principals, and teachers. As a result, a faculty member is teaching a principal preparation program in a neighborhood school so that teachers can earn their principal's license on site, saving them a long commute to campus. The community organizations have found that university faculty are interested in learning about their neighborhoods and are responsive to requests. These reciprocal relationships continue once GYO candidates graduate and are teaching. A GYO fifth-grade teacher organized a science fair and invited several NEIU faculty members and the director of Action Now Institute to be judges, allowing them to assess seventh and eighth graders as they discussed their hypotheses. Having faculty in the community and community members on campus reinforces the sharing of expertise and strong, collaborative relationships, and creates the conditions under which other community members and family members of GYO candidates see a college degree as an attainable goal.

GYO Today: Challenges

GYO IL faces a number of challenges, including the length of time it takes for candidates to graduate, candidate attrition, and lack of full commitment to the GYO mission by a few consortia. But two challenges are particularly difficult: state funding and passage of the Test of Academic Proficiency (TAP).

The state has provided more than $20 million—a steady stream of funding—for GYO since 2006, but state funding is definitely a mixed blessing, especially during severe fiscal crises. Illinois passes its budget annually, so the battle for funding is waged every January to June. This requires an enormous organizational effort for almost half of every year that drains time and energy from the program itself. GYO has never received sufficient funds to grow as originally planned. Instead, funding has been slowly declining, from a high of $3.5 million in 2009 to a dismal $1 million in 2013, increased to $1.5 million in 2014. One modest benefit of GYO's annual fight for funding is that GYO candidates graduate with personal knowledge of education as a legislative issue.

The TAP, similar to the Praxis in many other states, is an exam whose passage is required to enter a teacher preparation program. A candidate is limited to five attempts to pass all four sections of the test. In September 2010, with little public notice, the Illinois State Board of Education significantly increased the scores required for passage and allowed candidates to "bank" the scores of any subtest passed, an improvement over past practice which had required candidates to retake all four subtests each time until they passed.

Since September 2010, GYO IL has tracked the pass rates on this test. In almost 3 years, pass rates for all potential teacher candidates dropped by more than half (86% to 39% passers). But far more troubling, only 17% (737) of African American candidates and only 22% (912) of Latino candidates have passed in this 3-year period. African Americans and Latino teacher hopefuls represent 19% of all test takers but only 9% of those passing. These data strongly suggest that Illinois will not improve its standing as third worst in the country in the mismatch between teachers and students of color without a significant and innovative intervention. GYO candidates, who are 86% African American and Latino, struggle with this test, which is screening the great majority of people of color out of teaching.

GYO IL organized around the test results, joining forces with COE Deans. In 2012, we won a victory when the state board approved the use of two alternatives to the TAP: the ACT + Writing (score of 22 or better) or the SAT (composite score of 1030). As of this writing, some 4,000 people have used ACT and SAT in lieu of TAP. GYO IL's new campaign is to get the state board to collect data on race and ethnicity of those using ACT and SAT in order to determine if these alternatives are helping to solve the problem of racial disparity.

GYO: The Future

GYO's brand of excellent teacher education is embedded in the community, honors the expertise of parents and other community members, and mediates the experience for preservice teachers and other school professionals; it takes time, commitment, and money. After 8 years of work, we are beginning to see large numbers of GYO candidates graduate. GYO teachers will begin to address the significant problem of teacher turnover in underresourced urban and rural schools. Research (Carroll & Foster, 2008; Hunt & Carroll, 2003) demonstrates that teachers have to be on the job 3 or 4 years before they have honed their craft and can begin to see large gains in student achievement. The easy fix of a truncated route to teacher preparation results in teachers who leave the classroom in 2 or 3 years, creating a revolving door of teachers in struggling schools and instability in the lives of low-income children and their communities (Allensworth et al., 2009).

Do we as a nation have the political will to invest in GYO-like programs to prepare culturally competent teachers of color for the classroom? Are we serious about increasing the diversity of the teaching force? Addressing this issue is overdue and is both right and just. Most important, it is effective; research shows that teachers of color who know the culture and community of their students produce better academic results for students of color (Clewell, Puma, & McKay, 2001; Dee, 2004; Meier, 1993).

What will growing a GYO approach require? First, it requires viewing non-traditional teacher candidates who live in low-income communities as assets, seeing their strengths, their gifts, and their promise as teachers and leaders. Second, it requires community organizers who work in communities of color and who recruit candidates of color and develop their leadership. Organizers also develop the power and political will (Oakes & Rogers, 2006) to ensure that low-income students in the poorest neighborhoods benefit. Third, it requires personal support for candidates—coordinators who know them well, track their academic progress, and provide tutoring when needed—as well as financial help. Fourth, it requires the kind of rethinking of teacher preparation that the education faculty at NEIU is doing. They have recognized that preparing highly effective teachers for low-income schools requires more than "book" knowledge—they must leave campus to learn about low-income communities and schools firsthand and their students must do their clinical practices in these schools. This in turn will begin to change curricula and traditional practices. Fifth, it requires funds coupled with policy commitment. Cultivating nontraditional candidates who know the language, culture, and community and, with support, will become highly effective teachers requires money and is an investment well worth making.

To prove the value of the investment, GYO IL commissioned an independent assessment of new GYO teachers (Rasher & Gould, 2012). GYO teachers scored in the exemplary range on content knowledge, pedagogy, classroom management, and student and family engagement. It is clearly an experiment that is working.

The GYO community partners developed GYO to cultivate teachers of color who know the language and culture of their students—who look like them. If teachers for urban schools are prepared in a vacuum, without taking the realities of the community into consideration, preparation programs are doing a huge disservice to low-income students of color. In GYO@NEIU, teacher candidates, university faculty members, and community organizers share the same vision—one of urban neighborhood experience grounded in assets and addressing issues of racism and classism. The GYO@NEIU partners see the school as a key factor in stabilizing and revitalizing low-income neighborhoods. They work together to heal the wounds of systemic racism and to bring about equality and justice that communities deserve. Authentic transformation happens from the inside out, not the outside in. GYO's teacher preparation program is built on the soul of the community and is transformational. GYO points the way toward the hope and promise for true transformation of schools in the nation's most challenged communities.

Notes

1 Soo Hong (2011) has written about LSNA's parent engagement work in her book *A Cord of Three Strands,* providing insight into how Nueva Generación was conceived.

2 The six GYO community-based organizations are Action Now Institute, Enlace Chicago, Kenwood Oakland Community Organization, Logan Square Neighborhood Association, Organizing for Neighborhood Equality: Northside, and Southwest Organizing Project.
3 One school district–led consortium fell victim to the state's fiscal crisis; one very small consortium graduated its final candidate and went out of business.

References

Allensworth, E., Ponisciak, S., & Mazzeo, C. (2009). *The schools teachers leave: Teacher mobility in Chicago public schools.* Chicago, IL: Consortium on Chicago School Research, University of Chicago Urban Education Institute.

Boser, U. (2011). *Teacher diversity matters: A state-by-state analysis of teachers of color.* Washington, DC: Center For American Progress.

Carroll, T., & Foster, E. (2008). *Learning teams: Creating what's next.* Washington, DC: National Commission on Teaching and America's Future.

Clewell, B. C., Puma, M. J., & McKay, S. A. (2001). *Does it matter if my teacher looks like me? The impact of teacher race and ethnicity on student academic achievement.* Washington, DC: Urban Institute, Education Policy Center.

Dee, T. S. (2004). Teachers, race, and student achievement in a randomized experiment. *Review of Economics and Statistics, 86,* 195–210.

Hong, S. (2011). *A cord of three strands: A new approach to parent engagement in schools.* Cambridge, MA: Harvard University Press.

Hunt, J., & Carroll, T. G. (2003). *No dream denied: A pledge to America's children.* Washington, DC: National Commission on Teaching and America's Future.

Ingersoll, R. M. (2003). *Is there really a teacher shortage?* (Report co-sponsored by the Center for the Study of Teaching and Policy and the Center for Policy Research in Education). Seattle: University of Washington, Center for the Study of Teaching and Policy.

Mediratta, K., Shah, S., & McAlister, S. (2009). *Community organizing for stronger schools: Strategies and successes.* Cambridge, MA: Harvard University Press.

Meier, K. J. (1993). Latinos and representative bureaucracy: Testing the Thompson and Henderson hypotheses. *Journal of Public Administration Research and Theory, 3,* 393–414.

Miner, B. (2010). Looking past the spin: Teach for America. *Rethinking Schools, 24.* Retrieved from www.rethinkingschools.org/archive/24_03/24_03_TFA.shtml

Oakes, J., & Rogers, J. (2006). *Learning power: Organizing for education and justice.* New York, NY: Teachers College Press.

Payne, C. (2008). *So much reform, so little change: The persistence of failure in urban schools.* Cambridge, MA: Harvard University Press.

Rasher, S., & Gould, R. (2012). *Grow your own teachers: An evaluation of teaching effectiveness,* Chicago, IL: Grow Your Own Illinois.

Skinner, E., Garreton, M. T., & Schultz, B. (2011). *Grow your own teachers: Grassroots change for teacher education.* New York, NY: Teachers College Press.

8

PATHWAYS2TEACHING: BEING AND BECOMING A "RIDA"

*Madhavi Tandon, Margarita Bianco,
and Shelley Zion*

> Before I entered this class I had never thought of becoming a teacher . . . it was the
> first time that teachers actually talked to me about becoming a teacher.
>
> (Francisco, Latino)

This chapter describes Pathways2Teaching, a precollegiate program designed to engage high school students of color[1] in exploring the teaching profession as an avenue for engaging with, giving back to, and righting wrongs within their communities. In order to increase the number of teachers of color in our nation's schools, we must first develop students' sociopolitical and critical consciousness as a means of disrupting the educational inequities they have experienced, for themselves and for their communities. Students with a strong sociopolitical consciousness not only view the world critically and understand the complexity of systems of oppression and privilege but also intentionally develop skills and a commitment to action to rectify those unjust systems (Watts, Williams, & Jagers, 2003). Furthermore, students begin to see teaching as a way to impact change in and for their community—an opportunity to become what Duncan-Andrade (2007) described as "Ridas"—a reference to a popular hip-hop term describing someone's loyalty and commitment to their people. When describing highly effective urban teachers, Duncan-Andrade stated, "Ridas are consistently successful with a broad range of students. . . . The depth of their relationships with students allows them to challenge students and get notable effort and achievement" (p. 623). Developing Ridas is the primary goal of the Pathways2Teaching program, which is an academically challenging course for students attending low-performing high schools.

Pathways2Teaching: Guiding Principles

Pathways2Teaching was founded on six guiding principles, which were informed by national issues in urban education and are organized in two clusters. The first cluster focuses on activities for students that build agency and skills; the second focuses on what adults in the program do to create access and success for students. Table 8.1 highlights key programmatic activities that support each guiding principle. In this chapter, each principle is explained in detail and illustrated with examples and student quotes.

TABLE 8.1 Guiding Principles and Key Activities

Guiding principles	Key activities
	Student activities
Critical lens	• Readings and discussions • Examination achievement gap data • Urban education research project: Counter narrative writing project
Promote the teaching profession	• Weekly elementary school field experience • Field experience reflection journal
College access and readiness	• Skill building (e.g., essay writing, research report writing, public speaking, presentation development) • Earn college credit for course • College search and application support • Scholarship application support • Campus visits and information sessions
	Adult activities
Inclusion	• Provide *all* interested 11th- and 12th-grade students an opportunity to earn college credit while engaging in a rigorous curriculum.
Role models and mentors	• Students are provided with opportunities to establish mentor–mentee relationships with community members, teacher candidates, master's level students, doctoral students, and faculty of color. • Nationally recognized scholars of color are invited to guest speak via Internet video conference call.
Family and community engagement	• Regular communication between family members and teachers of the course • Parents are regularly informed of the work of the class and invited to learn about it through student led presentations. • Family and community evening for students' research presentations.

Critical Lens: Focus on Educational Justice

> Teachers are really a gateway to success or failure. A good teacher makes learning fun, positive . . . being in that field gives you a chance to change a lot of lives, make a stand on things like the education gap, like segregation.
>
> (Jada, African American female)

The first guiding principle of the Pathways2Teaching program is the intentional focus on developing a curriculum informed by a critical theoretical framework. More specifically, the curriculum is informed by (a) critical race curriculum (Yosso, 2002), (b) critical pedagogy (Duncan-Andrade & Morrell, 2008; Giroux, 2011), and (c) sociopolitical development (SPD) theory (Watts et al., 2003). By incorporating these theoretical frameworks into our curriculum, we seek to empower students with emancipatory knowledge in order to develop what Freire (1990) described as critical consciousness, a means to connect knowledge to agency and power. In thinking about how to operationalize the development of critical consciousness toward the end goal of liberation, we draw on Watts et al.'s (2003) conceptualization of SPD as emphasizing

> an understanding of the cultural and political forces that shape one's status in society. We use it to describe a process of growth in a person's knowledge, analytical skills, emotional faculties, and capacity for action in political and social systems.
>
> (p. 185)

SPD directs attention to how people develop critical responses to injustice, and supports the development of resiliency in youth from oppressed communities (Ginwright, 2010). Two key elements of SPD that are relevant to the Pathways2Teaching program include understanding the self within systems and exercising agency within those systems (Kirshner, Zion, & Hipolito, 2010).

To help explain the concept of understanding the self within systems, scholars working within traditions of liberation psychology argue that true well-being comes when people gain a critical consciousness of the historical and material forces shaping their lives, see suffering as human-made and alterable, and shift from accepting the ways things are to envisioning a new order (Watts et al., 2003). SPD specifically addresses the need to move beyond awareness that the world is unjust into the development of skills and dispositions that support taking action to rectify experiences or situations that are unjust—to exercise agency within systems.

> I've had an understanding that as minorities we're set up to fail for some time. This class made the thought more apparent. . . . We are getting a second rate education in a second rate educational system. And people wonder why a lot of us no longer take it seriously? This has got to change and it's up

to us to change it. We can't sit back and expect the world to fix it. It's the same world that put us in this situation. They don't care. We are the only ones who can make a difference. Become a mentor, donate, do something productive! We spend all this time trying to get out of the hood but never wanna do anything to change it.

(Darius, African American male)

Through the explicit introduction of these theoretical frameworks, students are encouraged to critically examine institutional racism and the policies and practices in schools that label, sort, marginalize, and oppress. This approach engages the political and socioeconomic realities in students' lives and guides them in challenging systemic structures that have shaped their lives and created barriers to a quality education (Duncan-Andrade & Morrell, 2008). Fostering SPD allows students to see themselves as agents of change and empowers them to seek ways of challenging the status quo. One of the ways in which we enact this aspect of our curriculum is through a required research project.

The student research project illustrates how aspects of SPD and critical pedagogy are incorporated while building important college readiness skills. Students are taught to conduct research and explore problems that are consequential in their own lives and communities. After exploring a number of educational issues that have had a personal impact on their lives (e.g., the opportunity–access gap, effects of poverty on learning, disproportionality, underrepresentation of teachers of color), students select a topic of interest for further inquiry, then delve into their own life experiences and validate their narratives. Once topics are selected, students (a) develop research questions, (b) locate and organize reliable information for a literature review, (c) identify a method for collecting and analyzing data, (d) write a research report and cite sources, (e) identify possible solutions, and (f) present their findings and suggestions for change to an authentic audience.

The power of acquiring emancipatory knowledge and agency through the research project is best illustrated by way of example. The following two of the many student research projects illustrate the power of learning how to interrogate a system of oppression and acquiring the necessary knowledge and skills to enact change. Although their topics were very different from each other, both had very personal meaning, and each culminated in achieving the desired result of informing teachers and impacting change for their community.

What Do Teachers Know About Foster Care?

Darryl, a 12th-grade student in our first cohort, wanted to explore teachers' understanding of the foster care system and its impact on students. More specifically, he wanted to know what training and experience, if any, teachers had in this area. As a 17-year-old African American young man who had been placed in foster care at age 10, he frequently shared his frustrations that teachers knew nothing of the emotional distress he and other students in foster care experienced or how this impacted their learning and underachievement. Understanding teachers' knowledge and training about children in the foster system became his research project.

Darryl conducted a comprehensive literature review about foster care and then developed a 13-question survey consisting of a mix between Likert scale and open-ended response questions. The survey was disseminated to teachers at his high school as well as faculty in one urban education teacher preparation program. Darryl's research findings validated his hypothesis and exposed how very little teachers (and many university faculty) know about students in foster care and how infrequently (if at all) the topic is addressed in teacher preparation programs. Darryl was able to share his research findings in various forums, including a research symposium at a local university and a statewide conference for teachers. His findings provoked interest in the topic of foster care in the teacher preparation program, and as a result, several courses now include readings and assignments related to the system and the experiences and needs of children placed in foster care.

Taking on Immigration Reform

Francisco, an active school leader and class president, had great hopes of attending a 4-year college and a sincere interest in becoming a teacher. However, as an undocumented student who entered the United States at the age of 12, his path to college and future dreams had many legal, emotional, and financial barriers, many of which he felt teachers did not understand. Francisco's research project focused on exploring the experiences, frustrations, and hopes of other undocumented students and community members.

> I researched experiences of undocumented students and the DREAM Act. I wanted to find out why they're keeping us from attending college just because we're from a different country—we have the same dreams of going to college and being somebody and having a better future.
>
> (Francisco, Latino)

Francisco completed a comprehensive literature review examining the chronology of proposed DREAM Act legislation, developed an interview protocol, and videoed his interviewees as they recounted personal experiences and frustrations with unrealized plans. His research revealed that undocumented students felt a sense of hopelessness without comprehensive immigration reform that includes tuition equity, the right to work, and a path to citizenship.

Francisco created a short digital movie with music, images of the American flag, and video clips of his interviews. He presented his research findings and the accompanying movie at the Colorado University Denver Research Symposium.

His presentation caught the attention of a local Latina community advocate who requested permission to use his movie with Latino students and their teachers around the country.

Promote the Teaching Profession

> I never noticed the impact teaching had. Teachers are essential to schools and to life really. I think I saw more about the importance of teaching.
>
> (Reggie, African American male)

Children's dreams for the future are often based on the visions and hopes bestowed on them by the adults in their lives, including their teachers (Gordon, 2000). Children are also influenced by media representation and community conversations they hear about the particular benefits and challenges of any given profession. These factors, among others, have a profound influence on how children and youth view their career options. Despite a long history among communities of color in which the teaching profession has been held in high regard (Foster, 1998; Lewis, 2006), Gordon's (2000) research highlights an unfortunate reality that students of color are not encouraged to enter the teacher workforce by their communities and families and, in many cases, their own teachers.

Based on the research of Gordon and others, the second guiding principle of the Pathways2Teaching program is an intentional focus on countering the current narrative about teaching by promoting the teaching profession as an act of social justice—a way of disrupting educational inequities experienced by students of color and creating positive change in and for their communities. Research illustrates that most teachers of color are attracted to the profession because of their awareness of and personal experiences with racial injustices in the educational system; like Ridas, they enter the field with strong visions of social justice and an explicit intent to remedy existing inequities in schools (Su, 1997). As such, throughout the program we emphasize the role of teachers as social justice advocates and activists.

In order to help students understand the critical need for diversifying the teacher workforce, they are exposed to a growing body of literature illustrating how and why teachers of color play significant roles in the lives and education of students of color (see Introduction and Chapter 3 of this book). Through readings, discussions, assignments, and research projects, students explore how teachers of color are committed to issues of social justice, multicultural education, and making sure their students are exposed to an academically challenging curriculum. We encourage students to understand how teachers of color act as cultural mediators with insider knowledge, thereby improving students' overall school experiences (Gay, Dingus, & Jackson, 2003; Gordon, 2000; Sleeter & Milner, 2011; Villegas & Irvine, 2010) and sense of community in the classroom. In many ways we are simply providing students with academic language to articulate what they already know.

> I feel like my teachers that are like the same race as me, or are just minority, we have a deeper connection with each other. Like we could talk about more things like from where we're from . . . and we just connect more on like the culture levels I guess.
>
> (Teresa, Latina)

In addition to promoting the teaching profession through readings and reflecting on their own experiences, we know the value of hands-on experience and real-world knowledge of the potential impact teachers make on children's lives and so require a weekly field experience in which high school students engage in teaching practices through tutoring elementary students from their community. Early on, high school students are taught the benefits and methods of engaging younger students in read-alouds. Decades of research document the numerous benefits of read-aloud experiences with children (Beck & McKeown, 2001), and hence Pathways2Teaching students are trained to conduct read-alouds that focus on vocabulary development and reading comprehension skills.

> I really liked being able to help somebody learn instead of the one being taught. I liked how I saw growth in the time I was with my two students. When we worked with vocabulary and they really struggled with it. I liked having fun ways to help them learn it.
>
> (Jasmine, African America female)

Through this structured field experience, Pathways2Teaching students begin to develop effective pedagogical practices that support high levels of literacy development as well as a personal understanding of the powerful and rewarding aspects of building relationships with their students. On their path to becoming Ridas, students take on the roles of mentors, role models, and teachers who contribute to their students' success. This has been a powerful motivator for students to seriously consider entering the teacher workforce and returning to contribute to their community.

> It's helped my thinking because I want to help kids and it's made me think about the kind of change I can make if I'm a teacher. I can teach other young males such as myself about being teachers. It's not always about the pay. You have to do what you love. It's like a selfless act to achieve that self-actualization. . . . I think I would want to teach in this area. I know all the ins and outs; I know all the tricks that I've done and all. I would want to come back here and give back to the community.
>
> (DeShawn, African American male)

College Access and Readiness

> Well I'm Hispanic so a lot of Hispanics think they can't succeed, so they always rate you as you're not going to graduate, you're not going to go to college.
>
> (Lucas, Latino)

The pathway into teaching for students of color is directly influenced by the number of students of color who graduate from high school and persist through college. Unfortunately, the pathway that moves students of color from public school to public school teaching is in disrepair (Bianco, Leech, & Mitchell, 2011). Decades of research have exposed systemic issues perpetuating low achievement for students of color, especially those from high-poverty communities (Berliner, 2006; Schott Foundation, 2009). Thus, any discussion of the underrepresentation of teachers of color must also acknowledge how the public school system has failed the very population we need most as classrooms teachers—and this is especially true for Latino and African American males.

This rigorous course equips students with college access and readiness skills as well as an appreciation of the importance of academic success. As part of the course curriculum, Pathways2Teaching students tour local colleges, spend time in college classes, interact with undergraduate and graduate students, and learn about the college application and admission process. These college experiences, although initially daunting, build a level of confidence and comfort in gaining a sense of familiarity with college life and demystify college expectations, thereby allowing students to see themselves as college worthy and ready.

Inclusion

> Growing up and going to the schools I went to I assumed college was impossible for a Black poor kid out of the projects and only for rich kids in good situations. . . . I was able to take college courses even with a low GPA. . . . My decision to go to college was completely based on Pathways2Teaching. Before this class I never really thought about college.
>
> (Darryl, African American male)

Far too many bright and talented students of color, especially those living in poverty, are excluded from high-quality, rigorous curricula such as those found in advanced placement courses, International Baccalaureate (IB) programs, or college credit precollegiate experiences (Ford, 2011, 2013). Instead, they are relegated to remedial classes or disproportionately represented in special education programs (Artiles, Kozleski, Trent, Osher, & Ortiz, 2010; Blanchett, 2006) and grossly underrepresented in gifted programs and advanced level courses. Ford (2011, 2013), Oakes (1985, 1990), and many others have written extensively about the harmful effects of deficit thinking and limited opportunities this stratification of resources creates. Without access to quality education in the early school years and college preparation courses in high school, it is no surprise, then, that of students who do persist through high school, many are unprepared for college.

For these reasons and more, we are unapologetic about maintaining an inclusive approach to our program by abolishing entrance criteria that limit students' access. Unlike other teacher pipeline programs (e.g., Teacher Cadet), we are inclusive of *every* interested student, regardless of grade point average (GPA), disciplinary record, English language proficiency, or any other exclusionary criteria. All interested students have access to the Pathways2Teaching program and can receive college credit on successful completion of the course.

Role Models and Mentors

> Having a graduate student in the class allowed us to view the college perspective from their view and help us be more prepared for college. . . . If more urban communities had more role models and mentors like these three women, students will have an arsenal of information about college and the importance of it.
>
> (Darryl, African American male)

Providing role models and informal mentoring relationships has been recommended as a strategy to increase high school graduation and college-going rates (Erickson, McDonald, & Elder, 2009) for students of color who are first-generation high school graduates with college aspirations (Flores & Obasi, 2005). Through the Pathways2Teaching program, high school students are introduced to a network of college students at the undergraduate, graduate, and doctoral levels. The informal mentoring relationships take many forms. Undergraduate and graduate student mentors regularly visit the classroom in order to develop informal relationships with students, and doctoral students volunteer with the program and accompany students on their weekly field experience. We are also intentional about our efforts to engage faculty of color by inviting them to speak in our classes or join us for lunch during campus visits. Additionally, scholars of color from around the country are invited to guest lecture via Skype. Our intent is to make sure that Pathways2Teaching students meet and interact with college students at every level of their academic trajectory as well as provide multiple opportunities to learn from local and national scholars of color.

Family and Community Engagement

> It would be exciting to see that your teacher lives in the same community as you do . . . [to] live right across the street from him. And not be like "oh yeah I live across town so I have to wake up early just to get here."
>
> (Darius, African American male)

Duncan-Andrade (2007) identified a sense of duty and commitment to students and the community as a practice of effective teachers—or Ridas. Ridas are "not afraid of the community and consequently built relationships with parents, siblings, families, and the broader community" (p. 628). These partnerships demonstrate a moral commitment to educational equity and social justice (Auerbach, 2007, 2009), something we strive to model for our Pathways2Teaching students.

There are many examples of how Pathways2Teaching instructors engage with students, their families, and the local community beyond the schools' walls. As Ridas, the instructors know where students live, shop, play, and worship and often share the same spaces and experiences. Pathways2Teaching instructors make frequent home calls and regularly attend school and community events (e.g., sports events, school plays, community meetings), which provide additional opportunities to interact with and cheer alongside families or advocate for the school and the community as partners with parents. We also invite families and community members to participate in the Pathways2Teaching program. School board members and retired district teachers volunteer in our classrooms, district administrators visit as guest speakers, and families and community members listen and learn from our students as they present their final research presentations. In sum, these collaborations strengthen our program by helping families and community members understand the need to diversify our teacher workforce. As we build relationships with families and the local community, we provide an exemplary model for our students in terms of what effective urban educators do to create a culturally responsive and collaborative learning environment.

Reflections: Successes, Challenges, and Future Direction

Pathways2Teaching is a work in progress; we continue to learn from our students and community partners about what works and what aspects of our program need further revision.

We have had many successes along the way, and first among them is our high school graduation rate. To date, 100% of seniors who have taken the course have graduated from high school. Many are currently attending local community colleges or state universities—even if only part time. This is in stark contrast to national, state, and district graduation and college-going rates for students of color from high-poverty communities. Through surveys and interviews we have learned that many students who had not considered a teaching career prior to taking this class now have an interest in pursuing teaching or related fields. As of December 2013, of the 17 seniors who graduated high school in 2011 (our first cohort), 100% were taking college courses (even if only one course per semester), and 18% had recently declared an education major. Several others from the same cohort acknowledged that although they were not pursing an education major at this time, their interest in serving the community remained strong as they explored other ways to advocate for children in fields such as social work, school counseling, and criminal justice.

Students now have a deeper understanding of an unjust educational system that has failed them, and this information has been liberating for many. This is not to suggest that students have shirked ownership of their poor academic performance during high school. In fact, many students have shared their frustrations and personal disappointment in their contributions to low GPAs and levels of college readiness. Through personal communication, students have expressed great regret at not working harder, studying more, and taking school more seriously. However, they now understand how attending under-resourced schools in high-poverty communities placed them at greater risk of school failure and contributed to academic underachievement. Additionally, they better understand how race and class influence teachers' deficit views and lowered expectations. They are also now equipped with a sociopolitical consciousness that allows them to see that change is possible and that they can participate in creating something better.

> A lot of the information that comes up in this class, a lot of what we read, the articles, it makes me sit back and think like wow, this is real, this really is a problem. Like you always know there's a problem with education . . . you know it's there and you see it because you never really see anything unless you're looking for it . . . but when you really start to think about what you need to change and stop the cycle that we live in, it helps make you create something new, something better.
>
> (Darius, African American male)

Another success of the Pathways2Teaching program has been its sustainability. As of 2013, the program has continued successfully for 3 consecutive years (with plans for continued expansion) without the support of large grant funding. Each stakeholder, including the university, school district, and individual schools, has contributed to the program's success without overburdening one institution or agency.

Although Pathways2Teaching has been successful on many levels, we do have challenges to address if we are to take this work to scale and truly have an impact on the demographic representation of teachers of color. We organize the discussion of challenges around the following core areas: (a) technical, (b) relational, (c) resistance, and (d) systemic.

At the technical level, we note similar challenges that many urban schools in poor communities face. The lack of resources and access to technology has hampered our ability to implement the program in optimal ways. For example, our schools cannot provide regular and reliable access to computers and the Internet for students' research or writing projects. Often students must handwrite assignments and wait, sometimes weeks, for computer access to type or conduct literature reviews. Obviously, this does not prepare them well for the quality of work required in college.

Another technical challenge includes creating a process for teacher training and professional development. This becomes imperative as we move into more schools, hire new instructors, and build our capacity for growth. Teachers' time for regular meetings and professional development is minimal. Although school principals and teachers have good intentions of supporting and participating in continuous professional development and shared vision making, their intentions quickly become subverted by district demands. A goal for 2014 is to develop a training model and a robust online resource center for teachers and school district personnel with a desire to replicate our program.

At the relational level, we experience challenges with staying connected to students for our longitudinal research and also supporting students while in college. Students' phone numbers and e-mail addresses change frequently once they graduate from high school. Fortunately, however, we have found that using social networking such as Facebook and Twitter has been fairly successful in maintaining contact.

At the resistance level, we have encountered two primary areas of opposition: a few teachers and funding agencies. First, although most teachers in our school settings are very supportive of the Pathways2Teaching program, we are aware of a handful of teachers' negative (in some cases caustic) reactions to students' research projects. This seems particularly true when those student projects have exposed the grim realities of students' school experiences with institutional racism and their lack of opportunities to learn. Thus far, the resisting teachers have been young, White, and inexperienced female teachers who have personalized students' research data and interpreted their findings as a personal attack. In one case, a student was told that her research was a "lie" and an "embarrassment." Referring back to Andrade-Duncan's (2007) description of teachers, clearly these few teachers are *not* Ridas. Instead, they represent the antithetical archetype—a "Gangsta":

> These teachers deliberately sidetrack or bully forthright discussions of racism, structural inequalities, and social and economic justice. Gangstas are the worst of our time-honored profession and they are present in virtually every school where students are suffering. Fortunately, they are not the majority of urban teachers.
>
> (p. 622)

In a follow-up interview with one student to support her and debrief this negative experience, she stated,

> I am glad that my presentation did what it was supposed to do. It got teachers thinking about an issue that is important to me and to all the students I surveyed as well as students of color around the country.
>
> (Elora, African American female)

We have learned several lessons from this type of rare resistance. We must prepare our students with the skills and confidence to respond to these infrequent criticisms in ways that honor their voice while also reminding them of teachers' positions of authority and power. Equally important, it is essential to provide a schoolwide professional development opportunity early in the school year so teachers understand the program's guiding principles and our focus on developing students' sociopolitical and critical consciousness.

Our second area of resistance has come from potential funding agencies. Although we have received consistent praise for our program's goals and success, funders often assume that students with low GPAs are not the "best and the brightest" and therefore might not make good teachers. As such, they resist funding the inclusive model we insist on. We have had to counter their arguments by providing the context to explain that our students *are* the best and the brightest but have been given limited opportunities to demonstrate their potential. Further, we argue that their experiences and persistence in an unjust educational system creates the perfect constellation of characteristics needed to meet their future students' needs.

At the systemic level, we note two primary barriers. We acknowledge that introducing college readiness skills and academic rigor in 11th or 12th grade might be too little, too late. Further, when students do get excited about college and teaching, access to funding and support is problematic. These barriers in particular threaten the long-term success of the program.

We identify a need for a spiraling curriculum that engages students in a social justice and college readiness curriculum beginning in ninth grade or earlier. Waiting until 11th and 12th grade to expose students to a rigorous curriculum with high demands in order to prepare them for college has posed challenges for our students. Further, career choice theorists and researchers suggest that certain cognitive competencies related to career development happen around the ages of 13 or 14 (Tang, Pan, & Newmeyer, 2008). Perhaps by beginning a Pathways2Teaching program in earlier grades we can build college readiness at a younger age while simultaneously addressing students' sociopolitical development and interest in teaching and related fields as an act of social justice.

At the systemic level we also must address our students' extreme economic challenges by seeking scholarship funds. Unlike many other college students, there are vast differences in our students' social, economic, and contextual factors that impede their pursuit of an undergraduate degree and teaching license in 4 or 5 years. After high school graduation, nearly all of our students have moved out of their homes, some by choice and others by necessity. Even with federal and state financial aid, many students must struggle to maintain full-time employment and navigate a new world of independent living while also taking college classes. This means that completing a degree and teacher licensure will take extraordinary effort, unwavering motivation, and more time to complete their undergraduate program.

Conclusion

The pipeline to teaching for students of color is in crisis. For various reasons, many students have simply never considered becoming a teacher and are also unprepared for the demands of college. We must respond to this crisis by finding ways to encourage their exploration of teaching while also addressing their academic needs. In many respects the Pathways2Teaching program is similar to other teacher pipeline programs (e.g., college visits, working with young children); however, we differ significantly in our approach in two important ways. First, we are adamant about maintaining an inclusive model that ensures access and opportunity to every interested student. Second, by developing a curriculum with a strong critical theoretical base, we include an intentional focus on building students' sociopolitical development and critical consciousness. With this focus we seek not only to diversify the teacher workforce but also to encourage our students to become future Ridas and change the landscape of urban schools and outcomes for students of color.

Note

1 We use the terms *students of color* and *teachers of color* throughout this chapter because given the demographic shift in the United States and specifically the demographic population in urban communities, it is a more accurate and contemporary description than the terms *ethnic* or *racial minority*.

References

Artiles, A. J., Kozleski, E., Trent, S., Osher, D., & Ortiz, A. (2010). Justifying and explaining disproportionality, 1968–2008: A critique of underlying views of culture. *Exceptional Children, 76*, 279–299.

Auerbach, S. (2007). From moral supporters to struggling advocates: Reconceptualizing parent roles in education through the experience of working-class families of color. *Urban Education, 42*, 250–283. doi:10.1177/0042085907300433

Auerbach, S. (2009). Walking the walk: Portraits in leadership for family engagement in urban schools. *School Community Journal, 19*, 9–32.

Beck, I. L., & McKeown, M. G. (2001). Text talk: Capturing the benefits of read-aloud experiences for young children. *Reading Teacher, 55*, 10–20.

Berliner, D. C. (2006). Our impoverished view of educational research. *Teachers College Record, 108*, 949–995. doi:10.1111/j.1467-9620.2006.00682.x

Bianco, M., Leech, N. L., & Mitchell, K. (2011). Pathways to teaching: African American male teens explore teaching as a career. *Journal of Negro Education, 80*, 368–383.

Blanchett, W. J. (2006). Disproportionate representation of African Americans in special education: Acknowledging the role of White privilege and racism. *Educational Researcher, 35*(6), 24–28.

Duncan-Andrade, J. M. (2007). Gangstas, Wankstas, and Ridas: Defining, developing, and supporting effective teachers in urban schools. *International Journal of Qualitative Studies in Education, 20*, 617–638. doi:10.1080/09518390701630767

Duncan-Andrade, J. M. R., & Morrell, E. (2008). *The art of critical pedagogy: Possibilities for moving from theory to practice in urban schools.* New York, NY: Lang.

Erickson, L. D., McDonald, S., & Elder, G. H. (2009). Informal mentors and education: Complementary or compensatory resources? *Sociology of Education, 82*, 344–367.

Flores, L. Y., & Obasi, E. M. (2005). Mentors' influence on Mexican American students' career and educational development. *Journal of Multicultural Counseling and Development, 33*, 146–164.

Ford, D. Y. (2011). *Multicultural gifted education* (2nd ed.) Waco, TX: Prufrock Press.

Ford, D. Y. (2013). *Recruiting and retaining culturally different students in gifted education.* Waco, TX: Prufrock Press.

Foster, M. (1998). *Black teachers on teaching.* New York, NY: New Press.

Freire, P. (1990). *Education for critical consciousness.* South Hadley, MA: Bergin & Garvey.

Gay, G., Dingus, J., & Jackson, C. (2003). *The presence and performance of teachers of color in the profession.* (Paper commissioned by the National Collaborative on Diversity in the Teaching Force). Washington, DC: National Education Association.

Ginwright, S. (2010). *Black youth rising: Activism and radical healing in urban America.* New York, NY: Teachers College Press.

Giroux, H. A. (2011). *On critical pedagogy.* New York, NY: Continuum.

Gordon, J. A. (2000). *The color of teaching.* London, England: Routledge Falmer Press.

Kirshner, B., Zion, S., & Hipolito, C. (February 2010). *Civic learning and action among non-college bound youth: A design-based research study.* Chicago, IL: Spencer Foundation.

Lewis, C. W. (2006). African American male teachers in public schools: An examination of three urban school districts. *Teachers College Record, 108,* 224–245. doi:10.1111/j.1467-9620.2006.00650.x

Oakes, J. (1985). *Keeping track: How schools structure inequality.* New Haven, CT: Yale University Press.

Oakes, J. (1990). *Multiplying inequalities: The effects of race, social class, and tracking on opportunities to learn mathematics and science.* Santa Monica, CA: RAND.

Schott Foundation for Public Education. (2009). *Lost opportunity: A 50 state report on the opportunity to learn in America.* Retrieved from www.otlstatereport.org/

Sleeter, C. E., & Milner, H. R., IV. (2011). Researching successful efforts in teacher education to diversify teachers. In A. F. Ball & C. A. Tyson (Eds.), *Studying diversity in teacher education* (pp. 81–104). New York, NY: Rowman & Littlefield.

Su, Z. (1997). Teaching as a profession and as a career: Minority candidates' perspectives. *Teaching and Teacher Education, 13,* 325–34.

Tang, M., Pan, W., & Newmeyer, M. D. (2008). Factors influencing high school students' career aspirations. *Professional School Counseling, 11,* 285–295.

Villegas, A. M., & Irvine, J. J. (2010). Diversifying the teaching force: An examination of major arguments. *Urban Review, 42,* 175–192.

Watts, R. J., Williams, N. C., & Jagers, R. J. (2003). Sociopolitical development. *American Journal of Community Psychology, 31,* 185–19.

Yosso, T. J. (2002). Toward a critical race curriculum. *Equity & Excellence in Education, 35,* 93–107. doi:http://dx.doi.org/10.1080/713845283

9

ADMISSION SYSTEM OF A TEACHER PREPARATION PROGRAM DESIGNED TO ALLOW ACCESS FOR DIVERSE TEACHER CANDIDATES

Robbie Burnett

The demographic makeup of the nation's teaching workforce continues to perpetuate a mismatch with the degree of racial–ethnic diversity in the population of prekindergarten through Grade 12 (P-12) students. Attempts to increase the diversity of teachers addresses the all-too-familiar achievement or "opportunity" gap in the P-12 educational system. In the state of Minnesota, the rapidly changing demographics (Minnesota Minority Education Partnership, 2012), and the fact that Minnesota has one of the largest achievement gaps between White and non-White students in the nation's K-12 system (Weber, 2009), have heightened the strategic imperative to intentionally seek faces that reflect those of our P-12 classrooms.

There are several factors identified at different stages in the recruitment pipeline that influence diversifying the teaching workforce. One prominent factor has been that the underachievement of minority students in P-12 education has resulted in fewer diverse students entering postsecondary education (Ingersoll & May, 2011). In addition, given the global economic workforce, employment opportunities for minorities have swelled, shrinking the share of diverse graduates entering university-based teacher preparation programs. According to Ingersoll and May (2011), "When minority candidates do seek to enter teaching, the growth of occupational entry tests, coupled with lower pass rates on these tests by minority teaching candidates, has meant that fewer minority candidates are successful" (p. 3). To attract students of color requires relational capacity within a network of multiple and nontraditional recruitment strategies, mentoring, support, and innovative partnerships that offer market-driven programs in high demand career fields.

This chapter examines how the College of Education (COE) at Minnesota State University (MSU), Mankato began to tackle this challenge. This midsize public institution within the Minnesota state colleges and universities system exists in a predominantly White community, which has historically lacked diversity in its teacher preparation program. In 2009, only 2.9% of students enrolled in the COE teacher preparation programs were from diverse backgrounds. To address this problem, the COE established a goal to increase the number of students of color in their teacher licensure programs to 25%. In order to achieve this ambitious goal, they invested in efforts to support both recruitment and retention in their program; this chapter discusses both efforts.

The first effort was the creation of the Maverick Teacher Recruitment Coordinator (MRC) position charged to provide organizational leadership to all aspects of teacher education recruitment and retention. The second was the development of the innovative Teachers of Tomorrow (ToT) initiative; this program was created to support students from traditionally underrepresented groups to address the particular challenges of sustaining candidates' interest and abilities (Bireda & Chait, 2011) in order to "keep them warm" as they completed general education requirements and applied for COE program admission.

Maverick Teacher Recruitment Coordinator

Prior to becoming the MRC, I was a graduate assistant who served in the COE student relations office while pursuing my master's degree and teacher licensure in special education. While in this role, I provided academic advising to 1st- and 2nd-year students, assisted them with course registration, and participated in regional and national recruitment and outreach events. These experiences allowed me to gain practical and personal experience in the work of recruitment and retention. Following the completion of my master's degree in special education, I was highly sought after to continue my relationship with the university but in a professional role—that of the MRC for the COE.

This role was designed and developed as part of the Network for Excellence in Teaching (NExT) Initiative—a partnership between the Archibald Bush Foundation and 14 university-based teacher preparation programs across Minnesota, South Dakota, and North Dakota, to innovatively transform teacher recruitment, preparation, support, placement, and assessment. The NExT initiative goal is to increase the number of students in the three states from prekindergarten through college who are on track to earn a degree after high school by 50% and to eliminate disparities among diverse groups. The MRC position was originally financially supported by the NExT initiative; however, due to the success, influence, and tremendous need for this role (and driven by an extraordinary and passionate leader), this position has now been moved to the academic base of the university for long-term financial support.

It is noteworthy to mention that around the same time the partnership came into fruition, the university identified recruitment, retention, and increased graduation rates of diverse students as a high strategic priority. Shifting the MRC position from "soft" to "base" funding is a result of the performance of the position. In addition, the shift showcases the alignment of unit practices to university strategic priorities and the institution's commitment to diversifying the teaching force.

The initial charge of the MRC position was twofold. First, the main task of the coordinator was to build meaningful and long-term connections with various offices and programs that are seen as relevant to recruitment and retention. Examples include the following:

- Units within the university (e.g., admissions, the Office of Institutional Diversity, faculty, etc.),
- P-12 partners, with a clear focus on identifying and recruiting the next generation of educators (e.g., through guidance counselors, administrators and teachers; various programs such as summer camps at the university campus and teacher candidate mentoring of P-12 students),
- Community college partners, especially for high-demand areas of licensure, and
- Community and academic agencies in various contexts serving potentially diverse teacher candidates such as the Minnesota Minority Education Partnership and the Minnesota College Access programs.

These networks connected our system of interacting with prospective students and their parents and families, involving them through various programs on and off campus, advising them regarding their options at MSU, Mankato, and then bridging their transitions from middle school to high school, high school to community college or university, community college to university, or from nonteaching careers into teaching.

Second, the coordinator is responsible for developing and implementing an extensive marketing campaign (electronic, print, visual media, etc.), emphasizing that the program is highly selective and competitive and that it offers real financial incentives for highly qualified candidates.

Moreover, the COE simultaneously hired another woman of color to serve as the student relations coordinator, a position that facilitates academic advising and registration, and leads the Academic Advising Office by managing professional education admissions for all teacher licensure programs, variance requests, and professional communications. The MRC and student relations coordinator work in tandem to recruit, support and graduate candidates of color.

I began my position in the fall of 2010 with limited direction and in uncharted territory. I was building the plane while flying it and selling seats to passengers while charting the course as I went along. This presented the opportunity for innovation, collaboration, and creative problem solving with building the recruitment infrastructure. Based on the goals of the NExT initiative, the design of our intentional recruiting efforts to target creative problem solvers, critical thinkers, excellent learners, and change agents consisted of the following:

- Creating the Maverick Teacher Recruitment Center to facilitate and manage partnerships with community colleges and P-12 schools,

- Designing and executing research to better identify high-potential teacher candidates, and
- Establishing a goal that 25% of its prospective teachers be students of color.

While I was laying the groundwork of the recruitment program, teacher education in Minnesota experienced numerous changes in state certification requirements. In 2010, the state moved away from the Praxis series and adopted the Minnesota Teacher Licensure Examination, a standardized assessment normed at the sophomore collegiate level of rigor. We also became an accelerated state in the adoption of the Teacher Performance Assessment (EdTPA) as we participated in a number of pilot studies in order to have more voice in the shaping of the instrument. EdTPA is a preservice assessment mechanism designed for the candidates to demonstrate their ability to effectively teach their content–subject to students through an electronic portfolio. It is comparable to entry level licensing tests such as the bar exam.

These changes prompted the urgency to learn what was coming down the pike and how such changes would impact the overall development of teachers of color. The lack of accessibility to specific content rubrics, scoring modules, and additional costs associated with the battery, coupled with the costs and pressures already established for passing the Minnesota Teacher Licensure Examination, presented another challenge in recruiting promising diverse candidates into the teaching profession.

Such complexities became influential components in decision making and planning around the design of how to retain and support our candidates of color. This caused me to reach out to the Office of Field and International Experience to begin conversations about how we might expose students to expectations of the EdTPA prior to them being accepted into their programs. As a result of these discussions, we began continuous dialogue across recruitment, placement, and support pillars to identify ways to share lessons learned to aid in preparing participants in ToT (described in the next section) to perform successfully. It was important for me, as the architect designing the recruitment and retention infrastructure, to keep my finger on the pulse. I attended a variety of national conferences across P-12 and higher education addressing college access, teacher education, and racial equity. Best practices learned from national symposiums were then applied to the construction of our teacher recruitment and retention model. One significant outcome of such new learning was the development of a diversity strategic recruitment plan.

To help focus and plan the use of resources and increase the number of diverse candidates recruited into the COE teacher preparation programs, the Office of Assessment and Research designed a diversity strategic recruiting plan. The approach the plan takes is to identify "clusters" of successful diversity candidates based on the high schools they attended and further (through other datasets) examine those schools and the school performance as defined through parameters identified by the Minnesota Department of Education. The results of the plan

TABLE 9.1 Biannual Diversity Enrollments

Year (fall semester)	2009	2011	2013
Diversity enrollment	2.9%	6.9%	9.5%

Note: Data from Minnesota State University, Mankato College of Education (2013).

provided clear and measureable identification of schools with significant diversity populations that are growing in numbers to allow for a more sustainable recruiting effort.

Approaching Year 4, the position has expanded. In my role as the MRC, I worked out of multiple sites and linked to a network of personnel that I coordinated. As the leader of this area, I directed efforts to build, organize, design, and plan the COE's recruitment infrastructure. As the key spokesperson for teacher recruitment within the COE, I represented the university and engaged with a variety of stakeholders to connect prospective students with various offices and programs. My work drives the college's ability to increase student enrollment, grow programs, and maintain quality. Progress is measured but consistent; the concerted efforts of the MRC are beginning to show results, as shown in Table 9.1.

Teachers of Tomorrow

The ToT program supports students from traditionally underrepresented groups who complete general education requirements and apply for admission into a teacher licensure program. Our vision is to prepare and engage teacher candidates of excellence in relevant and innovative opportunities that integrate collaborative and effective practices in order to produce real-world educators that ensure student success. Because quality teaching is complex and develops overtime, ToT was created for students from diverse backgrounds with the intent to "keep them warm" during their continual development while completing general education requirements and applying for COE program admission. Demographics of participants include African American males and females, Biracial females, White males, Somali males and females, Latina females, and Hmong females. These were 1st-, 2nd-, and 3rd-year students predominantly from metropolitan areas of Minneapolis–St. Paul Twin Cities, Minnesota; Milwaukee, Wisconsin; Chicago, Illinois; and St. Louis, Missouri. Students were seeking admittance into initial licensure programs of elementary and early childhood education, special education, and K-12 secondary education. In addition, we wanted to engage and immerse candidates of color with their White counterparts to create a safe space for each to learn from one another. Initially the ToT program offered the following benefits to participants:

- Weekly meetings on various academic and P-12 educational topics such as the importance of diversity in learning and teaching, the impact and influence of racial and social identities on the contribution of their future role as a teacher, and promoting equity;

- Participation in on-campus and recruitment outreach events;
- Academic advising;
- Assistance with preparation for program admission;
- Scholarship opportunities;
- Development and polishing of time management, organizational, communication, and study skills;
- Assistance in navigating the institutional experience such as learning to advocate for self, initiating student faculty contact, finding available support services, and modeling positive interactions with faculty and staff of different backgrounds; and
- Exposure to peers with similar interests to enhance a healthy and motivating learning atmosphere.

The COE supported the work of the MRC by allotting two graduate assistants (one funded through Institutional Diversity) to carry out the work. Graduate assistants operated as an extension of the MRC coordinating recruitment events, facilitating ToT weekly meetings and organizing study groups.

Some of these students did not possess the solid foundation, support, and guidance that I had been afforded. As a leader, I recognized the "cry in the land" from students who desired the map and tools to be successful. I designed the ToT program in 2010 for this reason. During my time at MSU Mankato and while developing the program, I had the experience and opportunity of viewing higher education through two lenses that contributed to my understanding of what ToT needs to do.

My first lens was as a student, when I lived with my father who was a previous faculty member at the university. In that context, I was afforded a strong foundation and guidance on how to navigate my higher education experience. Literature suggests that involvement, engagement, and affiliation are critical to students' development and progress in postsecondary education (Hurtado & Carter, 1997). Being equipped with this knowledge and support boosted my confidence, which made it easier for me to persevere through graduation.

The second lens is as a professional within the Minnesota State Colleges and Universities system. In this role I am developing an understanding of how structures and systems operate in teacher preparation programs. Continuing to learn in my own work, digest my findings, and reflect on my own student experience, I have developed a passion for teacher education admission policy work dedicated to race and equity, which I believe stems from completing a teacher preparation program myself and then becoming a professional working with teacher candidates of color.

In Year 1, the ToT program inherited six diverse students already in the pipeline and seeking admission into our teacher preparation programs. Retention rates increase when diverse teacher candidates receive targeted rigorous, purposeful support (Villegas & Rogers-Ard, 2012). Working with and learning from these students, I quickly found out that the backbone of recruitment is retention—if I was going to recruit more candidates of color, a regime of support needed to be in place to facilitate retention.

Establishing a welcoming and inclusive culture, the ToT program experienced a fluid number of participants. Active membership was measured by the number of meetings attended in a semester, the amount of study table hours acquired per semester, and involvement in recruitment outreach activities such as participating in on-campus student panels or speaking to middle and high school students during on-site school visits. ToT participants were supported through mentoring and Minnesota teacher licensure preparation, which serve as essential methods that facilitate retention. Policies surrounding program admission were also viewed as critical components to increasing and retaining the number of diverse candidates into programs. Such practices are described in the next sections in further detail.

Mentoring

The program began in 2010, but it was not until 2012 that we began to understand the types of support our students needed to be successful. What we discovered is that just like new teachers, teacher candidates also need to be mentored throughout their time in preparation. Literature suggests that strategic support from carefully selected and professionally trained mentors can accelerate the effectiveness of new teachers to ensure the success of all students (New Teacher Center, 2013). However, little is mentioned about pairing preservice teacher candidates with mentors during the early stages of their preparation, prior to field experience or student teaching. Perceiving the need for a mentoring framework that would motivate students to strive for excellence, improve and accelerate academic performance, and produce high-caliber teacher candidates, the MRC reached out to the college's Center for Mentoring and Induction, an affiliate of the New Teacher Center in Santa Cruz, California, to explore options of how to create a preservice mentoring model for teacher candidates in the ToT program.

Because mentoring was identified as the most critical component to the support system, the role of the graduate assistants in the ToT program was transformed from logistics and facilitation management to skillful mentoring of students in the program. Through the New Teacher Center and the Center for Mentoring and Induction, graduate assistants received formal training and participated in professional learning opportunities that would equip them with strategies needed to successfully support ToT participants. In addition, COE faculty also participated in the two centers' professional learning opportunities.

During fall of 2013, graduate assistants and COE faculty launched professional learning communities to foster increased communication and engagement in the spirit of collaboration for the support and success of ToT students. Each graduate assistant mentors four to five students. One-on-one meetings are scheduled according to the need of the student. For the first three to four meetings, the mentoring protocol (described in the following paragraphs) is used to guide the discussion and planning for the semester.

At the beginning of each semester, student and mentor engage in a reflective assessment. Mentors help the students complete and reflect upon their academic performance during a semester using reflection assessment tool. The tool is designed to review their academic progress, strengths and challenges they faced during a semester, and establish goal grade point average (GPA) for the upcoming semester. It is front-end intentional planning for the semester. Using the GPA calculator, the students calculate semester grades needed to achieve their goal GPA. This provides them an idea of what grade they would need for each course. Students have different study skills and strengths, and the mentors help them create a semester calendar and craft a weekly schedule (routine). This involves planning their week using a calendar or planner in which the students intentionally plan or identify the number of hours invested in each course and establish a goal for assignment submission using due dates from the course syllabi. The students are encouraged to craft a grade tracker using an Excel spreadsheet for all the courses they are enrolled in for the semester.

The components of the grade tracker include goal grade for an assignment, a section to record the achieved goal, and a comment section to reflect whether they achieved their goal and any potential reasons that helped them achieve and/or any challenges that contributed to any failure they may have experienced. The students are also encouraged to proactively connect with professors in the beginning of the semester. The students draft a letter to faculty sharing their participation in ToT and requesting the co-involvement of faculty to assist with tracking their academic progress throughout the semester. The mentor and mentee schedule follow-up meetings to review their progress in the action plan they created for the semester.

After the mentoring protocol is completed, the collaborative assessment log, adapted from the New Teacher Center, is used for remaining one-on-one meetings. It operates as collaborative work with the students and the mentees. The conversations are based on the four quadrants of the collaborative assessment log: reflection, addressing current challenges, identifying the next steps of the student, and next steps of the mentor. Goal setting is another process that is combined with the collaborative assessment log so that the students know what they want to achieve for the semester and then determine achievable next steps. At this point, the process has yielded higher motivation and elevated self-confidence in our students—the belief that they can achieve their goals.

Another New Teacher Center adapted tool we use guides a process called *selective scripting*, which involves observing a beginning teacher candidate to identify the areas of professional growth. The tool involves scripting teacher–student interaction during a classroom observation, focusing on the teacher's language and the students' response. After the observation, the mentor and teacher candidate collaboratively assess the area of focus. The selective scripting tool comes into play when our students approach admission into their respective programs and participate in TeachLivE Lab. This learning simulation activity builds failure and resilience into the program as teacher candidates are placed in a mixed-reality teaching environment to practice pedagogy and content. TeachLivE also allows ToT participants to practice their classroom management skills of engaging all learners via the simulation. To get ahead of the game, candidates must have opportunities to fail frequently during their time in teacher preparation programs while there are still supports in place (Marshall, 2013).

Minnesota Teacher Licensure Examination Support

Through experience and program maturation, we had discovered our desired destination and the tools necessary to equip us for a successful journey. Program participants were progressing through general education courses and approaching the point of making applications to their respective initial licensure programs. However, members began to voice their concerns about passing the new state exam requirement, the Minnesota Teacher Licensure Examination. As previously mentioned, this new exam has an increased level of rigor with a poor track record of passing both White and non-White teacher candidates. In 2010, the Minnesota Teacher Licensure Examination basic skills passing rate for COE teacher candidates was 59% in writing, 64% in reading, and 63% in mathematics respectively (Minnesota State University, Mankato College of Education, 2010). The exam's basic skills strict cutoff scores have become an additional stressor for ToT program participants. Literature suggests that licensure tests only provide a snapshot of teacher effectiveness and have the potential to both adversely affect diverse candidates outcomes and decrease workforce diversity (Goldhaber & Hansen, 2010).

Currently, students are only required to provide evidence of registering and taking the battery for provisional acceptance into their respective programs. However, it is being considered that in the near future, candidates will be required to pass the examination before entering their respective programs. Support for such a requirement comes from concerns that allowing students to enter programs when they are unable to pass the examination is "leading candidates on," which many traditional university teacher preparation programs view as unethical. Foreseeing this barrier, and with the assistance of a tenured senior literacy faculty member, the MRC and Student Relations Coordinator were able to reach out to members of the K-12 & Secondary Programs Coalition—faculty members from content (mathematics and English) departments to form a workgroup. The

Coalition discussed the "knowns" about the test, reviewed data, and shared what they believed from their content expertise would aid students in attaining successful scores on the assessment.

As a result, a collegewide Minnesota Teacher Licensure Examination advising protocol was developed. In the fall of 2013, four Minnesota Teacher Licensure Examination basic skills preparation courses were offered that focused on math, reading, writing, and general test overview. They were designed for students that have not passed the test, anticipate having trouble passing that particular section, or have never taken the test. To bolster support for ToT participants enrolled in the Minnesota Teacher Licensure Examination math prep course, the design of an explicit math study table was offered. ToT participants then register and take the Minnesota Teacher Licensure Examination basic skills math test as a group. We anticipate that ToT participants who enroll in the basic skills math prep course and participate in the basic skills math study table will pass prior to applying to their respective programs, strengthening the probability of gaining program admission.

The ToT program has become not only the catalyst for increasing and retaining the number of students of color enrolled in the COE's teacher preparation program but also a safe place for diverse candidates and their White counterparts to engage and immerse themselves in intercultural competency experiences by learning from each other. ToT provides support for students to persist with the intent and focus on excellence. The essential retention methods of mentoring, strategic support for licensure, and innovative solutions are showing promise in helping diverse teacher candidates persist, thrive, and become licensed graduates.

In collaboration with the COE Office of Assessment and Research, we are in the development stages of building a data system that captures demographics and analyzes data and persistence of ToT participants. The analysis of applicable data is ongoing; early indications include fall-to-fall retention rates as shown in Table 9.2. Looking across academic years from the inception of the ToT program to the present, we can see that retention rates have increased over time.

TABLE 9.2 Teachers of Tomorrow Fall-to-Fall Retention Rates

Year	2010	2011	2012	2013
Beginners	11	17 (9 from previous fall)	16 (14 from previous fall)	14 (12 from previous fall)
Additions	0	8	3	5
Attrition	2	3	2	2
Returners	9	14	14	12
Retention	61%	64%	81%	85%

Note: Data from Minnesota State University, Mankato College of Education (2013).

Program Admission

Demands for more qualified teachers, coupled with national efforts to improve and elevate the process of teacher preparation, have necessitated a reexamination of the admission and retention policies and practices of teacher preparation programs (Ginsberg & Whaley, 2003). Given that the COE has seen considerable change in state licensure, curriculum, and structures, combined with an increase of diverse candidates matriculating and preparing to apply for admission to major and program, the COE is now examining their admission policies and processes with a focus on undergraduate initial licensure admission.

The examination was conducted by the COE Admissions Policy Taskforce, comprised of representation from initial licensure programs that included faculty, field experience officials, and P-12 school partners. Our purpose was to revisit and take a step back to review procedures and strategies because it is best practice for adapting to the changing dynamics of our profession. The goal of this task force was to evaluate existing criteria for admission into majors and professional education, and to develop recommendations for improvement based on current student performance and other available data. In addition, the group explored options for aligning individual department admission criteria across the college. Discussions also developed around reviewing data on successful and unsuccessful teacher candidate performances during field experience. Our P-12 school partners felt this might aid in assessing student dispositions at point of admission. Work from the task force continues, and investigations strive to establish a language and rationale for an admissions policy statement as it relates to candidate selection for the academic year 2015–2016.

At the time when this chapter was written, investigations of the task force involved reviewing institution data and statewide data on Minnesota Teacher Licensure Examination pass scores. Thirteen out of 21 teacher preparation programs in Minnesota require students to pass the examination prior to program admission. Therefore, the task force recommended consideration of the same requirement. In addition, the group will continue to explore how pass rates impact enrollment for teacher preparation programs.

Conclusion

In recent decades much has been written about the growing need to diversify the teaching force (Ingersoll & May, 2011). The supply and demand of teachers of color in P-12 schools is center stage of the education profession, drawing the attention of scholars and policymakers alike (Villegas & Irvine, 2010). Given the historical context of this issue, addressing the demographic imperative of recruiting, preparing and retaining a diverse and highly effective teaching force over time continues to amplify shortages, deficits, and barriers. New research is needed to provide innovative solutions and produce culturally compatible teachers that reflect the faces of our nation's classrooms and challenge systemic policies and practices.

At the university level, recruitment and retention of diverse teacher candidates is only one strategy to tackle the issue. Such efforts may be considered technical solutions rather than adaptive change. Too often, entities tout having an increase in diversity, but how has such an increase transformed curriculum and practices to be inclusive and to recognize the contributions of this new and much-needed population of students?

Another implication for preservice university teacher preparation programs is that recruitment and retention not rest solely on the shoulder of one individual but rather that efforts to promote graduating diverse teacher candidates become the culture of the college. This may cause a need for a shift in paradigm (see, e.g., Chapters 11 and 12). According to Childs et al. (2011), teacher preparation programs' "willingness to change turns out to be around the edges" rather than at the core.

For instance, addressing teacher education program admission involves more than just candidate selection; admission challenges the policies, systems, and structures that reach the heart of COEs' duty to prepare and produce educators that reflect the demographics of our P-12 classrooms. According to Villegas and Irvine (2010), "Increasing the diversity of the teaching force is a crucial component of a comprehensive strategy for addressing the achievement gap that has historically existed between students of color and their White counterparts" (p. 187). Thus action causes COEs to look inward, adjust, and shift rather than making changes externally. Teacher education faculty and staff play integral roles in the success of recruitment, retention, licensure, and graduation of diverse teacher candidates.

Teacher preparation programs focused on increasing diversity should also consider aligning teacher recruitment and retention program efforts vertically—with university strategic goals and priorities—and horizontally—with units across the university that support underrepresented groups such as institutional diversity and equity offices. Such collaborations will assist with the development of recruitment, support, and retention infrastructure designed to produce teachers of color.

Once programs are established, faculty involvement with retention is a crucial component to the success of recruitment efforts. Faculty will appreciate their voices being heard in the shaping of retention efforts, thus strengthening their commitment to the work of responsive recruitment and retention that is needed to meet the rapidly changing dynamics of our profession required to be successful with all learners—both P-12 and university students.

References

Bireda, S., & Chait, R. (2011). *Increasing teacher diversity: Strategies to improve the teacher workforce.* Retrieved from www.americanprogress.org/issues/education/report/2011/11/09/10636/increasing-teacher-diversity/

Childs, R. A., Broad, K., Gallagher-Mackay, K., Sher, Y., Escayg, K.-A., & McGrath, C. (2011). Pursuing equity in and through teacher education program admissions. *Education Policy Analysis Archives, 19*. Retrieved from http://epaa.asu.edu/ojs/article/view/

Ginsberg, R., & Whaley, D. (2003). Admission and retention polices in teacher preparation programs: Legal and practical issues. *Teacher Educator, 38*, 169–189.

Goldhaber, D., & Hansen, M. (2010). Race, gender, and teacher testing: How informative a tool is teacher licensure testing? *American Educational Research Journal, 47*(1), 218–251.

Hurtado, S., & Carter, D. F. (1997). Effects of college transition and perceptions of the campus racial climate on Latino college students' sense of belonging. *Sociology of Education, 4*, 324–345.

Ingersoll, R. M., & May, H. (2011). *Recruitment, retention and the minority teacher shortage* (Consortium for Policy Research in Education Research Report # RR-69). Retrieved from www.cpre.org/recruitment-retention-and-minority-teacher-shortage

Marshall, L. (2013, July 23). Six elements for improving teacher prep. *Education Week*. Retrieved from www.edweek.org/tm/articles/2013/07/23/fp_marshall_prep.html

Minnesota Minority Education Partnership. (2012). *2012 state of students of color and American Indian students report*. Retrieved from http://mmep.org/policy/research

Minnesota State University, Mankato College of Education. (2010). *Office of Professional Education Minnesota Teacher Licensure Examination (MTLE) institution overall results report*. Mankato, MN: Author.

Minnesota State University, Mankato College of Education. (2013). *Bush Foundation milestone report*. Mankato, MN: Author.

New Teacher Center. (2013). *Professional learning series for mentors and coaches: Instructional mentoring field guide*. Santa Cruz, CA: Author.

Villegas, A. M., & Irvine, J. J. (2010). Diversifying the teaching force: An examination of major arguments. *Urban Review: Issues and Ideas in Public Education, 42*, 175–192.

Villegas, A. M., & Rogers-Ard, R. (2012, December 18). WANTED: A more diverse teaching force [*Education Week* webinar]. Retrieved from www.edweek.org/go/webinars

Weber, T. (Narrator). (2009, July 15). Study: Achievement gap persists in Minnesota, rest of U.S. [Radio broadcast episode]. K. Wurzer (Producer), *Morning Edition*. Retrieved from http://minnesota.publicradio.org/display/web/2009/07/14/achievement_gap

10

TACTICS AND STRATEGIES FOR BREAKING THE BARRIERS TO A DIVERSE TEACHING FORCE

William F. Ellis and Kitty Kelly Epstein

This chapter is intended to be practical. It does not analyze demographics, history, or theory because these topics are covered elsewhere in this book and in our own earlier writing (Epstein, 2012a, 2012b, 2005). The chapter has two purposes. (a) It can serve as a handbook of specific tactics to diversify the teaching force in a particular community or higher education institution. We discuss five barriers and suggest that readers address each of them with the recommendations at the end of that section. (b) The chapter outlines a strategic approach to creating a movement that can break down the barriers to diversifying the teaching force more broadly across the country. We argue that the teacher diversity problem is so pervasive that a movement for change, which can be started by virtually anyone, anywhere in the country, is badly needed. With the tactics we suggest, almost any group can produce some changes, thereby addressing two of the biggest problems for communities of color everywhere—lack of meaningful, stable employment and lack of enjoyable, affirming, and effective education.

The U.S. educational system has always had barriers to the employment of diverse teachers. There has never been an ethnically representative teaching force, and the legislators and policymakers with authority to mandate one have never been willing to do so. The argument of this chapter is that a diligent, passionate, enthusiastic effort using the tactics we propose can change the problem to some extent within particular communities. We agree with critical race scholars that racism is an ongoing aspect of the U.S. social order (Ladson-Billings & Tate, 1995), and we suggest that teacher-credentialing issues are one manifestation.

In light of these realities, it is also our view that the system, which essentially reserves jobs for Whites, is at the core of the U.S. credentialing process and will continue to exist until a powerful social movement pushes it aside in the same way that other overt forms of segregation and privilege have been pushed aside in the past; the second section of this chapter outlines that broader effort.

Our expertise results from our life experience, our professional work, and our activism. Along with many colleagues and allies, we have been able to create successful teacher diversity initiatives and activist support to sustain them. William F. Ellis led the Oakland Partnership Program, which recruited and prepared approximately 300 diverse teachers in two districts in the San Francisco Bay Area during the late 1990s (Epstein, 2012a). Before accomplishing this early victory in teacher diversity, Ellis attended segregated schools in the South and then graduated from a historically Black college, Morehouse College, where he received a thorough grounding in civil rights thinking and activity. Many of the individuals recruited through the Partnership Program have since become innovative teacher leaders and school district administrators (Epstein, 2012a).

Kitty Kelly Epstein also worked in the Partnership Program and has recently been part of Teach Tomorrow in Oakland, led by Rachelle Rogers-Ard (Sawchuck, 2013; see Chapter 2). In addition, she has helped to diversify the faculty and student body of several higher education institutions. Epstein served as Education Policy Director for Mayor Ron Dellums, and the mayor himself also made important contributions to developing this movement (Epstein, 2008). Epstein was recently awarded the Scholar-Activist Award by the Urban Affairs Association for her work in the area of teacher diversity, among other accomplishments in urban analysis and organizing. She has written earlier articles and a book that deal with these topics (Epstein, 2012a, 2012b, 2005).

Immediate Problems and Tactical Solutions to Diversify the Teaching Force Within a Particular Community

Through these experiences we have identified and dealt with five specific, ongoing barriers to the recruitment and credentialing of teachers of color: (a) reaching the people who would want to teach; (b) financing the credential process in light of requirements to work for free (i.e., student teaching), high test fees, the cost of test preparation, and the cost of graduate tuition; (c) teacher tests, which, like all other standardized tests, exclude more people of color than Whites; (d) higher education credentialing departments, which have their own set of barriers, fees, and requirements; and (e) other forms of personal support.

Recruitment: Reaching the People Who Might Want to Teach

The ongoing segregation of American society is the first reason Latinos, Asians, and African Americans do not enter the teaching force. Whites tend to network with other Whites in professional organizations, neighborhoods, schools, social events, and churches. The many networks and processes required to enter teaching are more available to Whites because they predominate within the relevant systems.

Solutions

All the programs with which we are associated welcome candidates of all races, but because of the lack of diversity in the teaching force and the segregated networks mentioned earlier, it is important to reach out to media and organizations that are likely to reach non-Whites. There are many ways in which this outreach can be done.

The Black and Latino press. Over the years we have requested and received a great deal of coverage in the Black and Latino press. In the San Francisco–Oakland Bay area, this has meant extensive support from the Post News Group, which has published numerous articles on individual Black and Latino college graduates who were entering teaching and specifics on how to contact us for recruitment and support. Black and Latino newspapers are generally small businesses with small revenue. Teacher programs that have funding should definitely spend some of it on paid ads, not just expect free publicity! At the same time, publishers of the ethnic press are often anxious to do news reporting on employment and education issues. Therefore, straight news on these issues is also possible. The Post News Group, which publishes seven Bay Area newspapers (www.postnewsgroup.com) and the Spanish language television station, Univision (www.univision.com) have been very helpful to our recruitment efforts.

Other community press and publicity. Other community newspapers, such as the *Montclarion* in Oakland, have also run articles. A single front-page article in the *Montclarion* newspaper produced a room full of diverse potential teachers in the era of the Oakland Partnership Program. The Pacifica news stations and National Public Radio have carried stories. There have been ads on the sides of buses, and there have been ads at the Bay Area Rapid Transit stations that featured the mayor saying, "We want you to teach Oakland children." In contrast, ads in the corporate press and traditional employment advertising do not seem to produce much.

Personal networks. If those organizing and staffing the teacher diversity efforts are diverse, they will have diverse e-mail, church, school, and business networks.

The "pitch." In this sort of campaign, the ads should not be seeking "diverse teachers" but rather individuals who want to explore the possibility of teaching. This is different. Because people without a credential do not think of themselves as "teachers," they are not likely to answer ads for teachers. Career-changers and recent college graduates who might consider teaching as a viable source of employment and a way to give back to their communities are the major target audience for your advertising.

Mass events. Mass events are a way to create a large group of potential teachers. If you host an event attended by a hundred people who are interested in exploring the possibility of teaching, five or six are likely to pursue the entire credentialing process through all the barriers. The event should be in a public space with good public transportation. It should be a place that conveys inclusiveness and that is a

familiar venue for diverse people. It should not be a personal home or a place associated with primarily White events. When the great African American progressive
Ron Dellums was mayor of Oakland, he was very interested in teacher diversity. So
we held a recruiting event in City Hall. It was inspiring to see hundreds of diverse
Oaklanders filling up City Council chambers to hear the mayor urge them to teach
children who were growing up in West and East Oakland with the same problems
and possibilities he had faced some 55 years earlier. We have also held events in
schools, colleges, churches, and auditoriums. Think big! And serve snacks!

On pipeline programs. Much of teacher recruitment focuses on something
called *pipelines*, often pipelines of high school or community college students (see,
e.g., Chapter 8). We are not opposed to these programs, and we mention an
important one later in this chapter. There should be many more of them, but
they take a long time to produce results. Therefore, we have focused our limited
resources on individuals who have a bachelor's degree or are about to obtain one.

Summary of Recommendations on Recruitment

We recommend that those wishing to diversify the teaching force take these steps:
(a) use the ethnic and community press and e-mail networks of diverse organization to publicize events, and (b) aim for events with large numbers of interested
college graduates and career-changers who may not already be thinking of teaching. Among these large numbers, some will be willing to persist through the various barriers to earning a credential.

Alternative Certification as a Way to Break Some Financial Barriers

In many states, including California, prospective teachers are expected to teach for
a year for free. This unpaid year is called "student teaching." There is a 20-to-1
racial wealth gap between Black and White families in the United States, and an
18-to-1 racial wealth gap between Latino and White families (Shapiro, Meschede, &
Sullivan, 2010). This means that the median White family has 20 times the accu-
mulated net assets of the median African American family and 18 times those of
the average Latino family. Although it is not easy for most people to finance student teaching, financing a year of unpaid work is possible for many White families
and not at all possible for many other families. African Americans and Latinos
generally do not have the money to work for a year for free. The best solution to
this problem thus far has been alternative certification, a process that allows individuals to work for a salary while learning to teach (McKibbin, 2001).

There are essentially two types of teacher certification programs: traditional and
alternative. Traditional credentialing is generally housed in a university. Most of
these credential programs rely on school districts, close to the college or university,
to provide the student teaching requirement of the certification process. Teachers
generally receive no remuneration for this work.

Alternative certification programs are often housed in school district or community facilities and often, but not always, involve a partnership with a university. Most of the teachers in these programs are interns and choose to practice teaching in a paid position while studying to complete their credentials. Alternative certification does, in fact, produce a larger number of non-White teachers than traditional certification (Nadler & Pederson, 2009; Shen, 1998). The alternative certification program called the Oakland Partnership created by Fred Ellis and other collaborators was credited with a likely impact on Oakland's teacher diversity; for example, Keleher and Libero (1999) reported that "the CSU/Hayward-Oakland Public School District Partnership has had approximately 60 to 80% candidates of color in its teaching program since 1995, an arrangement which may contribute to Oakland's relatively high proportion of teachers of color" (p. 35).

Summary of Recommendation on the Use of Alternative Certification

We recommend that individuals, community organizations, school districts, and colleges working to diversify the teaching force look into the alternative certification possibilities offered by the relevant state or local government. Based on our experience in California, the most viable and enduring model seems to be a collaboration between a school district and one or more higher education institutions. It can also be helpful to include a nonprofit community-based organization that can administer the "extras" like test preparation and test fees, the cost of which may create resistance within a school district. A good source of information is the National Association for Alternative Certification.

Dealing With the Tests

In the past two decades, U.S. education has moved from a system that assumed a college degree provided enough knowledge to teach elementary children to a system that requires up to five different standardized written tests, each with multiple sections, each with a hefty cost, and each administered by a private company, in order to establish sufficient knowledge to teach. In California, for example, these include the California Basic Educational Skills Test (CBEST), which consists of three separate tests; the California Subject Examinations for Teachers Multiple Subject (four sections); the Reading Instruction Competence Assessment; and either the Teacher Performance Evaluation or the Performance Assessment for California Teachers.

Because standardized testing began with the Eugenics movement, it is not surprising to discover that non-Whites pass less frequently than Whites on all standardized tests (Stoskopf, 2002). A glance at California's most recent report on passing rates makes clear that this is equally true of the many required teacher tests (California Commission on Teacher Credentialing, 2012).

There are four reasons that Black, Latino, Native American (and often Asian) people pass at lower rates. First, differential pass rates are acceptable to policymakers.

This may seem too obvious to be worth stating. But imagine a fair world where that was not acceptable and policymakers demanded changes in the content of the tests, the relevance of the content, or the assumptions behind the items and procedures. Imagine a test on which affluent suburban people failed more frequently than less affluent urban residents. Would this be tolerated?

Second (and highly related to the first point), the particular items are skewed. Here is just one example: There is not a single item in Spanish on the California tests, although half of the public school students are Spanish speaking. Might it not be fair to ask just one or two questions on the teacher tests that might privilege the Spanish-speakers over monolingual English speakers?

The third reason is the inadequate education often experienced by people of color in the United States. This means that prospective teachers of color have often received schooling that left gaps in their education. And finally, the tests are expensive. Because of the racial wealth gap, candidates of color are less likely to be able to pay for either test preparation or multiple opportunities to take the test.

We have taken five approaches to breaking this serious deterrent to teacher diversity. First, we have opposed the tests in public, legislative, and legal ways. This is important, because testing is a matter of public policy. We campaigned during the 1990s against the first of the teacher tests and helped to initiate a lawsuit in which the plaintiffs were the Association of Mexican American Educators and others. Although the plaintiffs did not prevail, the lawsuit did result in changes to the test, including extending the time available to test takers and changing some of the content on the math test. Such movements have had only slight successes thus far, but we think they should be pursued by coalitions of churches, civil rights organizations, teachers, and everyone else who cares about social justice (Epstein 2012a; Minorities, Citing Bias, Sue Over Test, 1992).

Second, we have discussed the biases within the tests with everyone to whom we present this material. We offer discussions, courses, and books that explain the Eugenics origins of testing and the ongoing biases. An understanding that this is not a personal problem but a social policy problem is critical to overcoming the feelings of inadequacy that years of testing failure may have engendered.

Third, the organizations we work with take a very particular and serious approach to test preparation on the information itself. No one is allowed to provide test support who is not "culturally competent." That means they are loving, patient, encouraging, knowledgeable, and frequently people of color themselves. Test prep is arranged to fit the schedules of the candidates, and it is given in small groups—not in huge impersonal classrooms. Brenda Mapp, the very successful teacher and test preparation support person for the Oakland Partnership program, met candidates in libraries and in their homes. She developed personal, friendly relationships and made it clear that she considered the test just a hurdle, not a mark of the candidate's intelligence. She was infinitely patient, and most candidates ultimately passed the tests. Teach Tomorrow in Oakland (see Chapter 2) has used many strategies, one involving a great organization called Teach Bar, which provides a personal, comfortable, relaxed space for group and individual test preparation.

Fourth, in some cases it is possible to have some tests waived. In California, for example, those seeking to teach a single subject in secondary school can show a pattern of classes that establishes competency in that subject. It is called an *approved program of study* and must be accepted by a higher education institution authorized by the Commission on Teacher Credentialing. Because many teacher credential personnel do not understand the impact of racism, they will not encourage this route. "If you know the subject, you can pass the test; no problem," they say in some cases. In other cases, the candidate never receives the information about this option at all, especially if the candidate did not begin college with a teaching career in mind. For many, it really is the best option, but each person needs very careful, frequent counseling to make it through this hurdle as well.

Finally, prospective teachers need financial assistance with both test fees and test preparation. Because of the racial wealth gap, we cannot assume that candidates of color have even the $41 needed to take the CBEST in California.

Summary of Recommendations for Dealing With the Tests

Conduct discussions on the biases of testing. Develop a fund to pay for test preparation and test fees. Encourage prospective teachers to seek what is called a *waivered major* or *approved program of study* in place of the tests where that is possible. Develop a personalized, culturally competent system of test preparation. And create a coalition to oppose the tests or aspects of them.

Dealing With Higher Education Institutions

In general, the credential that authorizes candidates to teach will come from a higher education teacher-credentialing program, even when candidates are prepared through alternative credentialing. Many higher education institutions have their own set of barriers that keep people out of teaching. They have complicated admission requirements and early application deadlines and often require that candidates pass all of the tests before they are admitted rather than allowing them to receive support, encouragement, and financial assistance to pass the tests while they are preparing to teach.

Although public institutions claim a mandate to prepare teachers, their education departments often have the least diverse student bodies (see, e.g., Chapter 12), and they are not always responsive to requests that they change policies in order to bring in a more diverse pool of teachers. The U.S. professoriate is 79% White (see the National Center for Education Statistics Fast Facts website: http://nces.ed.gov/fastfacts/). Whites are, on average, less sympathetic to policies that create diversity than people of color. The teacher education professoriate lacks diversity for the same reason that the K-12 teaching pool is not diverse—socially constructed barriers created in a system that is dominated on the one hand by business interests that seek areas of education spending that will provide them with profit, such as standardized testing, and on the other hand by White professionals who do not question the imbalance in ethnic composition. This, of course, creates a vicious circle. In addition, sometimes policies that prevent diversity in public institutions are mandated or condoned by state legislation. And, finally, because public institutions continue to receive funding no matter what their specific policies, they have little incentive to change unless a mass movement forces the change.

We have therefore sought an array of higher education partners. Sometimes public colleges will set up special programs; sometimes private colleges are more flexible than state institutions. Sometimes financial aid can make up for the differences in tuition, because of the existence of some loans that can be forgiven for service in urban schools.

Summary of Recommendations on Dealing With Higher Education Institutions

Hunt for institutions that are actually committed to diversity or that have created substantial diversity already. You will be asking institutions how they can help to create some flexibility in order to break down the barriers we have mentioned. So, for example, it is helpful to admit students "provisionally" so that they can take classes before they pass the teacher tests. We have worked with a private Catholic college that admits on this basis, and almost every admitted student has eventually passed the necessary tests. Enrollment in a program helps people to think of themselves as educators and to seek educational employment, even if it is not immediately full-time teaching.

Keep hunting, and sometimes you will find several higher education partners that you can recommend to candidates. In other cases, you will want one supportive partner so that you can create a collaborative in order to apply for various forms of funding.

Personal Support

Because of the barriers, becoming a teacher is a frustrating experience for many. People need a support network (KGO News, 2012). We recommend that you hold events to celebrate and communicate, develop "cohorts" that work together, provide a lot of community praise and acknowledgement, and hire staff who are completely devoted and willing to spend extra off-duty time with the candidates.

Longer Term Strategies for a Diverse Teaching Force

We do not see a diverse teaching force as one small issue among many. We see it as perhaps the most important change of all. Suppose that we actually succeeded in bringing thousands of Black, Asian, Native American, and Latino individuals into employment in the schools attended by their children and the children of their neighbors. What would happen?

Reducing Unemployment, Wealth Gaps, and Unpleasant Educational Environments

First, substantially reducing barriers to entering the teaching force would have an immediate impact on the unemployment in communities of color and a lesser but real effect on the racial wealth gap. Teaching is the largest profession in the world. If people of color were able to enter it, there would be an impact on the "minority" unemployment rate and income levels.

Changing the "Feel" of School

We are not arguing that every person of color would make a good teacher. The capacity to work effectively with young people is more complicated than that. But the feeling of comfort for parents and students gained through interacting with employees that speak the same languages; visit the same churches, schools, and supermarkets; and deal with the same local issues would be enormous.

Reducing Urban Incarceration

Employing urban young men in jobs where they have a chance to play with, entertain, and educate their younger neighbors would be far cheaper than the massive incarceration they now experience (Alexander, 2012). Creating pipelines, like the Cal-Grip program sponsored by the mayor's office and the Spanish Speaking Citizens Foundation in Oakland, can provide paid internships for high school students, reduce the likelihood of conflict with police, and allow youngsters to learn by teaching others (Students Celebrate Summer "High School Pathways," 2010).

Increasing the Male Presence

Our colleague Kimberly Mayfield Lynch is a teacher-educator and the mother of a 9-year-old son. She talks about teachers who "speak boy" and contrasts them with those who seem to make school a chore for male children. Preparing the fathers and older brothers of urban youngsters to enter the classroom as full-time instructors would resolve the desperate need for male voices in a setting that is increasingly unattractive to one gender.

Generating a Movement

We have been able to generate a city-sized movement in support of this issue. There are school board members, organization leaders, teacher educators, civil rights leaders, Black sororities, Asian and indigenous activists, parent groups,

Latino nonprofit organizations, the teachers' union, and others who are very committed to this movement. It needs to be national and it could be!

If, for example, all the Black sororities and fraternities, the immigration rights organizations, some church leaders, and some antiracist union locals committed to creating the coalitions that would take the steps we have outlined, teacher diversity programs could emerge in every city.

Conclusion: Taking the First Steps

Anyone—teacher, parent, activist, college student, college professor—can start a movement to diversity the teaching force. We suggest beginning with these steps:

1. Find out the percentage of students by ethnicity and the percentage of teachers by ethnicity in your school district or state.
2. Look closely at details about the programs featured in this book. They have solved, at least partially, many of the problems your community will face.
3. Invite some acquaintances to come together and discuss whether they think lack of teacher diversity is a problem.
4. Create a plan to bring together the kind of organizations we have mentioned in this chapter.
5. When these leaders have come together, provide the local statistics and perhaps a copy of this chapter or this entire book to those you have gathered. Help them to understand that the lack of diversity results from a set of institutional barriers, not from a lack of interest.
6. Call a public meeting for people with a bachelor's degree who would want to consider teaching. Use ethnic media and networks to publicize.
7. Talk with a school district and some higher education institutions to see what they will do to help break down the barriers and increase diversity. The college or district (or both together) can create an alternative certification program, if one does not exist. They may need written and oral information to understand how it works. Ask the college to change its admission deadlines and to admit candidates provisionally while they work on the tests. If you cannot find colleges or districts that are willing to do these things, start a petition expressing community desire for changes that will create diversity. If you cannot obtain any modifications, go forward anyway. Raising the issue and bringing together the potential candidates will begin to open some doors.
8. By this time, you will be seeing your own path emerge. Those who are interested in more details or a little advice are welcome to contact the authors at fredellis@gmail.com and kkepstein@gmail.com.

References

Alexander, M. (2012). *The new Jim Crow: Mass incarceration in the age of colorblindness.* New York, NY: New Press.

California Commission on Teacher Credentialing. (2012). *Report on passing rates of commission-approved examinations from 2005–2006 to 2009–2010.* Sacramento, CA: Author. Retrieved from www.ctc.ca.gov/commission/agendas/2011–06/2011–06–5c.pdf

Epstein, K. K. (2005). The whitening of the American teaching force: A problem of recruitment or a problem of racism? *Social Justice 32,* 89–102.

Epstein, K. K. (2008, September 18). Dellums task force, school district to recruit teachers. *Oakland Post,* p. 1.

Epstein, K. K (2012a). *A different view of urban schools: Civil rights, critical race theory and unexplored realities.* Revised edition. New York, NY: Peter Lang.

Epstein, K. K. (2012b). *Organizing to change a city.* New York: Peter Lang.

Keleher, T., & Libero, D. P. (1999). *Creating crisis: How California's teaching policies aggravate racial inequalities in public schools.* San Francisco, CA: Applied Research Center.

KGO News. (2012, February 3). *Aspiring teachers get guided through system.* Retrieved from http://abclocal.go.com/kgo/story?section=news/education&id=8529769

Ladson-Billings, G., & Tate, W. (1995). Toward a critical race theory of education. *Teachers College Record, 97,* 47–68.

McKibbin, M. (2001). One size does not fit all: Reflections on alternative routes to teacher preparation in California. *Teacher Education Quarterly, 28,* 133.

Minorities, citing bias, sue over test of teachers' skills. (1992, September 24). *Los Angeles Times,* p. 1.

Nadler, D., & Pederson, P. (2009). What happens when states have genuine alternative certification. *Education Next, 9.* Retrieved from http://educationnext.org/what-happens-when-states-have-genuine-alternative-certification/

Sawchuck, S. (2013). California program takes aim at "teacher-diversity gap." *Education Week.* Retrieved from www.edweek.org/ew/articles/2012/10/10/07diverse_ep.h32.html

Shapiro, T., Meschede, T., & Sullivan, L. (2010). *The racial wealth gap increases fourfold* (Institute on Assets and Social Policy Report). Waltham, MA: Brandeis University.

Shen, J. (1998). Alternative certification, minority teachers and urban education. *Journal of Research and Development in Education 31,* 9–16.

Stoskopf, A. (2002). Echoes of a forgotten past: Eugenics, testing, and education reform. *Educational Forum, 66,* 126–133.

Students Celebrate Summer "High School Pathways" Success. (2010, August 25). *Oakland Post,* p. 12.

PART IV

Diversity Plans, Demographic Trends, and Accreditation in Higher Education

11

ARCHITECTING THE CHANGE WE WANT: APPLIED CRITICAL RACE THEORY AND THE FOUNDATIONS OF A DIVERSITY STRATEGIC PLAN IN A COLLEGE OF EDUCATION

Joseph E. Flynn Jr., Rebecca D. Hunt, Scott A. Wickman, James Cohen, and Connie Fox

Institutional change is always a challenging endeavor. Within any educational institution a wide range of values, beliefs, dispositions, and opinions must be considered and validated lest change not take root. Change agents must be aware of effective communication and create a strategy that takes into account the broad range of factors that impede intended progress (Ellsworth, 2000). Regardless of whether the object of change is an entire system or a simple procedure, creation, introduction, and implementation of the change will have a significant impact on its success.

But consider for a moment a change that is more than surface or procedural. After all, a new data system or reimbursement procedure may be a nuisance but does not require any substantial cultural shift within the institution. Institutional change that challenges stakeholders' fundamental beliefs and values requires each individual to see and interact with the context in a new way. A more complex challenge than implementing a new data system is moving an institution to embrace diversity in order to advocate for social justice.

According to survey data, our graduates—graduates of the College of Education (COE) at Northern Illinois University—report "extremely positive" or "mostly positive" assessments of their abilities in low percentages: teaching English language learners, 32%; general multicultural and culturally responsive methods, 48%; addressing issues of socioeconomic diversity, 30%; and establishing equity in the classroom, 42% (Illinois Association of Deans of Public Colleges of Education, 2012). The reason these low percentages are a problem is simple. If current and future teachers do not understand theories, ideals, and attendant critical practices of diversity and multicultural education, then there is a higher probability that they will reproduce oppressive social and educative practices. Continuing to matriculate teachers not fully prepared to meet the demands of a diverse classroom will only perpetuate uncritical perspectives of diversity and multicultural education (heroes and holidays) and forgo practices that foster critical and empowering discourses for students and the further promotion of social justice (Sleeter & Grant, 2007).

As such, it is essential that students in teacher preparation programs are immersed in environments in which critical ideals and practices are both taught and modeled. Students must see that these practices are not additions or bracketed issues to consider; rather, they are fundamental to the education enterprise. As Sobel and Taylor (2005) stated, "Though promoting acceptance, tolerance, and respect for diversity are commendable goals, multicultural coursework in general can stop short of affirming one's own and other's diversity" (p. 84). When students are in programs in which there is a "diversity course" and the ideals of that course are not sustained across and throughout the curriculum, then students do not have the opportunity to have these key connections modeled and lived. They lose the opportunity to experience an educational space in which diversity, multicultural education, and social justice are not *part* of the fabric, but *are* the fabric of educational experiences. If education, at root, is not engaged in the pursuit of praxis, the building of community, the respecting of others along with the self, and the liberation of all, then education is reduced to a mere commodity and tool for the continued oppression of marginalized groups (Freire, 2000). Fostering an academic environment that fully promotes diversity and social justice requires colleges of education and other institutions to create a plan, a diversity strategic plan, that expresses both a vision and path for successful institutional change.

The remainder of this chapter explores the creation of a diversity strategic plan for the COE at Northern Illinois University, a Midwestern research-focused university. Ideas appropriated from critical race theory (CRT)—particularly *counter-story*, *intersectionality*, and *embracing social justice*—were indispensable to the development of this plan because they urged a focus on creating practices that foster equity and equality for all students—especially historically marginalized students. The chapter also explores institutional practices related to diversity and social justice before the plan and key initiatives of the plan. This chapter is not meant to offer a full theoretical exploration of ideas related to CRT but rather to display a practical application that connects its purposes and frameworks to a project of institutional change. Institutions may not always begin discussion with a specific bent toward CRT, but that does not necessarily mean those ideas do not weave in and out of the discourse. Our story is a case in point.

Critical Race Theory and Seeing a Need for a Diversity Strategic Plan

In the fall of 2011, the dean of the COE charged the College Curriculum Committee (CCC) with the responsibility of developing a comprehensive diversity strategic plan for the COE. *A Plan for Our Future: The College of Education Diversity*

Strategic Plan provides the blueprint to not only diversifying our faculty, staff, and student body but also fostering a curriculum that helps all stakeholders in the college understand and embrace a mission of respect for all group and individual identities.[1] Following a shared governance model, which embraces the voice of faculty in regards to curriculum matters (Tierney & Lechuga, 2004), the CCC formed the Subcommittee for the Diversity Strategic Plan Development (the Subcommittee). The Subcommittee, which included at least one member from all departments represented in the COE, took the lead in developing a document that could be reviewed by the larger CCC. Although the COE had developed a general strategic plan that included diversity as a part, it was determined by the dean that the COE's issues related to diversity were (and are) such a unique challenge unto themselves that a separate plan focusing on diversity was essential.

The project was given a short timeline. The dean issued the charge in September with the expectation that the plan would be approved before the end of the following spring semester, May of 2012. The Subcommittee took 3 months to deliberate a range of issues and an additional month to draft the document. Although a short timeline may seem daunting, the fact of the matter is that the urgency kept the Subcommittee focused, resulting in a more efficient process. During the following semester, the CCC reviewed and approved the draft document. Department representatives serving on the CCC then took the draft to their respective departments for further review, revision suggestions, and consent. Once all revision suggestions and concerns were noted and incorporated, the revised draft became the COE *Diversity Strategic Plan* and was then formally approved by both the College Curriculum Committee and the College Faculty Senate.

At the outset, the Subcommittee subscribed to the idea that teaching *inclusiveness, pluralism,* and *mutual respect for all peoples and cultures* as a humanistic imperative are requisite for (a) ethical living (Dewey, 1938; Hickman & Alexander, 1998) and (b) full civic participation in a multicultural democracy in a diverse world (Gay, 2010). The attempt to foster understanding and be more consciousness of diversity has been part of the fabric of education for decades under the guise of multicultural education (Banks, 2004; Boyle-Baise, 1999). Despite its persistence, Gay (1992) expressed that theories of multicultural education outpace its actual practice and it can be argued easily that this disjuncture persists. It was the Subcommittee's intention to challenge this.

As the *Diversity Strategic Plan* states, the primary purposes of the plan were as follows:

1. Improve our shared understanding and valuing of diversity in all its forms.
2. Increase the recruitment, retention, and completion rate of students of diverse backgrounds.
3. Increase the recruitment and retention of faculty and staff of diverse backgrounds.

4. Engage in diversity in our curriculum, scholarly and artistic endeavors, and daily operations (Flynn et al., 2013, p. 3).

With these purposes framing the design of the plan, the Subcommittee identified three intractable issues that needed to be addressed that had been regularly discussed across the COE but remained challenges nonetheless. First, there was a perceived lack of cultural awareness limiting our ability to recruit students of color into teacher education. Second, culturally and linguistically diverse students perceived unfriendliness or misunderstanding of faculty and staff. And finally, as stated above, through follow-up alumni surveys, it was found that our graduates in their 1st and 5th years of teaching felt unprepared to address a range of diversity needs in their classrooms.

Further complicating the COE's efforts at recruiting a more diverse student population were recent state-level changes in the scoring of the Test of Academic Proficiency (TAP), the state-required assessment for initial licensure. New changes to the test and its scoring resulted in a marked decline in pass rates across the state, especially for culturally and linguistic minorities. This trend held for the COE as well. For example, during the 2010–2011 school year, 4 out of 29 Latino students passed the test—that is only 14%—and 0 out of 5 Asian American students passed. Overall, 21.5% of our students passed the TAP, meaning that roughly 1 in 5 of our students were succeeding, far below the state average. Even though the performance gap between our African American and White students was minimal (21% and 22%, respectively), both groups were far below their group's state averages.

The Subcommittee quickly realized that this problem was not only a racial, ethnic, or linguistic issue but also an economic one. Many of our students are first-generation, working class, or nontraditional students. Using the ACT—the required standardized test for admission—as a predictor of success on the TAP, students scoring 24 or greater have a much higher probability of passing on the first attempt. Our students' average ACT score is 22. In effect, regardless of race, ethnicity, or language, many of our students did not have the preparation to pass the basic skills test for certification, nor the resources for test preparation classes. Thus, offering our students support on this paramount assessment was necessary both for increasing diversity and for ensuring the quality of our licensure graduates.

As the Subcommittee's deliberations ensued, there was sharp awareness of the underrepresentation and struggles of culturally and linguistically diverse students, but there was not a full understanding of exactly how the underrepresented population felt about their experience in the COE. Therefore, it was imperative that the COE reexamine and create a curriculum that actively encourages respect for diversity from and for all stakeholders, fosters students' ability to understand key ideas associated with diversity, and nurtures education professionals for whom the values of social justice are indelible characteristics.

Finding a Base: Critical Race Theory as Inspiration

Ideas emanating from CRT framed the Subcommittee's interpretation of the overarching problems and how to address them. Crenshaw, Gotanda, Peller, and Thomas (1995) stated two primary interests of CRT:

> The first is to understand how a regime of white supremacy and its subordination of people of color have been created and maintained in America, and . . . [the second is] a desire to not merely understand the vexed bond between law and racial power but to *change* it.
>
> (p. xiii)

The first interest is an important framing for the mission of a diversity strategic plan. It can be argued that the COE—most colleges of education for that matter—is a White space. Hodgkinson (2002) showed that while minority student enrollment in higher education has in fact increased, in colleges of education it has decreased as many minority students choose to enter other degree programs. This trend produces serious consequences for the composition of not only the national teaching force, but also college of education faculty and administrators. In a 2013 survey of more than 1,000 college of education faculty across the United States, Flynn, Kemp, and Page (2013) found that White teacher educators tend to promote essentialist and perennial approaches to curriculum, whereas non-White teacher educators tend to embrace postmodernist or social reconstructionist and progressive approaches. They explained the repercussions of this finding:

> If dominant perspectives about the purposes of education are firmly rooted in essentialist and perennialist philosophies then the kinds of cross-institutional reforms needed to fully and effectively marshal multicultural practices in schools is compromised. . . . It is easy to add diverse voices and perspective to the curriculum . . . but shifting pedagogy and policies to challenge notions of oppression and marginalization and encourage activism is something entirely different.
>
> (p. 68)

Our institution is predominantly White in terms of the student body, faculty, and staff. White epistemologies and ways of knowing establish the status quo, and there is not a critical mass of students or scholars who consistently challenge the assumptions of privilege and normativity of Whiteness. That does not mean that challenging White normativity does not happen in the COE; a steady cadre of faculty, students, and staff members are vocal about the assumptions of White privilege and the challenges of being non-White or culturally and linguistically diverse. Challenging White supremacy and normativity is not meant to chastise White students, faculty, or staff; rather, it is meant to call attention to the persistence of institutional privilege in the hopes of ameliorating marginalizing practices (Kinchloe & Steinberg, 2000). Hence, the importance of the second interest of CRT emerges—changing institutional policies and practices that impact race and other aspects of identity.

Sleeter and Bernal (2004) pointed out,

> One might think of CRT in education as a developing theoretical, conceptual, methodological, and pedagogical strategy that accounts for the role of race and racism in U.S. education and works toward the elimination of racism as part of a larger goal of eliminating other forms of subordination.
>
> (p. 245)

Although in deliberation of the diversity strategic plan there was not any direct naming of CRT, the ideas consistently underscored our discussions. In effect, theoretical perspectives derived from CRT became significant in the genesis and construction of the diversity strategic plan. Specifically, the concepts of counter-story and working toward social justice served as critical foundations for the motives and conceptual framing of the plan.

Oftentimes CRT scholars employ counter-stories to challenge or subvert dominant perspectives, revealing important alternatives for seeing and further complicating dominant narratives. Used as both a technique and a tool for analysis (Delgado, 1989), counter-storytelling is employed to challenge dominant narratives that make change difficult by uncovering or problematizing "their contingency, cruelty, and self-serving nature" (Delgado & Stefancic, 1993, p. 462). Included in the Subcommittee's deliberations were the findings of internal focus group interviews conducted the year before that sought to access how culturally and linguistically diverse students felt about their experiences in the COE. The focus group findings were sobering, to say the least. The following comments represent thematic trends that emerged:

- "When we are encouraged to pick groups in the classroom, the white girls most often pick each other, leaving us out to fend for ourselves."
- "People are comfortable with people who have something in common with each other. . . . It would be helpful if our instructors helped a little more with barriers of traditions or stereotypes."
- "Many of our peers are just not informed about how some of our lived experiences are valid because they belong to us."
- "I am an African American student who made it to my clinical blocks. I had trouble pronouncing one of the books when I was student teaching, and they placed me in an ESL [English as a second language] class."
- "I am an Asian student. I was also placed in [an ESL] class. I had three different dispositions, and I believe they were all because I come from a different place."

- "Most of the professors are really great, but some are not supportive and have trouble relating to me."
- "I respect teachers challenging me to do my best, but I do not like it when they talk down to me. Sometimes they single me out, saying things like, 'Do you understand so-and-so?' "

Common themes across the focus groups included isolation, marginalization, misunderstanding, lack of support, and even disrespect, validating what the Subcommittee felt was a challenging concern—the perception of a hostile environment for culturally and linguistically diverse students fostered by faculty, staff, and other students.

Student comments on the whole revealed an array of issues related to a lack of cultural competence and understanding. What emerged from the students' comments was a counter-story that directly challenged the prevailing perception about interacting with the COE. Although it can be argued that this is an appropriation of counter-story as theorized by CRT scholars, the Subcommittee felt that these collective testimonies served as both a challenge to the status quo and an argument for change. Research shows that students are more successful when they feel welcomed, valued, and challenged by material that builds on their prior knowledge, experiences, and interests (González, Moll, & Amanti, 2005). When these attitudes, behaviors, and curricular considerations are missing, students from culturally and linguistically diverse backgrounds may resist learning (Kohl, 1995) and experience the institution as a hostile or unwelcoming place. This, of course, leads to the attrition of culturally and linguistically diverse students.

Grounding Vision: Embracing Curriculum, Social Justice, and Identity for Equity

What is essential to consider when creating a strategic plan of any type is the fundamental idea and purpose that grounds the plan. Considering a diversity strategic plan elicits the need to wrestle with the question, "*Why* are we doing this?" As pointed out, a key issue the institution needed to address was the manifestation of institutional racism, evidenced by the low matriculation and certification rate of culturally and linguistically diverse students, the sluggish rate of hiring underrepresented faculty and staff, misunderstanding and mischaracterizing of linguistically diverse students and faculty, and student complaints about inadvertent marginalizing treatment and insensitivity from faculty and staff. In effect, there was a belief that the COE, like many institutions, inadvertently sustained a culture of marginality for non-White and linguistically diverse students. Through deliberation, the Subcommittee determined that at root the purpose of this diversity strategic plan was the promotion of social justice as a principle for ameliorating oppressive or marginalizing institutional practices.

Despite the possibility that some could deem social justice as a "radical, left-wing mission," the Subcommittee found inspiration in Noguera (2008) who expressed the responsibility of educators to explore social justice issues and create practices that mitigate these hurdles:

> Educators, who should be committed to helping young people realize their intellectual potential as they make their way toward adulthood, have a responsibility to help them find ways to expand identities related to race so that they can experience the fullest possibility of all that they may become.
>
> (p. 16)

Mirroring Noguera's (2008) sentiment, our recently retired university president consistently espoused the idea that graduates from the university *should* have an understanding of and commitment to social justice. The Subcommittee took his espousal to heart and set out to create an institutional commitment to socially just and equitable teaching pedagogy and the further encouraging of faculty and staff to be aware of how their actions can be marginalizing despite best intentions.

The Subcommittee recognized that although considering the content taught in courses was important, that alone would not suffice as a strategy for institutional change. An understanding of *curriculum* that incorporated *nontechnical* aspects of curriculum along with *technical* aspects (i.e., courses, content, assessments, standards, etc.) was necessary for a plan to be holistic and progressive. Lunenberg (2011) described nontechnical aspects of curriculum as follows:

> [Nontechnical curriculum theorists] like Eliot Eisner, Carol Gilligan, James Banks, Henry Giroux and Peter McLaren, William Reid, Maxine Green and Michael Apple, and William Pinar feel that the world is much more complex, involving *subjective, personal, aesthetic, heuristic, transactional,* and *intuitive* thinking and forms of behavior. The argument is that curriculum cannot be precisely planned—it evolves as a *living organism* as opposed to a *machine,* which is precise and ordered [emphasis added].
>
> (p. 5)

In effect, paying attention to both the taught and hidden curriculum is essential to the development of a diversity strategic plan. A significant part of the Subcommittee's deliberations aimed to reconsider both academic concepts and the overarching experience for all students. Every moment, every interaction, became the landscape of curriculum.

The idea of social justice has a number of interpretations. However, the common thread running through its various definitions, as applied to educational contexts and issues, is the exploration and amelioration of marginalizing and inequitable institutional practices. Miller and Kirkland (2010) described the mission of social justice as the "[unpacking] of truths that challenge master narratives and unveils counter-narratives that often go untold or ignored altogether" (p. 3). Similarly, Goodman (2011) said that social justice "involves addressing issues of equity, power relations, and institutionalized oppression . . . changing unjust institutional structures, policies, and practices, and challenging the dominant ideology" (p. 4). Grant and Agosto (2008) defined social justice as a process, goal, and stance. This particular construction frames social justice as a position the institution takes, encourages sustained engagement, and defines a guiding purpose for the institution. As the definitions taken as a collective show, the promotion of an institutional context that embraces both diversity and the reduction of institutional inequity and marginalization are missions directly related to social justice. For the Subcommittee it became clear that sustaining or disregarding institutional practices that have deleterious effects on access to resources and opportunities is an affront to social justice. Furthermore, not focusing efforts on the systematic redressing of marginalizing practices sustains the institution's complicity in injustice.

Despite the urgency of addressing institutionally marginalizing practices, it can be challenging to talk explicitly about institutional inequality (Delpit, 1995; Pollock, 2005). As stated, the majority of the institution—faculty, staff, and students—is White. Although there are actors from all racial backgrounds within the institution—and beyond the Subcommittee—who are understanding and proactive toward critical issues like racism, being told your institution can be a racist place is nonetheless a bitter pill to swallow. It is key to privilege the humanity of others and recognize that oftentimes folks exercise a dysconscious racism (King, 1991) rather than being overtly racist. As King described, "Dysconsciousness is an uncritical habit of mind (including perceptions, attitudes, assumptions, and beliefs) that justifies inequity and exploitation by accepting the existing order of things as given" (p. 135). Rhetorically the Subcommittee did not want to attack institutional racism head-on for fear of disillusioning or insulting fellow faculty and staff members, especially those that neither see nor understand how their own actions can be indicative of the problem. That could have increased the possibility that some would dismiss the *Diversity Strategic Plan* altogether. With that strategic hurdle in mind, the desire to recognize the entrenched presence of institutional racism persisted. It is a fine line to walk, and although CRT, especially the strategy of counterstory, offers inroads to addressing racism, that always happens in a context, and there must be an awareness of the real possibilities of resistance and rejection.

Another important issue in the Subcommittee's deliberations was the role of identity in diversity and social justice. Our identities are multiple, dynamic, and intersected (Anzaldúa, 1999). That is to say, not only do we view ourselves and engage these multiple identities differently depending on the context, but also our multiple identities change with the experiences we have. Both power and oppression are affiliated with the various multiple identities we have (Goodman, 2011). Within the context of the U.S. social structure, some of our identities are considered dominant and privileged (White, Christian, heterosexual, male, able-bodied). Those not reflecting these designations are considered subjugated identities (Goodman, 2011), which in the context of the U.S. are anything but white skin, any religion or belief system that is not Christian, any sexual orientation that is not heterosexual, any nonmale, and any disabled-bodied individuals. How society places immediate, unconscious judgments on each of us depends on the matrix of privileged and subjugated identities we have. This *intersection* of identities is essential to understanding diversity and social justice.

Crenshaw (1991) used the theory of intersectionality to explore how aspects of identity mix and collide to create experiences that are not easily identified in dominant discourses of identity. Employing a Black feminist framework, she pointed out in her exploration of violence against women and rape that her "focus on the intersections of race and gender only highlights the need to account for multiple grounds of identity when considering how the social world is constructed" (p. 1245). These considerations are both deliberate and necessary, or else important experiences are eclipsed. Crenshaw elucidated,

> Although racism and sexism readily intersect in the lives of real people, they seldom do in feminist and antiracist practices. And so, when the practices expound identity as woman or person of color as an either/or proposition, they relegate the identity of women of color to a location that resists telling.
> (p. 1242)

Crenshaw warned us that disregarding the complex interplay of identities in favor of focusing on a single aspect of identity can silence narratives that challenge status-quo assumptions regarding the experiences of marginalized groups. In blunt terms, there is a qualitative difference between a White middle class female compared with a working class Latina. Although both may be female, the lived experience of being Latina is not the same as being White. The experience of being female may be common between the two, but the added identity of being a Latina for the latter may carry a different set of cultural capital (Bourdieu & Passerson 1977; McLeod, 2008) and a unique experience that is not told when engaging an a discourse about the marginalization of women. For example, although the first-wave feminist movement of the 1960s made significant inroads for all women, it largely catered to the issues of White, middle-class females. Its agenda did not necessarily address the distinct issues of non-White women (hooks, 2000). As a result, a second wave of feminism paid closer attention to the needs of racially and ethnically oppressed women.

Embracing the notion of intersectionality presents a nuanced understanding that begins with the complexity of the self as a means of understanding the complexity of others (Bennett, 2011). Crenshaw (1995) summarized the importance of intersectionality like this: "Through an awareness of intersectionality, we can better acknowledge and ground the differences among us and negotiate the means by which these differences will find expression in constructing group politics" (p. 378). Teacher candidates should understand that all are products and reflective of culture. Our identities are socially constructed within the context of the U.S. social system. And each of us is a matrix of identities (some of which are privileged, some of which are marginalized) that intersect in unique ways. If colleges of education do not create contexts and curricula in which these ideas are central, their students' abilities to fully connect with others and create their own culturally responsive practices may be hamstrung.

A Long Look in the Mirror: Seeing Successful Institutional Practices and Shortfalls

The creation of the *Diversity Strategic Plan* was not meant to convey the notion that the COE had not been attendant to or caring of these issues. In fact, the COE is a strong community of faculty, staff, and students who see the value of diversity. Conveying to institutional stakeholders a recognition and respect for the work people do is necessary for creating an embraceable document. After all, recognition is gratifying, and no one wants to be told that her or his efforts are worthless at best and racist at worst. However, putting into practice the values of diversity and social justice with clear goals—observable, measurable, *and* achievable actions—had been elusive. The final *Diversity Strategic Plan* focused on the needs of *all* stakeholders in the COE—students (regardless of class status and/or program), faculty, and staff—while staying rooted in theoretical imperatives and goals associated with CRT.

Given the charge from our COE as well as our ethical and moral responsibilities as professional educators to transform the *Diversity Strategic Plan* from yet another idealized academic, ivory-tower conceptualization into specific actions, four overarching goals targeting specific operational changes as we move forward were identified:

1. Faculty and staff members in the COE will acquire and practice the knowledge, skills, and dispositions that reflect cultural competence and a commitment to social justice.
2. Students enrolled in COE degree and certificate programs will experience curricula that encourage the valuing of social justice as well as knowledge, skills, and dispositions that reflect cultural competence.
3. The COE will actively recruit and retain students from diverse groups.
4. The COE will actively recruit and retain faculty and staff from diverse groups. (Flynn et al., 2012, p. 15)

To fulfill these goals, we are acting on a list of specific initiatives as outlined in the *Diversity Strategic Plan*, organized in terms of their focus on (a) faculty and staff, (b) students, and (c) the institution, that represent a comprehensive approach to reconsidering the COE's curriculum. The implementation of the recommended initiatives will be an ongoing, challenging endeavor that will have many successes as well as some failures. Regardless, the COE has committed itself to the implementation of the *Diversity Strategic Plan*; what is vitally important is the continued persistence and determination of the administration, faculty, and staff. Following is a sample of key initiatives contained in the *Diversity Strategic Plan*.

Faculty and Staff Initiatives

We believe that faculty and staff need to model and provide leadership in creating an environment that promotes, supports, and encourages a community of diverse learners, as exemplified in the following initiatives. Central to this belief are the execution of the following activities:

- Assess, in a systematic way, faculty and staff professional development needs in relation to issues related to identity, social justice, and diversity, leading to regular and consistent professional development offerings as well as engaging diverse learners in a supportive academic environment.
- Aggressively recruit and hire underrepresented faculty, staff, and administrators.

Student Initiatives

We believe that social justice in a university and college setting must ultimately be student centered. Therefore, the following initiatives reflect this imperative:

- Assess, in a systematic way, student understanding about social justice, identity, and diversity issues.
- Ensure curriculum infusion of ideas related to cultural competence, identity, and social justice.
- Expand themed learning communities that focus on understanding the intersection of identity, multicultural and social justice education, and culturally relevant pedagogies.
- Increase the number of courses utilizing service-learning requirements and initiate community service days focusing on projects in underserved communities.
- Continue and expand student recruitment and retention efforts.

Institutional Initiatives

In order for the preceding sets of initiatives to be successful, they must be executed in an institutional context that supports and encourages practices that foster an understanding of diversity and social justice as both a priority and an organizing set of principles. This imperative is reflected through the following institutional-level initiatives:

- Increase and foster university–school–district partnerships with area urban school districts.

- Establish an informed, focused, and ongoing plan for helping students succeed on the required assessments for teacher certification.
- Adopt provisional admittance policies for programs where there is an underrepresentation of culturally and linguistically diverse students that show an ability to be great teachers.
- Institute a cooperative teacher orientation that expresses clearer expectations for school partnerships in relation to clinical and student teaching experiences that focuses on differentiating cultural differences from dispositional or intellectual weakness.
- Increase the number and frequency of speakers, lectures, workshops, and presentations with themes related to diversity, social justice, culturally relevant teaching, and identity that are open to all members of the COE and university community.
- Increase utilization of the college and department websites to promote issues related to diversity and social justice locally, regionally, nationally, and internationally.
- Institutionalize an effective faculty–student mentoring program.

This is a sampling of the initiatives proposed in the plan. What is most important regarding these proposed initiatives is budget allocation and follow-through. It is one thing to suggest that initiatives need to happen; it is quite a different thing to make them a budgetary priority. In fact, as of the writing of this chapter, many of the suggested actions have been included in the COE's budget, and the Office of the Dean, College Curriculum Committee, College Faculty Senate, and department chairs are involved in ongoing oversight of implementation of the plan. In order for any strategic plan to work, there must be a critical mass of institutional resources invested and engaged with the vision of the plan.

The spirit of this plan is squarely aligned with the values and ideals of CRT. Essential tools of CRT, specifically counter-story and intersectionality, served as theoretical buoys that helped guide the deliberations and theorization of the plan. Most important, though, is that CRT's fundamental mission of fostering social justice served as the primary underpinning and goal of our *Diversity Strategic Plan*. All too often when conversations about diversity and social justice commence, the necessary discourse around needs and purposes can be assumed and make the creation of a strategic plan into another empty institutional exercise. However, as the tenets of CRT point out, understanding and ameliorating social injustice, especially racism, must be an intentional act. On seeing and knowing the marginalization and underrepresentation of culturally and linguistically diverse students within our institution, it became our intention and responsibility to create change. *A Plan for Our Future: The College of Education Diversity Strategic Plan* is our institution's architectural blueprint for the change we want to see.

Note

1 The complete plan can be found at the College of Education website (http://cedu.niu.edu/aboutus/dean/diversityplan.pdf).

References

Anzaldúa, G. (1999). *Borderlands, la frontera: The new mestiza.* San Francisco, CA: Aunt Lute Books.

Banks, J. A. (2004). Multicultural education: Historical development, dimensions, and practice. In J. A. Banks & C. A. McGee Banks (Eds.), *Handbook of research on multicultural education.* San Francisco, CA: Jossey-Bass.

Bennett, C. I. (2011). *Comprehensive multicultural education: Theory and practice* (7th ed.). Boston, MA: Pearson.

Bourdieu, P., & Passerson, J. (1977). *Reproduction in education, society, and culture.* London, England: Sage.

Boyle-Baise, M. (1999). Bleeding boundaries or uncertain center? An historical exploration of the field of multicultural education. *Journal of Curriculum and Supervision, 14*(3), 191–215.

Crenshaw, K. (1991). Mapping the margins: Intersectionality, identity politics, and violence against women of color. *Stanford Law Review, 43*, 1241–1299.

Crenshaw, K. (1995). Mapping the margins: Intersectionality, identity politics, and violence against women of color. In K. Crenshaw, N. Gotanda, G. Peller, & K. Thomas (Eds.), *Critical race theory: The key writings that formed the movement.* New York, NY: New Press.

Crenshaw, K., Gotanda, N., Peller, G., & Thomas, K. (1995). *Critical race theory: The key writings that formed the movement.* New York: New Press.

Delgado, R. (1989). Storytelling for oppositionists and others: A plea for narrative. *Michigan Law Review, 87*, 2411–2441.

Delgado, R. & Stefancic, J. (1993). Critical race theory: An annotated bibliography. *Virginia Law Review, 79*, 461–516.

Delpit, L. (1995). *Other people's children: Cultural conflict in the classroom.* New York, NY: New Press.

Dewey, J. (1938). *Experience and education.* New York, NY: Touchstone.

Ellsworth, J. B. (2000). *Surviving change: A survey of educational change models.* Washington, DC: Office of Educational Research and Improvement.

Flynn, J., Armstrong, S., Curry, L., Hunt, R., Johnson, L.-R., Johnston-Rodriguez, S., . . . Fox, C. (2012). *A plan for our future: The College of Education diversity strategic plan.* DeKalb: Northern Illinois University College of Education.

Flynn, J. E., Kemp, A. T., & Page, C. S. (2013). Promoting philosophical diversity: Exploring racial differences in beliefs about the purposes of education. *Journal of the Texas Alliance for Black School Educators, 5*(1), 53–71.

Freire, P. (2000). *Pedagogy of the oppressed.* New York: Bloomsbury Academic.

Gay, G. (1992). The state of multicultural education in the United States. In K. A. Moodley (Ed.), *Education in plural societies: International perspectives* (pp. 47–66). Calgary, Alberta: Detselig Enterprises.

Gay, G. (2010). *Culturally responsive teaching: Theory, research, and practice* (2nd ed.). New York, NY: Teachers College Press.

González, N., Moll, L., & Amanti, C. (Eds.). (2005). *Funds of knowledge: Theorizing practices in households, communities, and classrooms.* Mahwah, NJ: Lawrence Erlbaum.

Goodman, D. (2011). *Promoting diversity & social justice: Educating people from privileged groups* (2nd ed.). New York, NY: Routledge.

Grant, C., & Agosto, V. (2008). Teacher capacity and social justice in teacher education. In M. Cochran-Smith, S. Feinman-Nemser, J. McIntyre, & K. Demers (Eds.), *Handbook of research on teacher education: Enduring questions in changing contexts.* Mahwah, NJ: Lawrence Erlbaum.

Hickman, L., & Alexander, T. (1998). *The essential Dewey volume I: Pragmatism, education, democracy.* Bloomington, IN: Indiana University.

Hodgkinson, H. (2002). Demographics of teacher education: An overview. *Journal of Teacher Education, 53*(2), 102–106.

hooks, b. (2000). *Feminist theory: From margin to center* (2nd ed.). Cambridge, MA: South End Press.

Illinois Association of Deans of Public Colleges of Education. (2012). *Teacher graduate assessment: 2011 survey results.* Charleston, IL: Author.

Kinchloe, J., & Steinberg, S. (2000). Constructing a pedagogy of Whiteness for angry White youth. In N. Rodriguiz & L. Villaverde (Eds.), *Counterpoints: Studies in the postmodern theory of education: Vol. 73. Dismantling White privilege: Pedagogy, politics, and Whiteness.* New York, NY: Peter Lang.

King, J. E. (1991). Dysconscious racism: Ideology, identity, and the miseducation of teachers. *Journal of Negro Education, 60*(2), 133–146.

Kohl, H. (1995). *I won't learn from you: And other thoughts on creative maladjustment.* New York: New Press.

Lunenburg, F. (2011). Theorizing about curriculum: Conceptions and definitions. *International Journal of Scholarly Academic Intellectual Diversity, 13,* 1–6.

McLeod, J. (2008). *Ain't no makin' it: Aspirations and attainment in a low income neighborhood* (3rd ed.). Denver, CO: Westview Press.

Miller, sj, & Kirkland, D. (2010). Introduction: Teaching social justice. In sj Miller & D. Kirkland (Eds.), *Change matters: Critical essays on moving social justice research from theory to practice* (pp. 1–18). New York, NY: Peter Lang.

Noguera, P. A. (2008). *The trouble with Black boys.* Hoboken, NJ: John Wiley & Sons.

Pollock, M. (2005). *Colormute: Race talk dilemmas in an American school.* Princeton, NJ: Princeton University Press.

Sleeter, C. E., & Delgado Bernal, D. (2004). Critical pedagogy, critical race theory, and antiracist education: Implications for multicultural education. In J. A. Banks & C. A. McGee Banks (Eds.), *Handbook of research on multicultural education* (2nd ed., pp. 240–260). San Francisco: Jossey-Bass.

Sleeter, C., & Grant, C. (2007). *Making choices for multicultural education: Five approaches to race, class, and gender* (6th ed.). New York, NY: Wiley.

Sobel, D. M., & Taylor, S. V. (2005). Diversity preparedness in teacher education. *Kappa Delta Pi Record, 41*(2), 83–86.

Tierney, W. G., & Lechuga, V. M. (Eds.). (2004). Restructuring shared governance in higher education. *New Directions for Higher Education,* 127. San Francisco, CA: Jossey-Bass.

12

DIVERSIFYING TEACHER EDUCATION AT A PREDOMINANTLY WHITE INSTITUTION: A PUBLIC SCHOLARSHIP FRAMEWORK

Jill Ewing Flynn, Deborah Bieler, Hannah Kim, Rosalie Rolón Dow, Lynn Worden, and Carol Wong

> I appreciate that kids can automatically be like, "Okay, somebody looks like me." I may not be able to do anything for them, but, right off the bat, they may sense some empathy.

> In our classes, you have these little blips about minorities. You learn about them from a book, which kind of bothers me, honestly. You can't learn about kids from a book, people from a book.

> I don't think that ignoring differences is good. You're black, or you're German, or you're whatever you are. Me saying, "I don't see color," that is absolutely—pardon my French—bullshit. That's absolutely ridiculous because it exists, and stuff happened.

These comments were made by University of Delaware (UD) undergraduate teacher education majors in focus groups made up of students of color, first-generation college students, and students from low-income backgrounds in their teacher education programs. As these students noted, recruiting and preparing a diverse teaching force benefits all teacher candidates as well as the prekindergarten to Grade 12 (P-12) students they serve. Their comments also highlight a palpable problem in so many teacher education programs: the lack of racial and socioeconomic diversity.

This chapter documents the initial efforts of a group of teacher educators to address diversity issues in teacher education programs at UD. This group began as a dispersed cadre of concerned colleagues and eventually became a grant-funded organization, the Collaborative to Diversify Teacher Education. The authors of this chapter are all members of the Collaborative and are committed to addressing the issues raised by our students in the opening of the chapter. Our mission is to cultivate teacher candidates from groups historically underrepresented in access to and successful completion of teacher education programs. Our goal is to recruit and prepare teachers who better match the demographics of students in Delaware public schools and nationwide, with a focus on race, ethnicity, and socioeconomic class.

The challenges we face at UD reflect a nationwide problem that some scholars call the *demographic imperative*, which encompasses three related issues in teacher education:

> 1) the increasing diversity of the students enrolled in U.S. public education; 2) the gap between such students and their teachers in terms of their lived experiences; and 3) the disparity in educational outcomes between students of color, low-income students, and their White middle-class peers.
>
> (McDonald, 2007, p. 2049)

In Delaware, ample evidence indicates persistent achievement and opportunity gaps between students of color, low-income students, and their White middle-income counterparts (Flores, 2007; Ware, 2004), which echoes national data on educational disparity (Milner, 2012).

UD's awareness of the demographic imperative was heightened by its reaccreditation process in 2011 by the Middle States Commission on Higher Education. The Middle States report indicated that the university lagged behind its peer institutions in nearly every measure of diversity, criticizing especially its poor retention and graduation rates of students of color. In response to this report, the university funded activities that foster diversity on campus, including the creation of the Collaborative.

There are three central challenges to the Collaborative's efforts to diversify teacher education. First, our teacher education programs are not centrally located or administered in a school or college of education. At UD, there are 11 undergraduate teacher preparation programs housed in 11 departments within six colleges across the University, a structure that can lead to fragmentation of teacher education faculty and can make it difficult to coordinate efforts. Second, neither the teacher education programs nor the university student body reflect the population of our state. In 2012, only 14.5% of our undergraduates were students of color,[1] compared with the state of Delaware, which had 31.1% people of color.[2] UD faculty are disproportionately White as well. The third challenge is particularly troubling. Members of the Collaborative analyzed institutional data to compare UD teacher education majors with the larger university population from 2006 to 2013. The rate of increase of racial-ethnic minorities enrolled in teacher education programs since 2006 is 7.9% slower than it has been at the university overall (see Table 12.1). Racial-ethnic minority students currently make up only 10.3% of the teacher education major population compared with 21.7% of the overall undergraduate population (including international students). In contrast to these troubling findings, teacher education programs do enroll 5% more first-generation college students than are enrolled on average at UD. Although the number of low-income and first-generation college students has remained fairly constant at the university, the number of first-generation teacher education majors has increased by almost 9% in the past 8 years.

With respect to race-ethnicity, income status, and first-generation status, teacher education majors between 2006 and 2013 graduated at higher rates than did the undergraduate student population overall (see Table 12.2). With respect to low-income status, however, teacher education majors graduated at much lower

TABLE 12.1 Comparison of Underrepresented Student Enrollment Overall Versus in Teacher Education Programs, 2006 to 2013

Group	Program	Spring 2006	Spring 2007	Spring 2008	Spring 2009	Spring 2010	Spring 2011	Spring 2012	Spring 2013	Average difference between groups	Average difference over time
Ethnic minorities[1]	Univ	14.7%	15.8%	16.4%	17.3%	18.3%	20.1%	20.6%	21.7%	+7.9%	+7.0%
	TEd	8.9%	9.0%	8.8%	10.8%	11.2%	11.2%	11.2%	10.3%	−7.9%	+1.4%
Low income	Univ	n/a	5.8%	5.6%	5.4%	6.2%	6.8%	7.4%	7.5%	+1.4%	+1.7%
	TEd	n/a	3.8%	3.9%	5.3%	5.1%	5.2%	6.1%	5.3%	−1.4%	+1.5%
First generation	Univ	4.0%	3.9%	4.0%	3.8%	3.8%	3.9%	3.9%	3.7%	−5.1%	−0.3%
	TEd	n/a	2.3%	6.1%	9.3%	11.6%	11.1%	11.0%	11.2%	+5.1%	+8.9%

Note: Univ = university overall; TEd = teacher education programs; n/a = not applicable.

[1] Includes all students who identified as American Indian, Asian, Black, Hispanic, Multi-Ethnic, Non-Resident Alien, or Pacific Islander. Does not include students who identified as "Unknown."

TABLE 12.2 Comparison of 4- and 5-Year Graduation Rates for Underrepresented Students Overall Versus in Teacher Education Programs, Entering Classes of 2007 and 2008

Group	Program	Number in original cohort		4-year graduation rate		Average 4-year graduation rate	5-year graduation rate		Average 5-year graduation rate
		Fall 2007	Fall 2008	Fall 2007	Fall 2008		Fall 2007	Fall 2008	
				Ethnicity					
Racial minority	TEd	32	42	20 (62.5%)	26 (61.9%)	62.2%	23 (71.9%)	28 (66.7%)	69.3%
Racial minority	Univ	554	511	317 (57.2%)	291 (57.0%)	57.1%	386 (69.7%)	343 (67.1%)	68.4%
White	TEd	298	214	220 (73.8%)	156 (73.0%)	73.4%	250 (83.9%)	170 (79.4%)	81.7%
White	Univ	2286	2354	1604 (70.2%)	1642 (69.8%)	70.0%	1857 (81.2%)	1812 (77.0%)	79.1%
				First-generation status					
First generation	TEd	53	32	28 (52.8%)	22 (68.8%)	60.8%	37 (69.8%)	23 (71.9%)	70.9%
First generation	Univ	321	262	197 (61.4%)	153 (58.4%)	59.9%	232 (72.3%)	176 (67.2%)	69.8%
Not first generation	TEd	293	232	223 (76.1%)	164 (70.7%)	73.4%	248 (84.6%)	180 (77.6%)	81.1%
Not first generation	Univ	2625	2726	1805 (68.8%)	1856 (68.1%)	68.5%	2099 (80.0%)	2068 (75.9%)	78.0%

Note: TEd = teacher education programs; Univ = university overall.

rates than their undergraduate counterparts overall. It is particularly alarming that for teacher education students, the income gap in terms of the 4-year graduation rate (a difference of 38.7%) was twice that of the overall UD student population (a difference of 19%; see Table 12.3).

One of our first tasks was to assess past efforts by various UD stakeholders to address the demographic imperative. We discovered that many efforts overlapped and/or operated independently of one another. However, many relied heavily on grant funding, making them challenging to sustain. Although separate initiatives sometimes create programs that benefit individual students, such efforts do not necessarily change institutional practices. In addition, teacher education program coordinators felt the lack of diversity was too large an issue for an individual program to take on, indicating a cooperative effort across all teacher education programs was needed.

Addressing the demographic imperative in contexts such as ours is best accomplished by connecting our efforts to a public scholarship framework that links diversity work to public engagement, seeking to create and nurture a university community that is reflective of and responsive to the demographics, needs, assets, and interests of constituent communities (Sturm, Eatman, Saltmarsh, & Bush, 2011). Public scholarship is a form of scholarly activity that conceptualizes academic work as an inseparable, unified combination of research, teaching, and service (Colbeck & Michael, 2006). The Imagining America's Tenure Team Initiative report noted that public scholarship "encompasses different forms of making knowledge about, for, and with diverse publics and communities, . . . contributes to the public good and yields artifacts of public and intellectual value" (Ellison & Eatman, 2008, p. 6).

Although our self-study was internal, its aim—to diversify teacher education and, ultimately, the teacher workforce—concerns the public good. The next section of this chapter focuses on the methodology and results of our public scholarship research project. Based on these results, the final section describes implications.

TABLE 12.3 Comparison of 4-Year Graduation Rates for Low-Income Students Overall Versus in Teacher Education Programs, Entering Class of 2009

Income status	Program	Number in original cohort Fall 2009	4-Year graduation rate Fall 2009
Low Income	TEd	13	4 (30.8%)
Low Income	Univ	195	81 (41.5%)
Not Low Income	TEd	305	212 (69.5%)
Not Low Income	Univ	2,969	1,795 (60.5%)

Note: Income data are not available for earlier cohorts. TEd = teacher education programs; Univ = overall university.

The Collaborative's Public Scholarship Research Project

Methodology

We designed and implemented a research project during the 2012–2013 academic year utilizing a mixed-methods approach (Johnson & Onwuegbuzie, 2004) that allowed us to triangulate data (Mathison, 1988) about how our teacher education programs consider diversity and how underrepresented students perceive or experience diversity. Our project included four data sources:

- Interviews with the 10 faculty members who coordinate our teacher education programs;
- Three student focus groups: two included four current teacher education majors each, and one included three former teacher education majors;
- A survey of undergraduates from underrepresented groups across the university; and
- Institutional data.

Each of the faculty program coordinator interviews and focus groups lasted 30 to 60 minutes and was recorded, transcribed, and analyzed using grounded theory (Corbin & Strauss, 2008). Of the 4,000 undergraduates invited to participate, 626 completed the online survey, including 102 (16.5%) current teacher education majors. All participants were from one or more underrepresented groups (students of color, first-generation college students, and/or low-income students). Finally, raw institutional data comparing the enrollment and graduation rates of teacher education majors with that of our overall undergraduate population since 2006, reported earlier in this chapter, were collected and analyzed, with special attention to trends related to student ethnicity, income status, and first-generation status.

Findings

Three major themes emerged in our analysis of the data from the survey, focus groups, and interviews: concerns about the profession, institutional issues, and supports for current students.

Concerns About the Profession

We examined students' concerns, beliefs and perceptions that might explain why individuals from underrepresented group choose not to enter the teaching profession. Understanding students' preconceptions about the profession is vital to developing a recruitment plan.

Given the negative public discourse about education and teaching—including all too many indictments of lazy, unprofessional, underperforming teachers (e.g., Kumashiro, 2012)—young people from underrepresented groups may choose other careers. Moreover, although youth from middle-income or predominantly White schools may have positive learning experiences (e.g., exemplary teaching, meaningful learning, extracurricular academic experiences, role models) that counteract the negative discourse, youth who attend high-needs schools are less likely to have access to these opportunities and may be less familiar with the positive aspects of public education. As a result, parents, peers, and even teachers may encourage youth to pursue a career that they see as more favorable or prestigious. Survey data from students who had considered but did not pursue teacher education indicated that 16% had family members who discouraged them from becoming teachers. One focus group participant discussed her parents' lack of support for her career choice: "My parents . . . didn't like the education program. . . . My mom was like, 'Why are you going to be a teacher? Why can't you be an architect or be something with a title?' "

On the survey, students who were non–teacher education majors listed reasons for not wanting to enter teaching that related to this theme, such as the amount of stress in the field, the lack of prestige, a belief that the job is not fulfilling, the perception that teaching entails doing repetitive work, the view that there are limited opportunities for advancement, and the need to work with "obnoxious" children and/or parents (47% of responses fell under one of these categories). In focus groups, students who changed their majors from teacher education said they were discouraged by school systems' insufficient focus on "real learning." All of these responses reveal a negative view of the profession.

Another common concern is the financial remuneration of teachers. On the survey, the second most frequent reason for not going into teaching was "salary too low" (43%). One participant said that both she and her family recognized that "I'm probably not going to make that much money" in teaching. Coupled with this issue was the concern that the effort necessary to be a teacher compared with the salary—the return on investment—was not rewarded. As one student wrote on the survey, "Teachers do not make enough money for the amount of work they do." Program coordinators echoed these same concerns.

Institutional Issues

Data from program coordinators and students indicated that many of the difficulties involved in diversifying the pool of teacher candidates have to do with attracting students to UD and making a college education affordable to them.

The literature suggests a need for institutionalization of diversity outreach (e.g., Henry, Fowler, & West, 2011). Although UD does have several such programs, these initiatives work largely in isolation and do not have consistent funding or institutional support. Program coordinators identified lack of time, resources, and institutional reward as major obstacles to recruiting a more diverse group of teacher candidates. All of the coordinators recognized that they have a role and a responsibility in diversifying our teacher candidates, but many already feel overburdened. Furthermore, outreach and community service do not receive as much weight in the university tenure/promotion structure as research and other academic activities.

Nine of the 10 program coordinators identified limited funds for scholarships and financial aid as a barrier to diversifying their teacher education student body. Survey data revealed that teacher education students identified "financial obligations: tuition and housing" as the number one barrier to their degree progress, with more than 40% of respondents identifying it as "very or extremely challenging" and 30% more identifying it as "moderately challenging." The survey also asked students who left teacher education what might have helped keep them in the major; the top two responses were student loan forgiveness for going into teaching and scholarships for teacher education majors.

Supports for Current Students

Data from program coordinators and students revealed a number of student needs related to financial, academic, and social support. Funding for teacher education program costs, campus climate, and academic support opportunities need to be addressed to recruit and retain a more diverse pool of teacher candidates.

With increased emphasis on rigorous standards, teacher education programs have implemented costly testing requirements, criminal background checks, and other fees. Approximately 29% of the surveyed students felt the additional fees associated with teacher education programs were very or extremely challenging, and 33.7% felt they were moderately challenging, to degree progress. After tuition and housing costs, teacher education fees were the second most frequently rated barrier to advancing through their major, more than Praxis or grade point average requirements. Furthermore, those with family income at or below the poverty line perceived teacher education fees as being more challenging to their degree progress. Combined with the low graduation rate of low-income students discussed earlier, we see that the additional costs of teacher education programs are a serious issue that needs attention.

A number of studies point to the need to consider the influence of campus climate on the recruitment and retention of a diverse body of students (e.g., Hurtado, Milem, Clyton-Pedersen, & Allen, 1999). Half of the program coordinators and some student respondents expressed concern about the homogeneity of students and staff in teacher education programs. In the focus groups, students of color expressed overall feelings of satisfaction with their majors but repeatedly made reference to the predominantly White context of teacher education's students and faculty. As is the case with students, teacher education faculty at UD are less diverse than the population at large (see Figure 12.1).

During focus groups, several participants joked about being the only person of color in their classes, stating that "it's beneficial because the teachers learn my

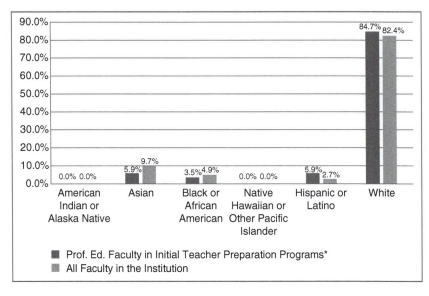

FIGURE 12.1 Racial/Ethnic Percentage of Teacher Education Faculty and Overall UD Faculty

name easier" or that teachers "would know if you're absent." These comments, although humorous, reveal concerns about being hypervisible as a student of color in predominantly White classes. The deleterious effects of being a student of color in predominately White classrooms are documented in the literature and include negative cognitive consequences (Lord & Saenz, 1985) and a tendency for the stereotypes of majority group members to be reified rather than dismantled (Gurin, Dey, Hurtado, & Gurin, 2002). One participant stated that the underrepresentation of students of color should be an area of concern and inquiry at the university:

> If you walk into a classroom and . . . you're the only black student of 20 kids, that should be concerning to you. . . . You have to ask yourself why this is happening. You shouldn't just say, "Oh, it's okay, though, because everybody loves teaching the children." No. [Laughter] That's ridiculous because why is it that way?

In the focus groups, students of color shared varied meanings attached to diversity; these meanings also revealed how they think the university values their presence as students of color, including the feeling that they were merely a token. One participant explained, "You're filling that quota. You're doing what the school wants you to do. You're this minority student, and they're increasing diversity."

Despite limited racial and ethnic diversity shown by our survey results, the results also indicate that many students reported feeling welcomed and included in their teacher education programs. However, it is worth noting that all of the students who indicated they had been treated unfairly were first-generation college students. Questions about socioeconomic status and general climate of teacher education programs revealed that first-generation college students were the most likely to feel isolated or left out because of their family's financial background.

A positive campus climate must not foster merely tolerance; it should actively support and reflect students' diverse racial/ethnic identities. Survey results also revealed areas of concern regarding the experiences of students of color at UD and campus climate. Racial-ethnic minority students, particularly Latino and Asian students, were more likely to say that their teacher education program never strengthened their sense of racial-ethnic identity, with lower means than the overall group of teacher education students. African American students were more likely to say they felt the need to minimize an aspect of their culture in order to fit in. These results are similar to those reported from a broader survey on UD's racial climate: "White students more frequently expected and found the campus climate to be welcoming for all people and groups than students of color" (UD Campus Climate Survey, 2011, p. 4). African American students in our survey were also more likely to say that they felt they were expected to speak on behalf of all members of their racial-ethnic group, that they felt left out because of their race-ethnicity, and that they witnessed their race being stereotyped.

Academic support and advisement in teacher education programs emerged as a third area in which support is needed. In our focus groups, first-generation college students explained that although they often had to negotiate experiences at the university on their own, they simultaneously developed independence and were highly motivated because they were the first in their families to attend a university. For this group of students, support once they are in college is extremely important, as other research has found (Park, Denson, & Bowman, 2013). One focus group participant explained, "For me, my advisor acted as a mentor going through the program. Maybe my parents weren't able to help, but she was. I think that having good advisors is a big key."

Although the majority of students did not identify a lack of academic support as a barrier to their degree progress, a question about resources on campus yielded surprising results. The survey asked how familiar students were with various support and enrichment services available at UD. More than 80% of current or former teacher education students were moderately, slightly, or not at all familiar with the Academic Enrichment Center, which provides services such as tutoring and study skills workshops for undergraduates. Students were just as unfamiliar with other academic and campus community resources such as disability services, work-study, and career services. Even the organization that specifically targets teacher education students, the Academic Support Program Inspiring Renaissance Educators, was not fully recognized, with 79.2% of current or former teacher education students being moderately, slightly, or not at all familiar with the program. All of these resources and programs are operating on UD's campus and serve as potential supports to students from underrepresented groups; however, clearly they need to be better publicized and utilized.

Implications and Next Steps

Our findings reflect our local context but can be useful to similar universities and/or programs and have implications for recruiting, preparing, and retaining a diverse pool of teacher candidates. Our results, informed by the national literature, suggest three primary areas of focus: student success and campus climate, advocacy for the teaching profession as a whole, and coordination and institutionalization of diversity efforts as public scholarship.

Student Success and Campus Climate

The graduation gaps, including the difference between racial minority and White UD students as well as the larger difference between low-income teacher education majors and those who are not low income, reveal that addressing student success and campus climate is imperative.

Our research shows that financial aid is the most important consideration for underrepresented groups in attending college and selecting teacher education as a major. Some students believe that a teacher education degree does not provide enough return on investment, especially given that teacher education majors have additional program expenses. For that reason, they may be more likely to consider entering, and more likely to successfully complete, a teacher education program if costs are manageable and they are not overburdened with debt. We advocate seeking long-term solutions such as student loan forgiveness for students who become teachers. Institutions could work to establish more 4-year scholarships for teacher education majors from underrepresented groups with financial need. In addition, having field placements in schools close to campus, helping students with transportation to field placements, and eliminating or subsidizing program fees could ease the financial burden for teacher candidates.

Teacher education programs, individually and collectively, should be a part of any university efforts to improve campus climate. Our research indicates that although students felt welcome in teacher education classes, they were also aware of the predominantly White nature of teacher education at UD, and they welcomed opportunities for further engagement in multicultural learning contexts (e.g. local schools with diverse demographics). The numerical and proportional representation of underrepresented students, known as *structural diversity*, is a key factor in a university's racial campus climate (Hurtado et al., 1999). Neither the teacher education student body nor the program faculty reflects the population of our state. In the same way that a negative campus climate can have harmful effects on the ability to recruit and retain a diverse student population, a more diverse student and faculty body can lead to a more positive racial campus climate, creating a welcoming environment where students from non-White backgrounds do not feel alienated and hypervisible. Institutions must address practices related to the recruitment and admission of a diverse student body and hiring of a diverse faculty. Deans and department chairs should require that faculty searches be conducted in ways that draw a diverse applicant pool with expertise in equity and diversity in addition to their other areas of scholarly expertise. To positively impact the racial climate, however, efforts at addressing structural diversity should be accompanied by attention to pedagogies and policies that support students as they negotiate differences and that foster sustained interaction among diverse classroom peers (Gurin et al., 2002; Hurtado, 2007).

Advocacy for the Profession

Teacher education programs can impact the recruitment and retention of diverse teacher candidates by better promoting the field of teaching, particularly showing it as a vibrant career related to social justice and making a difference in the world. As Cantor (2003) suggested, when university gates are opened to "many publics," university communities can "remain connected to the concerns of the day, the critical societal issues and the voices pushing them" (p. 5). One of the most promising ways to achieve this goal is for universities to provide long-term support for teacher education faculty to create partnerships with community members. We need to respond to the public's negative perceptions of schools. Teaching is, in fact, a dynamic and changing profession, not "doing the same thing every day" as one survey participant thought. We can make students more aware of what opportunities for advancement exist, from building to department to district (team leaders, department chairs, instructional coaches, principals, superintendents) as well as regional, state, and national positions. Because the negative public discourse about teaching influences students and their support system, we need to educate the whole community. Although this would not be a direct goal of teacher educators' public scholarship, it is a likely and important byproduct of it.

As part of their efforts to advocate for the teaching profession, teacher education programs should partner with communities to prevent underrepresented youth from feeling alienated from public school education. National research, particularly on Latino/a teachers, can provide some helpful insights in this area. For example, Irizzary and Donaldson (2012) found that many of their participants were actually motivated to go into teaching because of the difficulties they faced in school and saw teaching as a way "to combat the negative experiences they had as K-12 students" (p. 166). These prospective teachers saw "schools as sites of transformation and possibility" and entered teaching so that they could give back to their communities and "address systematic injustices in their own educational backgrounds" (pp. 166–167). Teacher education programs can work to promote the profession as a vehicle for social and institutional change, which is important to many students when selecting a career path.

One possibility for addressing this issue would be for universities to provide financial support for efforts, such as our own Success Through Education conferences, which brought high school students who had expressed an interest in pursuing a teaching degree to campus to attend classes, meet faculty, and learn more about teacher education. The main purpose of this conference series is to initiate the creation of a "pipeline," whereby Delaware youth from historically underrepresented populations will enroll in UD's teacher education programs, which in turn will increase the diversity of teachers in our local schools (see, e.g., Chapter 8). This conference also helps make the college admissions process more transparent.

Another step may be revisiting UD's undergraduate admissions requirements. In their interviews, program coordinators raised concerns about UD. They felt that admissions criteria focused too much on SAT scores, a focus that can hinder recruiting more diverse students. Coordinators also expressed concern that underrepresented students often come from underresourced schools whose coursework is not viewed as suitably rigorous by Admissions.

Another related recommendation is to follow the examples of universities that have developed grow-your-own programs, like those highlighted in several chapters of this book, in which teacher education programs partner with local schools to recruit, mentor, and train culturally diverse and low-income high school students through college and place them in employment as teachers in their communities. (National Education Association, 2009). Finally, teacher educators need to take advantage of our many interactions with teachers in the field to encourage them to be advocates for the teaching profession and to recruit their own students to consider education as a potential career.

Institutionalization of Diversity Efforts as a Public Scholarship Project

According to Sturm et al. (2011),

> Most colleges and universities have undertaken pipeline initiatives and efforts to achieve greater diversity and participation . . . and many have undertaken various forms of community engagement and service-learning in order to inculcate citizenship values and connect the institution to the community. But these efforts are often pursued piecemeal; they are not conceptualized or coordinated across systems in the integrated way necessary to have broad-scale impact. Because of this, they tend to operate at the periphery of core institutional strategies and practices. . . . The realization of full participation in higher education thus requires building an architecture of full participation—an institutional transformation strategy that sustains ongoing improvement and integrates publicly engaged scholarship, diversity, and student success with each other and with core values and priorities.

(pp. 9, 11)

A public scholarship framework seeks to engage communities both inside and outside university walls because "full participation incorporates the idea that higher education institutions are rooted in and accountable to multiple communities" (Sturm et al., 2011, p. 4). Active institutional support of publically engaged scholarship entails changing institutional practices and policies (e.g., tenure reward systems) to ensure that public scholarship work in which faculty partner with diverse communities is rewarded (Eatman, 2009; Ellison & Eatman, 2008). We recommend that a broader range of workload configuration options be possible for faculty who work to recruit and retain underrepresented students in teacher education.

In addition, many institutions with a serious commitment to diversity have an administrator who coordinates outreach and retention. The program coordinator interview data clearly articulate the need for an administrative position, a coordinator–director of diversity for teacher education at UD whose resources are not grant dependent but rather linked to a dependable annual budget. A coordinator could assist teacher education programs in becoming advocates for culturally relevant teaching practices and more directly involved in helping students become college ready. There are multiple ways to conceive of this work, but it is important that the university create a formal, institutional structure for community engagement and public scholarship.

Conclusion

The multifaceted, longitudinal work needed to diversify our teaching force—and our campus—can only be accomplished with serious attention to issues raised in our research: the improvement of campus climate, advocacy for the teaching profession, and coordination and institutionalization of diversity efforts as a public scholarship project. Sturm et al. (2011) explained three important features of public engagement work:

1. Public engagement encourages and enables full participation of diverse groups and communities;
2. Full participation of diverse communities is a critical attribute of successful and legitimate public engagement; and
3. The systems that take account of these synergies are likely to enable the successful pursuit of both public engagement and full participation/diversity, and to enhance the legitimacy, levels of engagement, and robustness of higher education institutions. (p. 6)

For these reasons, the public scholarship framework provides an important lens for recruiting, preparing, retaining, and supporting a diverse and highly effective teaching force. As previously articulated, such a teaching force is not only a valid end in and of itself but also develops a productive cycle in which strong collegiate teacher candidates from underrepresented groups go on to become strong teachers, who educate P-12 students from underrepresented groups, who will then become strong college applicants. The Collaborative to Diversify Teacher Education at UD looks forward to using the public scholarship framework in partnership with the university as a whole to address these issues, and we welcome the opportunity to connect with other teacher education programs ready to take on this challenge.

Notes

1 Data drawn from UD's Office of Institutional Research (www.udel.edu/IR/fnf/ethnc. html). International students are not included in this number.
2 Data drawn from U.S. Census Bureau 2010 statistics (http://quickfacts.census.gov/qfd/states/10000.html).

References

Cantor, N. (2003). *Transforming America: The university as public good*. Retrieved from http://imaginingamerica.org/wp-content/uploads/2011/07/Foreseeable-Futures-3-Cantor.pdf

Colbeck, C. L., & Michael, P. W. (2006). The public scholarship: Reintegrating Boyer's four domains. *New Directions for Institutional Research, 129,* 7–19.

Corbin, J., & Strauss, A. (2008). *Basics of qualitative research* (3rd ed.). Thousand Oaks, CA: Sage.

Eatman, T. K. (2009). Engaged scholarship and faculty rewards: A national conversation. *Diversity & Democracy, 12,* 18–19.

Ellison, J., & Eatman, T. K. (2008). *Scholarship in public: Knowledge creation and tenure policy in the engaged university*. Syracuse, NY: Imagining America. Retrieved from http://imaginingamerica.org/research/tenure-promotion/

Flores, A. (2007). Examining disparities in mathematics education: Achievement gap or opportunity gap? *High School Journal, 91,* 29–42.

Gurin, P., Dey, E. L., Hurtado, S., & Gurin, G. (2002). Diversity and higher education: Theory and impact on educational outcomes. *Harvard Educational Review, 72,* 330–366.

Henry, W. J., Fowler, S. R., & West, N. M. (2011). Campus climate: An assessment of student perceptions in a college of education. *Urban Education, 46,* 389–718.

Hurtado, S. (2007). ASHE Presidential Address: Linking diversity with the educational and civic missions of higher education. *Review of Higher Education, 30,* 185–196.

Hurtado, S., Milem, J., Clyton-Pedersen, A., & Allen, W. (1999). *Enacting diverse learning environments: Improving the climate for racial/ethnic diversity in higher education*. ASHE-ERIC Higher Education Report (Vol. 26, No. 8). Washington, DC: Graduate School of Education and Human Development, The George Washington School.

Irizarry, J., & Donaldson, M. (2012). Teach for América: The Latinization of U.S. schools and the critical shortage of Latina/o teachers. *American Educational Research Journal, 49,* 155–194.

Johnson, R. B., & Onwuegbuzie, A. J. (2004). Mixed methods research: A research paradigm whose time has come. *Educational Researcher, 33*(7), 14–26.

Kumashiro, K. (2012). *Bad teacher! How blaming teacher distorts the bigger picture*. New York, NY: Teachers College Press.

Lord, C. G., & Saenz, D. S. (1985). Memory deficits and memory surfeits: Differential cognitive consequences of tokenism for tokens and observers. *Journal of Personality and Social Psychology, 49,* 918–926.

Mathison, S. (1988). Why triangulate? *Educational Researcher, 17*(2), 13–17.

McDonald, M. (2007). The joint enterprise of social justice teacher education. *Teachers College Record, 109,* 2047–2081.

Milner, H. R. (2012). Beyond a test score: Explaining opportunity gaps in educational practice. *Journal of Black Studies 43,* 693–718.

National Education Association. (2009). *Strengthening and diversifying the teacher recruitment pipeline: Current efforts.* Washington, DC: Author.

Park, J. J., Denson, N., & Bowman, N. A. (2013). Does socioeconomic diversity make a racial difference? Examining the effects of racial and socioeconomic diversity on the campus climate for diversity. *American Educational Research Journal, 50,* 466–496.

Sturm, S., Eatman, T., Saltmarsh, J., & Bush, A. (2011). *Full participation: Building the architecture for diversity and public engagement in higher education.* Retrieved from www.fullparticipation.net

UD Campus Climate Survey. (2011). Retrieved from www.udel.edu/prominence/pdfs/DECExecutiveSummary.pdf

Ware, L. (2004). Brown's uncertain legacy: High stakes teasing and the continuing achievement gap. *University of Toledo Law Review, 35*(4), 841–855.

13

THE POTENTIAL OF ACCREDITATION TO FOSTER DIVERSITY IN TEACHER EDUCATION PROGRAMS

Doyin Coker-Kolo

Accreditation has considerable capacity to regulate higher education for quality assurances if it lives up to its potential. Accrediting agencies ensure rigor, effectiveness, and continuous improvement by verifying that institutions meet or exceed prescribed norms and standards (Gafoor & Khabeer, 2013). In return, they bestow integrity and legitimacy on the institution and its programs and protect them from unwarranted criticisms (Head & Johnson, 2011). Institutions of higher education strive for excellence, equity, and innovation. In fact, most institutions include diversity in their mission statements or strategic goals indicating their desire to promote a diverse and inclusive environment that values, respects, and cares for all its members. Yet most campuses still struggle with ways to negotiate differences, maintain civility, and ensure equal opportunity for all their constituents (Clark, Fasching-Varner, & Brimhall-Vargas, 2012). Accreditation can assist institutions in actualizing their commitment to democracy and true excellence by setting clear and rigorous standards that demand that institutions produce measurable outcomes to support their claims.

This chapter describes the potential of accreditation and accrediting agencies in promoting diversity, focusing primarily on the standard and elements for diversity in the National Council for the Accreditation of Teacher Education (NCATE) with regard to their responsiveness to the trends in demographics of the student population and the teaching force. The chapter also discusses ways in which the strengthening of accreditation standards on diversity can promote the overall effectiveness of teaching and learning processes as well as the effectiveness of the institutions. It must be noted that in 2011, NCATE embarked on a merger with the Teacher Education Accreditation Council (TEAC) to develop a common and more rigorous set of standards for the accreditation of teacher education preparation institutions, which became the Council for the Accreditation of

Educator Preparation (CAEP). Teacher preparation institutions may continue to use the NCATE standards until 2016, after which they must all migrate to the new CAEP standards established in August 2013. Although this chapter focuses mainly on the soon to be phased out NCATE standards, it briefly examines the veracity of the proposed CAEP standards and their responsiveness to holding institutions accountable for diversity. The significance of this chapter lies in its attempt to examine the potentials of accreditation as an instrument for promoting and enforcing diversity in teacher education programs and in the teaching workforce.

Since the multicultural education movement began in the 1970s, attention to diversity has been mandated by most accreditation agencies for professional programs not only in teacher education but also in programs like social work and business administration (Jani, Pierce, Ortiz, & Sowbel, 2011). However, the degree to which different aspects of diversity are emphasized and enforced in accreditation standards varies from program to program. As is explained later in the chapter, diversity accreditation standards often serve as a vehicle for promoting the recruitment and retention of ethnic minority faculty and students (Siegel, Abushanab, & Holliday, 2010). Additionally, institutions are required to provide evidence for students' knowledge, skills, and dispositions in diversity from developing culturally responsive curricula and implementing culturally responsive pedagogy. In teacher education programs, there are additional expectations to produce graduates who have the confidence to work in diverse settings and the ability to assure high performance for all students (NCATE, 2008).

Although accreditation is primarily about making threshold decisions, the potential of accreditation increases when the emphasis is on continuous improvement rather than compliance. Proitzl, Stensaker, and Harvey (2004) asserted that accreditation assures quality and promotes excellence and continuous improvement where "diversity is seen as a positive characteristic to be fostered, not a disadvantage to be reduced or minimized" (p. 737). Additionally, accreditation tends to promote diversity and continuous improvement if it has more flexibility and negotiable standards (Miretzky & Stevens, 2010). Accreditation agencies must keep a balance between setting prescriptive standards that mandate institutional compliance in core areas with more general goals that take into account the individual institutions' mission and resources.

The Council for Higher Education Accreditation (2012) defined accreditation in higher education as "a collegial process of self review and peer review for improvement of academic quality and public accountability of institutions and programs, usually occurring every 3–10 years" (p. 3). AdvancED (2013), a global accreditation agency, agreed with the quality assurance definition but suggested that it has a broader purpose: "Accreditation examines the whole institution—the programs, the cultural context and the community of stakeholders—to determine how well the parts work together to meet the needs of students" (p. 1). This emphasis on continuous improvement and the collective effort of the institution and its constituents to produce evidence of positive impact on student performance makes accreditation uniquely positioned to directly benefit not just the institution but also the individual students.

The two main types of accreditation are institutional and programmatic (or professional). Most higher education institutions, private and public, must be accredited by their state department of education or a designated body. Additionally, these institutions seek national or regional accreditation. This type of accreditation focuses on the effectiveness of the overall operations of the institution, including their level of productivity in terms of students' retention and graduation, faculty qualifications and their engagement in continuous improvement (Council for Higher Education Accreditation, 2012). Regional accreditation agencies such as the Middle States Commission on Higher Education and the Southern Association of Colleges and Schools are recognized by the Council for Higher Education Accreditation. Specialized programmatic or professional accreditation focuses on particular aspects of a department, school, program, or specialized academic field. For colleges of education or teacher preparatory programs, the NCATE, now referred to as CAEP, provides institutional accreditation at the divisional level. Although NCATE provides accreditation for the school or college of education (also referred to as a *unit*), its Specialized Professional Associations provide recognition for the specific programs within the departments in the school or college.

Demographic Shifts and Implications for Higher Education

Educational institutions are a microcosm of society. As explained in the Introduction to this book, there has been a dramatic shift in the demographics of the population of the United States, and the nation has become multidimensional in race, ethnicity, class, language, and religion. Nowhere is this shift more apparent than in our public schools, where by 2020, children of color will comprise nearly half of the school-aged population (U.S. Department of Education, 2010). The disparity between the demographics of the P-12 students and the teaching workforce is problematic because many preservice teachers report that they lack the cultural knowledge and experiences of working or living in diverse environments yet will be faced with teaching a very diverse student population (Miretzky & Stevens, 2010). To effectively impact the learning of the diverse P-12 student population, preservice teachers must demonstrate a significant understanding of diversity and the ability to face the challenges of a diverse classroom. It is therefore important to examine how accreditation, a key driver of effectiveness, can be leveraged to facilitate institutional or program responsiveness to the current demographic shifts and ensure the success of all students regardless of their backgrounds.

Teachers of color bring a rich cultural perspective to the classroom and provide opportunity for cultural exchanges that benefit not only the students but also their colleagues and the community. However, the literature is replete with concerns from educators, politicians, and others about the underrepresentation of minorities in higher education institutions in general but particularly in colleges of education (Gollnick & Chinn, 2009; Shudak, 2010). This lack of access leads to the mismatch between the diverse P-12 student population and the teaching workforce and its attending consequences of poor graduation rates, high dropout rates, and low achievement in general for students from underrepresented groups. Shudak (2010) defined *cultural mismatch* as a situation whereby minority students are paired with teachers of dissimilar backgrounds in terms of skin color, cultural tastes, life experiences, languages, and so on. Such mismatches, he asserted, can harm minority students because "they cannot give meaning to their lives when they do not see themselves represented in the institutions (like schools) that comprise the larger context that surrounds them" (p. 350). An example would be the inadequate representation of minority cultures and identity in curriculum and textbooks. However, cultural matching between a teacher and his or her students eliminates the barriers of cultural misunderstanding and miscommunication and leads to higher student achievement. Shudak further described cultural mismatch as a cycle that creates a phenomenon of underachievement for minority students who fail to achieve success in P-12 schools and are unable to pursue postsecondary education where they might become teachers. American Association of Colleges for Teacher Education (AACTE) Chief Executive Officer Sharon Robinson decried the mismatch and called on policymakers, school district leaders, and those responsible for teacher preparation to do a better job in examining the staffing needs of K-12 classrooms and to target financial aid and support to minority students with an interest in the teaching career (AACTE, 2010).

According to Valentin (2012), teacher education programs have a moral responsibility to prepare preservice teachers to become competent in facing the challenges of today's diverse classroom settings. Wiggins, Follo, and Eberly (2007) suggested programs can meet this obligation by the integration of diversity into their curriculum and field experiences. They further claimed that such a curriculum is paramount to teacher candidates becoming not only highly qualified, but highly effective teachers. Valentin argued that an institution's conceptual framework should include a description of the diversity competencies in the curriculum because the conceptual framework is the foundation for the unit's operations. Valentin also charged that infusing the curriculum with diversity may not be enough but should be coupled with an assessment of candidates' prior dispositions, effective and collaborative pedagogy, and opportunity to interact with students from diverse backgrounds during field and clinical experiences. An examination of NCATE (2008) standards also reveals the requirement of these attributes of diversity in the conceptual framework and curriculum of any teacher preparation program that seeks its accreditation.

Effective teaching is the single most important factor in student learning (Danielson, 2007; Wiggins & McTighe, 2011). If, as Wiggins et al. (2007) suggested, diversity experiences help to produce more highly qualified and effective teachers, then diversity should be the hallmark of every teacher education program. Given the increasing diversity of today's student body and the mismatch of these students with the teaching workforce, measuring the effectiveness of a college of education and, indirectly, the university that houses it must include a measure of their effectiveness in maintaining not just quality but equality of access. The scholarship of diversity in teacher education is sparse on the specific issue of assessing teacher preparation institutions for their recruitment efforts (Shudak, 2010).

Accreditation agencies can play an important role in establishing clear and unambiguous standards to hold institutions accountable for recruiting faculty and students of color. According to Akiba, Cockrell, Simmons, Seunghee, and Argawal (2010), accreditation standards drive the prospects for multicultural education in teacher education programs and provide the guidelines for them to develop or revise the diversity components in their curriculum. Additionally, they influence the perceptions and understandings of faculty members who create multicultural education courses and program leaders who oversee the implementation of the programs for diversity. However, it is not clear how rigorously accrediting agencies enforce a requirement for diversity in candidates' recruitment and retention and in hiring of faculty and staff.

NCATE and Diversity Requirements in Teacher Education Accreditation

Diversity has always been a standard in teacher accreditation since the inception of NCATE in 1954. NCATE is considered the gold standard of teacher education accreditation (Akiba et al., 2010; Miretzky & Stevens, 2010; Shudak, 2010; Valentin, 2012). As noted on its website, NCATE is the teaching profession's mechanism to help establish high quality preparation of teachers and other school professionals. As of 2012, nationally and internationally, 656 institutions were accredited by NCATE. Seventy others were candidates or precandidates for accreditation (NCATE, 2012). NCATE's accreditation is standards based. Its current six standards were established in 2008 and designed to assess teacher candidates' performance (Standards 1 and 2) and institutional capacity (Standards 3–6; Gujjar, 2011). The agency requires those institutions seeking its accreditation to meet a diversity standard, which is the fourth of its six standards. NCATE (2008) defines *diversity* as "differences among groups of people and individuals based on ethnicity, race, socioeconomic status, gender, exceptionalities, language, religion, sexual orientation and geographical area" (p. 86). NCATE's diversity standard also has four elements, but in general, it requires that the college of education "designs, implements, and evaluates curriculum and provides experiences for candidates to acquire and demonstrate the knowledge, skills, and professional dispositions necessary to help all students learn" (NCATE, 2008, p. 34). Furthermore, the institutions must also show how they provide opportunity for candidates to interact with diverse students on campus and in P-12 schools and with diverse university and clinical faculty.

It is disconcerting to note here that CAEP, the accreditation body replacing NCATE for teacher preparation institutions, does not have a standalone diversity standard in its newly developed set of unit standards (CAEP, 2013). CAEP includes diversity as elements in two out of its five standards but did not bring in all the elements in the former NCATE diversity standard nor integrate diversity throughout the other standards.

The Potential of Accreditation to Monitor Diversity in Teacher Education Programs

As an externally controlled process, accreditation is often feared on college campuses for its stringent requirements, demands on faculty's time, and judgment on an institution's reputation (Head & Johnson, 2011). The process could be perceived as complex and perfunctory for any institution that does not strategize. Shudak (2010) suggested that accreditation gives teacher education programs "a free pass" to act with impunity in relation to diversity and that this laissez-faire attitude goes unchallenged by the academic community. Akiba et al. (2010) conducted a content analysis of state certification and program accreditation standards in 50 states and the District of Columbia, examining the types and characteristics of diversity related requirements contained in these standards and employed a conceptual framework based on Sleeter and Grant's (2009) five approaches to multicultural education. This framework places the diversity efforts in an institution on a continuum from a deficit model, which sees minority students as deficient and needing correction in order to fit into the mainstream culture, to the highest approach, which not only educates students about social justice, equity, and structural equality but raises their consciousness and encourages students' active participation in ameliorating social injustices. Specifically, the approaches are "(1) teaching the exceptional and culturally different, (2) human relations, (3) single-group studies, (4) multicultural education and (5) education that is multicultural and social reconstructionist" (Akiba et al., 2010, pp. 447–448).

The study found that although accreditation standards vary from state to state, the diversity standards typically focus on three main areas: (a) diversity-related candidate performance, (b) program or curriculum design, and (c) field experience and internship. Additional requirements found, but not as commonly as the preceding, were diverse faculty (found in 16 states), assessment of diversity related knowledge and skills of teacher candidates (in nine states), and faculty knowledge of diversity (found in eight states). It is not surprising that these findings closely align with the diversity guidelines listed in NCATE accreditation standards (NCATE, 2008, pp. 34–37). Whether institutions are NCATE- or state-accredited, the good news is that almost all have some minimum diversity requirements in their certification or accreditation standards. The bad news is they set few or no requirements for diversity in candidate recruitment and faculty hiring.

As noted by Akiba et al. (2010), the majority of states (43 out of 50) set their requirements at the level of Sleeter and Grant's (2009) second multicultural education approach called *human relations*. This approach is described as "helping students to develop an appreciation for and understanding of differences and similarities between cultural and ethnic groups with an aim to improve individual and group interactions across cultures and ethnicity" (Akiba et al., 2010, p. 448). In Coker-Kolo's (1993) dimensions of global understanding ranging from knowledge to affective and participatory domains, these guidelines rank at the basic level of knowledge acquisition, lower than the affective and participatory dimensions. Akiba et al. (2010) concluded that "these standards are ambiguous in nature since they focus on the goals rather than on approaches or methods to achieve the goals" (p. 423). These criticisms are based on the global nature of the standards, the lower expectation set for students' activism as social agents, and the requirement for programs to only set goals but not to guarantee the implementation or integration of multicultural ideals in their programs. Last and most important, less than a third of the states require institutions to address candidate and faculty diversity as part of their requirements. Given this scenario, it is questionable if the accreditation requirements are responsive enough in addressing the challenges associated with the rapidly changing demographics of our society and the P-12 student population.

Although many multiculturalists (such as Shudak, 2010, and Akiba et al., 2010) have argued for more stringent diversity criteria in accreditation and more rigorous process, research conducted by Miretzky and Stevens (2010) indicates that most colleges of education endorse the current NCATE diversity standard and some even struggle to adequately meet all of its elements. Miretzky and Stevens argued that the diversity standards set for institutions are broad and all encompassing, but accreditation reviewers tend to enforce them inappropriately from a narrow perspective. Their study, which examined rural institutions' capacity to respond to NCATE's definition of diversity and its associated accreditation standard, confirms that in spite of good-faith efforts, rural education programs do experience problems with meeting NCATE diversity requirements for ensuring candidates' interaction with ethnically diverse faculty and students in the university and K-12 environments. Miretzky and Stevens suggested that most reviewers focus more on the racial and ethnic dimensions of diversity and ignore other evidences like exceptionality, gender and social economic status. The latter are said to be more universal and locally relevant, while having the greatest impact on the classroom environment, and cut across other areas of diversity.

Additionally, respondents felt that candidates could transfer their competency in those diversity characteristics to other areas of diversity such as culture. Miretzky and Stevens (2010) posed some insightful questions. For instance, they asked if there are particular experiences that regardless of setting should or must be met to maximize the likelihood of developing educators who are effective in teaching diverse student populations. They also questioned if a rural school's claim that their focus on, say, socioeconomic status as the most important and the most relevant for their region is comprehensive enough to adequately prepare candidates to teach students of color or English language learners. The authors acknowledged the need to address the challenges of the changing demographics and the dominance of majority and female teachers in P-12 classrooms. However, they argued for flexibility in the accreditation process so that programs would not have to choose between what they know are strong experiences versus a diverse setting that may provide less than desirable experiences just to meet the standards. Moreover, addressing standards is important, but creativity and adaptability should not be abandoned in supporting teacher education programs to effectively prepare their candidates to succeed in diverse P-12 classrooms.

The argument from Miretzky and Stevens's (2010) study that institutions can focus on any aspect of diversity in which they have strength is predicated on the fact that all the diversity characteristics are actually interrelated. Valentin (2012) indicated that there are common threads among all aspects of culture; hence, diversity should be looked at in a broader sense and not only on the basis of race and ethnicity. This fact aligns with Cushner, McClelland, and Safford's (2003) theory that teaching and learning are influenced by 12 sources of cultural identity: race, ethnicity/nationality, social class, sex/gender, health, age, geographic region, sexuality, religion, social status, language and ability/disability. Although the argument of a "piecemeal approach" to implementing diversity requirements may be tenable, the evidence for the transferability of one diversity skill to the other is unclear. For example, could one claim that a student who is competent in working with individuals with disability can transfer that skill into working with English as a second language students? Additionally, it would have been helpful if Miretzky and Stevens (2010) had discussed the sources of the diversity experiences for teacher candidates in their study. Was the source through a single course or were the experiences embedded throughout the curriculum? What kinds of field and clinical experiences were provided? How was disposition assessed? It is not enough to focus on the geographical location; it is more helpful to discuss the program curricular initiatives that offer the diversity experiences for the students and how those experiences translate into learning achievement for P-12 students.

As Shudak (2010) suggested, accreditation may actually have the opposite effect on diversity in an institution if it is treated in a perfunctory manner. If an institution does not ensure equal access to its teacher education programs and address what he terms as the cultural mismatch between teachers and students in schools, the result is this opposing force of accreditation.

Fortunately, examples abound of institutional creativity in addressing the need for diversity of their candidates regardless of their geographical location. At Central Washington University, faculty partnered with a school district to establish a "grow-your-own" program to recruit students of color from high schools (Schmitcz, Nourse, & Ross, 2012). Like the grow-your-own programs discussed in several chapters in this book, the unique feature of the program is that the future teachers are paired with master teachers in the P-12 schools for a year for an ongoing mentor relationship. This program not only helps address the historic underrepresentation of minority teachers in P-12 schools, it also creates an enduring partnership between higher education and P-12 schools and faculty.

Changes in the Teacher Education Accreditation Standards and the Impact on Diversity

The merger between NCATE and TEAC to form CAEP could enhance the credibility of the teaching profession because it provides a unified body for its accreditation and allows the profession to speak with a common voice. Scholars of multicultural education and culturally responsive teaching therefore awaited the new CAEP standards with great anticipation. Unfortunately, many of these scholars may find their expectations unmet because the new CAEP standards do not have diversity components as strong as those of its predecessor (NCATE). The standards have stirred up a debate about their impact on diversity in the teaching workforce (Hawkins, 2013). There are two major areas of concern with the new CAEP standards, and they are interrelated. The first is the absence of a standalone standard for diversity.

That absence is very disappointing for many reasons. As described in the Introduction to this book and in articles by other concerned educators, the lack of diversity emphasis is a missed opportunity to address the demographic imperatives in the teaching workforce. This omission sends a clear message that we, as a profession, do not take the changing demographics of the student population seriously, despite the overwhelming data pointing to the inadequacy of teacher preparation institutions to produce a matching diverse workforce. These data are strong, compelling, and most available to and collected by AACTE (Racial Ethnic Distribution of Education Students, 2013). We need to use accreditation to leverage change in teacher preparation, to represent diverse role models of success, and to help ensure that our students are prepared to compete in today's increasingly diverse global society. Additionally, the national accrediting body should set a higher standard than the state. Most state departments of education and professional associations have diversity standards in their frameworks for program review and development; there should be no reason why CAEP, a national accrediting body, should require any less. It is insufficient to say that "diversity" is integrated into all other standards. In fact, it is understated and only appears within two standards: (a) as 1.9 under "Standard 1: Content and Pedagogical Knowledge" and (b) as 3.2 under "Standard 3: Candidate Quality, Recruitment and Selectivity." In another area (2.3), it was added under an explanation showing that it was not clear enough and could be missed (CAEP, 2013).

The second concern is the apparent conflict between the recruitment of diverse candidates and the selectivity "bar" that CAEP is attempting to establish with particular reference to Element 3.2, which states,

> The provider ensures that the average GPA of its accepted cohort of candidates meets or exceeds the CAEP minimum GPA of 3.0 and a group average performance in the top third of those who pass a nationally normed admissions assessment such as ACT, SAT or GRE.

(CAEP, 2013, p. 8)

Although it is important to set high standards as a profession (in fact, many states already do), we should acknowledge that quantitative requirements as set forth in the preceding will preclude otherwise potential high-quality candidates from being able to enter into the teaching profession! As Hawkins (2013) aptly pointed out, "We should be wary about the unintended consequences of setting the bar too high for minority students in a profession that is already less diverse than the population it serves" (p. 1). I suggest that other measures of potential success, such as motivation, perseverance, and commitment to diversity, must and can be considered if a candidate is strong in these qualitative areas but underprepared in other quantitative measures.

"NCATE unit standards constitute the critical knowledge, skills and professional behaviors that teacher candidates and other professionals are expected to know and are able to do in order to improve academic and social experiences for PK-12 students" (NCATE, 2008, p. 10). Decades of research show that great teaching is the single most important factor affecting student achievement in the classroom, and there is a link between diversity competencies and effectiveness in the classroom (Danielson, 2007; Wiggins & McTighe, 2011). Having a standalone diversity standard not only holds institutions accountable for providing candidates with appropriate knowledge, skills, and dispositions but also prompts institutions to increase the diversity of the teaching workforce to address the demographic imperatives in our P-12 schools. The vision of effective teaching and what young people need to succeed in the 21st century should include a clear knowledge of diversity in its broad definition. It is strongly suggested that CAEP consider the restoration of the former diversity standard and all its elements. Additionally, they should include a strong emphasis on diversity in faculty, student recruitments, and in student teaching placements. CAEP should be praised for setting up a body to redefine the standards for accreditation for educator preparation providers that focus on rigorous assessments, continuous improvement, innovation, clinical practice, and strong evidence of what candidates are able to do to impact the learning and social development of P-12 students. However, it should set a higher bar for diversity in student and faculty recruitment and should create clearer, more measurable, and outcome-based diversity standard.

Conclusion

There is no question that the shifting demographics in age, race, gender, and socioeconomic status have had significant implications for the education being offered to P-12 students and the preparation of those who teach them in the United States. Questions have been asked about the adequacy of diversity education in teacher preparation programs and their responsiveness to the demographic shifts. As noted by Ingvarson, Beavis, and Kleinhenz (2007),

> Teacher education is high on many states' political agendas and the colleges of education are often criticized for not responding fast enough to changing

societal needs so candidates are well prepared for the demands of teaching in a diverse and demographically changing world.

(p. 353)

Accreditation agencies at all levels play a significant role in ensuring that teacher education programs equip teacher candidates with the knowledge, skills, and dispositions to work with P-12 students from diverse backgrounds. All accrediting agencies responsible for ensuring quality in teacher education programs have some diversity standards or elements, although it is not at all certain that the standards are rigorous enough, are effectively enforced, or adequately hold institutions accountable for the recruitment and retention of candidates and faculty from minority groups. Additionally, the accreditation processes are perceived as complex and perfunctory on many campuses (Head & Johnson, 2011; Shudak 2010). Faculty find them onerous and resource intensive. That, coupled with constricting resources at most institutions, has created a perfect storm for those in the professional education unit who want to get their programs accredited beyond compliance.

Typically, accreditation standards focus on candidates' knowledge of diversity, the design of the curriculum, and field experiences. Young (2010) argued for a multicultural curriculum with an emphasis on culturally relevant pedagogy, which Ladson-Billings (1995) described as focusing on student academic achievement and the ability to accept and affirm their cultural identity while developing critical perspectives that challenge inequities that schools and other institutions perpetuate. The capacity of the colleges to adequately implement accreditation standards also varies and sometimes is impacted by their geographical locations and local resources. It is hard to argue for selective implementation of accreditation requirements based on an institution's context (Miretzky & Stevens, 2010). The use of creativity, however, is understandable and should be encouraged as long as institutions are achieving the desired outcome. For instance, if an institution has a hard time recruiting diverse faculty and has presented hard evidence of its good faith effort, they could collaborate with a more diverse institution in their area for course delivery and ensure clinical experience placements occur in diverse, multicultural, multiethnic settings. As opined by Ingvarson et al. (2007), "Accreditation standards are more likely to lead to innovation and improvement if they focused on clarifying the expected outcomes of teacher education, rather than stipulations about inputs, such as curriculum content and processes" (p. 353).

In *Out of Our Minds: Learning to Be Creative*, Ken Robinson (2011) suggested that

the standards that we are using to raise academic standards are "tired mantra," standards designed for other times and other purposes. We will not succeed in navigating the complex environment of the future by peering relentlessly into a rear view mirror.

(p. iv)

Accreditation agencies and educators need to seriously consider this statement and ask themselves if the current standards go far enough, if they are responsive to the dramatically changing demographic imperatives, and if they lead to successful outcomes for all students. Finally, do they require evidence of institutional or programmatic policies designed to recruit and retain strong candidates including those from historically underrepresented groups? Although it is essential to prepare prospective candidates to work with diverse students, it is also imperative to address the need to diversify the teaching workforce. This may be the area in which accreditation standards do not go far enough.

References

AdvancED. (2013). *What is accreditation?* Retrieved from www.advanc-ed.org/what-accreditation.

Akiba, M., Cockrell, K., Simmons, C., Seunghee, H., & Argawal, G., (2010). Preparing teachers for diversity: Examination of teacher certification and program accreditation standards in the 50 states and Washington, DC. *Excellence in Education, 43*, 446–462.

American Association of Colleges for Teacher Education. (Producer). (2010, April 15). *Teacher preparation: Who needs it? What the numbers say* [Video]. Retrieved from http://aacte.org/digital-media/event-recordings/videos-from-aacte-briefing-teacher-preparation-who-needs-it-what-the-numbers-say.html

Clark, C., Fasching-Varner, K., & Brimhall-Vargas, M. (Eds.). (2012). *Occupying the academy: Just how important is diversity work in higher education?* Lanham, MD: Rowman & Littlefield.

Coker-Kolo, D. (1993). *A description of the level of global understanding of students in the undergraduate elementary teacher education program and faculty perceptions about global education at four universities in South Carolina* (Unpublished doctoral dissertation). University of South Carolina, Columbia.

Council for the Accreditation of Educator Preparation. (2013, August). *CAEP 2013 standards for accreditation of educator preparation*. Retrieved from http://caepnet.files.wordpress.com/2013/09/final_board_approved1.pdf

Council for Higher Education Accreditation. (2012). *Accreditation serving the higher interest.* Retrieved from www.chea.org/pdf/chea-at-a-glance_2012.pdf

Cushner, K., McClelland, A., & Safford, P. (2003). *Human diversity in education approach* (4th ed.). New York, NY: McGraw-Hill.

Danielson, C. (2007). *Enhancing professional practice: A framework for teaching* (2nd ed.). Alexandria, VA: Association for Supervision and Curriculum Development.

Gafoor, S., & Khabeer, Q. (2013). Role of ICT in review of accreditation, assessment and academic audit in today's higher education. *Indian Streams Research Journal, 2*, 1–9.

Gollnick, D. M., & Chinn, P. C. (2009). *Multicultural education in a pluralistic society* (8th ed.). Upper Saddle River, NJ: Pearson Education.

Gujjar, A. A. (2011). Comparison of the standards for accreditation of teachers developed by ACTE & NCATE. *Articlesbase.* Retrieved from www.articlesbase.com/international-studies-articles/comparison-of-the-standards-for-accreditation-of-teacher-education-program-developed-by-acte-ncate-4131152.html

Hawkins, D. (2013). Teaching failure? *Diverse Issues in Higher Education, 30*(10), 14–15.

Head, R., & Johnson, M. (2011). Accreditation and its influence on institutional effectiveness. *New Directions for Community Colleges, 2011*, 37–52. doi:10.1002/cc.435

Ingvarson, L., Beavis, A., & Kleinhenz, E. (2007). Factors affecting the impact of teacher education programmes on teacher preparedness: Implications for accreditation policy. *Australian Council for Educational Research European Journal of Teacher Education, 30,* 351–381.

Jani, J., Pierce, D., Ortiz, L., & Sowbel, L. (2011). Access to intersectionality, content to competence: Deconstructing social work education diversity standards. *Journal of Social Work Education, 47,* 283–301.

Ladson-Billings, G. (1995). Toward a theory of culturally relevant pedagogy. *American Educational Research Journal, 32,* 465–491.

Miretzky, D., & Stevens, S. (2010). How does location impact meaning and opportunity? Rural schools and the NCATE diversity standard. *Teachers College Record, 114,* 1–36.

National Council for the Accreditation of Teacher Education. (2008). *Professional standards for the accreditation of teacher preparation institutions.* Washington, DC: Author.

National Council for the Accreditation of Teacher Education. (2012). Quick facts. *NCATE: The standard of excellence in teacher preparation.* Retrieved from www.ncate.org/Public/AboutNCATE/QuickFacts/tabid/343/Default.aspx

Proitzl, T. S., Stensaker, B., & Harvey, L. (2004). Accreditation, standards and diversity: An analysis of EQUIS accreditation reports. *Assessment and Evaluation in Higher Education 29,* 735–750.

Racial ethnic distribution of education students pursuing initial certification 2011–2012. (2013, September). *AACTE Advisor.* Retrieved from http://aacte.org/pdf/Publications/Advisor/Advisor092013.pdf

Robinson, K. (2011). *Out of our minds: Learning to be creative.* Chichester, England: Capstone.

Schmitcz, S., Nourse, S., & Ross, M. (2012). Increasing teacher diversity: Growing your own through partnerships. *Education Digest, 133,* 181–187.

Shudak, N. J. (2010). Diversity in teacher education: A double helix. *Academic Quest, 23,* 348–355.

Siegel, S., Abushanab, M., & Holliday, B. (2010). Accreditation bodies and diversity standards. *American Psychological Association Communique.* Retrieved from www.apa.org/pi/oema/resources/communique/2010/04/accreditation.aspx

Sleeter, C. E., & Grant, C. A. (2009). *Making choices for multicultural education: Five approaches to race, class and gender* (6th ed.). New York, NY: Wiley.

U.S. Department of Education, National Center for Education Statistics. (2010). *Status and trends in the education of racial and ethnic groups* (NCES Publication No. 2010–015). Retrieved from http://nces.ed.gov/pubs2010/2010015.pdf

Valentin, S. (2012). Addressing diversity in teacher education programs. *Education, 127,* 196–202.

Wiggins, R., Follo, E., & Eberly, M. (2007). The impact of a field immersion program on preservice teachers' attitudes toward teaching in culturally diverse classrooms. *Teaching and Teacher Education, 23,* 653–663.

Wiggins, G., & McTighe, J. (2011). *Understanding by design: Guide to creating high quality units.* Alexandria, VA: Association for Supervision and Curriculum Development.

Young, E. (2010). Challenges to conceptualizing and actualizing culturally relevant pedagogy: How viable is the theory in classroom practice? *Journal of Teacher Education, 61,* 248–270.

CONTRIBUTOR BIOGRAPHIES

Jeff Bartow has been a community organizer for over 30 years. Since 2002, he has served as Lead Organizer and Executive Director of the multi-issue group, Southwest Organizing Project, which works on issues important to the 27 member organizations in their low-income Chicago Lawn neighborhood. Mr. Bartow has led critical work on the foreclosure crisis and on immigration issues.

Margarita Bianco is associate professor in the School of Education and Human Development at the University of Colorado Denver and executive director of Pathways2Teaching. Her research interests include the underrepresentation of teachers of color and students of color and twice-exceptional learners in gifted programs. Professor Bianco is the recipient of several awards, including the Outstanding Researcher Award from the Council for Learning Disabilities, University of Colorado Denver's Rosa Parks Diversity Award, the 2011 University of Colorado President's Diversity Award, and the University of Colorado's 2012 Teaching Excellence Award.

Deborah Bieler is associate professor in the Department of English and coordinator of the English education program at the University of Delaware. Dr. Bieler's research concerns the preparation and retention of socially responsive secondary English teachers. Her current projects include a study of discourse patterns in new teachers' interactions with struggling students and a study of the effects of service learning in English education.

Robbie Burnett serves as Maverick Teacher Recruitment Coordinator within the College of Education at Minnesota State University, Mankato. She specializes in diversity recruitment and retention. Her interests include designing equitable support mechanisms that promote graduation for diverse teacher candidates. Currently, she is in the educational leadership doctorate program at Minnesota State University, Mankato.

Anne Burns Thomas is assistant professor in the Foundations and Social Advocacy Department in the School of Education at State University of New York College at Cortland. Additionally, she is coordinator of Cortland's Urban Recruitment of Educators (C.U.R.E) program. A former middle school teacher, her research interests include the nature of support for new teachers in urban schools, urban teacher education programs, and recruitment of teachers from groups underrepresented in teaching.

Lorena Claeys is executive director of the Academy of Teacher Excellence, the University of Texas at San Antonio. Dr. Claeys's research interests include teacher recruitment, preparation, and retention, and teachers' motivation to teach culturally and linguistically diverse students.

James Cohen is assistant professor of English as a second language (ESL)–bilingual education at Northern Illinois University. His research interests lie in the areas of bilingual and ESL education, literacy instruction of immigrant and nonnative English speakers, nonparallel schooled immigrant students, and undocumented immigrants.

Doyin Coker-Kolo is associate dean, coordinator, and certification officer for the School of Education at Millersville University of Pennsylvania. Dr. Coker-Kolo's research interests focus on gender equity and diversity in education, middle level education, African higher education, and multicultural education. Besides contributions to edited books, her works have been published in *Multicultural Perspectives* (a journal of the National Association of Multicultural Education), *Journal of Third World Studies*, and *National Social Science Technology Journal*.

William F. Ellis was born to a family enmeshed in the U.S. sharecropping system in an agricultural region of Georgia. Dr. Ellis graduated from the most prestigious of historically Black colleges and universities, Morehouse College, and participated in the Southern civil rights movement. He taught in the San Francisco School District, and then later organized one of the most successful programs in the United States to diversify the teaching force. He has led struggles and written articles about discriminatory aspects of the U.S. education system, including the inaccurate presentation of U.S. history. His doctoral dissertation utilized action research to create a more accurate representation of African American history.

Kitty Kelly Epstein is an academic, an author, and an activist. Dr. Epstein has prepared hundreds of urban teachers; helped to create two successful programs for teacher diversity; led a thousand-person participatory action process; supervised dissertation studies using critical race theory, participatory action research, autoethnography, and alternative dissertation methods; served as education policy director for Oakland Mayor Ron Dellums; hosted an education talk show; and presented workshops in Norway, South Africa, Nicaragua, Jordan, Ethiopia, China, and other locations. She is author of two books: *A Different View of Urban Schools: Civil Rights, Critical Race Theory and Unexplored Realities* and *Organizing to Change a City*. She was recently named scholar-activist of the year by the Urban Affairs Association.

Belinda Bustos Flores is chair and professor, Department of Bicultural–Bilingual Studies at the University of Texas, San Antonio. Her research focuses on teacher development including self-concept, ethnic identity, efficacy, beliefs, teacher recruitment and retention, and high stakes testing. Dr. Flores is lead editor for *Teacher Preparation for Bilingual Populations: Educar para transformar* and for *Generating Transworld Pedagogy: Reimagining La Clase Mágica*.

Jill Ewing Flynn, a former high school English teacher, is currently associate professor of English education at the University of Delaware. Her research and teaching interests include critical multicultural education and teacher preparation. She is the student teaching coordinator for the English education program.

Joseph E. Flynn Jr. is associate professor of curriculum and instruction at Northern Illinois University. Dr. Flynn teaches courses related to social justice and multicultural education, curriculum studies, and the nature of educational change and reform. His scholarship offers critical examinations of Whiteness studies, media and popular culture, and curriculum. Previously, he has guest-edited a special edition of *The Black History Bulletin* on the role of African Americans in popular culture. Currently, he is coeditor of the *Woodson Review* and is coediting a book entitled *A Rubric Nation: Critical Inquiries Into the Impact of Rubrics on Education.*

Connie Fox is associate dean of the College of Education at Northern Illinois University (NIU). In that role, she is responsible for curriculum leadership and assessment, and she champions the College Diversity Plan. Dr. Fox was the first president of the American Association for Physical Activity and Recreation and has held leadership positions in a number of other professional organizations. She has received several honors and awards, including the Honor Award from the American Association for Physical Activity and Recreation and the Young Scholar Award from the Midwest Association for College and University Physical Education. At NIU, she has received the College of Education Excellence in Teaching Award.

Maureen Gillette is dean of the College of Education at Northeastern Illinois University in Chicago. She is coauthor (with Carl A. Grant) of *Learning to Teach Everyone's Children: Equity, Empowerment, and Education That Is Multicultural.* For the past 13 years, Dr. Gillette has been engaged in designing, implementing, and evaluating programs that recruit, prepare, and graduate first-generation, community-based teacher candidates for urban schools. She holds bachelor's and master's degrees from Northern Illinois University and a doctoral degree from the University of Wisconsin–Madison.

Conra D. Gist is assistant professor of curriculum and instruction at the University of Arkansas. Her research focuses on teacher diversity, culturally responsive pedagogy, and teacher learning and development.

Anne Hallett served as executive director of Grow Your Own Illinois from 2005 to 2013. She founded and directed the Cross City Campaign for Urban School Reform, a network of school reform leaders in large cities, and the Chicago Panel on School Policy. She serves on the board of directors of the Center for Neighborhood Technology–Energy and as a life member of the Interfaith Youth Core.

Rebecca D. Hunt is assistant professor in the Department of Educational Technology, Research and Assessment at Northern Illinois University. Postdoctorate, as a 2008 American Library Association Spectrum Scholar, Dr. Hunt received a master's degree in library and information science from the University of Alabama. Her research interests focus on school library services for K-12 students, diversity in literature for children and young adults, and media literacy.

Mona Ivey-Soto is assistant professor in the childhood and early childhood education program at State University of New York Cortland and has also been involved with coordinating their urban education program. She holds an affiliate faculty position in Africana studies. Dr. Ivey-Soto is actively involved in her local urban community, advocating for educational opportunities and policy changes for refugee and immigrant children and families, and is cofounder of the Syracuse Children's Mental Health Consortium group. Through her teaching, scholarship, and service, Dr. Ivey-Soto is committed to providing teacher candidates with meaningful opportunities to engage their own biases and understand systemic oppression and how to advocate for social change in urban schools.

Katelyn Johnson has been a community organizer for nearly 10 years, working as a housing organizer, parent organizer, and Grow Your Own Teachers coordinator. Named as executive director of Action Now Institute in 2010 and executive director of sister-organization Action Now in 2012, Ms. Johnson continues to work to build power for low-income communities and affect policies changes around equitable public education, living wage jobs, affordable housing, and other community issues.

Hannah Kim is assistant professor of history and co-coordinator of social studies education at the University of Delaware. Her research and teaching interests include teacher preparation, world history curriculum, and U.S. and Korean relations.

Kevin K. Kumashiro is dean of the School of Education at the University of San Francisco, and president (2012–2014) of the National Association for Multicultural Education. He is the author or editor of nine books on education and social justice, including the award-winning *Troubling Education* (2002); *Against Common Sense: Teaching and Learning Toward Social Justice* (2004/2009); and most recently, *Bad Teacher! How Blaming Teachers Distorts the Bigger Picture* (2012).

Christina L. Madda is assistant professor in the Department of Literacy Education at Northeastern Illinois University where she teaches courses in literacy instruction for elementary grades, assessment and diagnosis, and technology integration. Her research interests include writing instruction in bilingual classrooms, teachers' instructional responses to policy, and university–community partnerships that strengthen teacher preparation. Dr. Madda is also involved with the Illinois Grow Your Own Teachers program. Her most recent publication in the *New Educator* journal addressed the potential of university–community partnerships like Grow Your Own Teachers to strengthen teacher preparation.

Kimberly Mayfield Lynch is associate professor and chair of the Education Department at Holy Names University in Oakland, California. From 2006 to 2011, Dr. Lynch served as the co-convener of the Effective Teaching Task Force for the Oakland Unified School District. Her research interests and activism focus on diversifying the teaching force.

La Vonne I. Neal is dean of the College of Education at Northern Illinois University. Dean Neal is a teacher–educator whose work in the design and implementation of culturally responsive teaching methods has earned wide recognition both among educators and in the popular press. For example, her research on the correlation between African American male students' walking styles and their placement in special education courses has been featured in *USA Today*, the *Atlanta Journal-Constitution*, DiversityInc.Com, and radio and television stations across the country. She coedits the *Black History Bulletin*, a publication for teachers of the Association for the Study of African American Life and History.

Rachelle Rogers-Ard manages Teach Tomorrow in Oakland within the Oakland Unified School District. Dr. Rogers-Ard is also a regional director for the National Association of Multicultural Education, a visiting professor in the Urban Education program at California State University East Bay, and the author and coauthor of several publications. To learn more about her, access her blog, and/or read her publications, visit her website (www.rachellerogersard.com).

Rosalie Rolón Dow is associate professor in the School of Education at the University of Delaware. An ethnographer of education, Dr. Rolón Dow studies how race, ethnicity, gender, and social class dynamics shape the educational opportunities and experiences of urban families, with particular attention on Latino/a students. Her teaching and research endeavors aim to address issues of educational (in)equity and seek to promote socially just educational practices and policies that draw on the strengths and cultural resources of families and communities.

Flynn Ross is associate professor of teacher education at the University of Southern Maine. Dr. Ross is the university-based coordinator of Extended Teacher Education Program (ETEP) in Portland. She is also the faculty coordinator of the Newcomer-ETEP program. Her areas of research include professional development, school programs, and multicultural education.

Imelda Salazar is a graduate of Universidad Francisco Marroquin in Guatemala City, Guatemala. She has experience as a pastoral worker on the U.S.–Mexican border and has been organizing in the United States with the Southwest Organizing Project (SWOP) in Chicago, Illinois, for the past 6 years. She directs the Grow Your Own Teacher program at SWOP.

Robert W. Simmons III is director of the Center for Innovation in Urban Education at Loyola University Maryland as well as associate professor in the School of Education and an affiliated faculty member in the African and African American studies program. Additionally, Dr. Simmons is a member of the nationally recognized social justice collaborative Edchange and a contributor for the Village Celebration. He has been a fellow with the Woodrow Wilson Fellowship Foundation and has participated in the Japan Fulbright Memorial Fund. He recently coedited *Talking About Race: Alleviating the Fear* with Steve Grineski and Julie Landsman.

Christine E. Sleeter is professor emerita in the College of Professional Studies at California State University Monterey Bay, where she was a founding faculty member. Her research focuses on antiracist education and multicultural teacher education. She has published numerous articles in edited books and journals such as *Journal of Teacher Education*, *Race Ethnicity & Education*, and *Teaching and Teacher Education*. Her recent books include *Power, Teaching and Teacher Education* and *Creating Solidarity Across Diverse Communities* (with E. Soriano). Awards for her work include the American Educational Research Association Social Justice Award and the Chapman University Paulo Freire Education Project Social Justice Award.

Madhavi Tandon is a doctoral candidate at the University of Colorado Denver. Her research focuses on marginalization of learners at the intersection of immigration, language, and race, with a specific focus on multilingual learners. Ms. Tandon works closely with schools that have a large population of multilingual learners to enhance instruction and outcomes for English language learners.

Omiunota N. Ukpokodu is professor in the Division of Curriculum and Instructional Leadership at the University of Missouri–Kansas City. She teaches courses in multicultural education, urban education, social justice, and social studies with research interests in quality teacher preparation, critical multicultural education, global/citizenship education, immigrant education, transformative learning and pedagogy, culturally responsive teaching, and social justice pedagogy.

Victor Manuel Valle is an education organizer and the Grow Your Own Teachers coordinator at Organizing Neighborhoods for Equality: Northside.

Audra M. Watson is director of mentoring and induction at the Woodrow Wilson National Fellowship Foundation based in Princeton, New Jersey. She also serves as director for the Woodrow Wilson–Rockefeller Brothers Fund for Aspiring Teachers of Color and as a program officer for the teaching fellowship program. In her primary role, she is responsible for designing—and ensuring the continued quality of—the foundation's mentoring programs across all fellowships. A 19-year veteran of the New York City Department of Education, she was previously executive director of teacher development, where she planned and executed strategy for preservice through early-career teacher support. Ms. Watson is a 3rd-year doctoral student in urban education policy at the City University of New York Graduate Center.

Scott A. Wickman is associate professor in the Department of Counseling, Adult and Higher Education at Northern Illinois University. Dr. Wickman has written about advocacy, spirituality, and the coconstruction of therapeutic meaning through intentional language use. He also has served as president of the Illinois School Counselor Association, Illinois Counseling Association, Coalition of Illinois Counseling Organizations, and North Central Association of Counselor Education and Supervision. Most recently, Dr. Wickman was executive producer of the documentaries "Color Me Obsessed: The Potentially True Story of the Replacements" and "Every Everything: The Grant Hart Story" as well as associate producer of "A Dog Named Gucci."

Carol Wong is associate professor in the School of Education at the University of Delaware. Her research is in the area of the learning sciences. Dr. Wong focuses on examining the intersection of (a) normative adolescent and academic development, such as self-regulation of learning, motivation, and college readiness and access, and (b) cultural phenomena and psychological processes related to race or ethnicity, including adolescents' experiences of stereotypes, prejudice, and discrimination.

Lynn Worden is assistant professor in the Department of Human Development and Family Studies at the University of Delaware (UD). Dr. Worden is the early childhood education coordinator for UD's blended early childhood and early childhood special education program. Dr. Worden is currently working on research in coteaching in early childhood student teaching experiences.

Shelley Zion is executive director of the Center for Advancing Practice, Education & Research and assistant research professor in the School of Education at the University of Colorado, Denver. In that role, she teaches in the EdD program and conducts research on topics related to student voice, school reform, and social justice. Dr. Zion is founder of the CRUE center, which provides training to schools working to address issues of equity. She is co–principal investigator on two funded projects focused on youth voice and empowerment for students of color in Grades 6 through 12: the Critical Civic Inquiry Project (Spencer Foundation) and the Compugirls Project (National Science Foundation). She is the 2013 recipient of the American Educational Research Association Leadership for Social Justice Teaching Award and University of Colorado Rosa Parks Faculty Diversity Award.

INDEX